ALGONQUINS.

From the Hebert Group before the Palais Legislatif, Quebec.

PIONEER PRIESTS

OF

NORTH AMERICA

1642-1710

BY THE

REV. T. J. CAMPBELL, S.J.

VOL. III.

AMONG THE ALGONQUINS

Second Edition

NEW YORK

THE AMERICA PRESS

1916

Copyright, 1911, by

THE AMERICA PRESS

The Frank Meany Co., Printers, Inc.

This volume of the

PIONEER PRIESTS OF NORTH AMERICA

is respectfully dedicated to the

RIGHT REVEREND BISHOP OF PORTLAND,

LOUIS SEBASTIAN WALSH, D.D.

in whose diocese, on the banks of the Kennebec,
the venerable remains of

FATHER SEBASTIAN RÂLE, S.J.,

lie buried

Nihil Obstat.

REMIGIUS LAFORT, S. T. L.,
Censor.

Imprimatur.

JOHN M. FARLEY, D.D.,
Archbishop of New York.

New York, April 25, 1911

TABLE OF CONTENTS

TABLE OF CONTENTS

GABRIEL DRUILLETTES.

CHARLES ALBANEL.

TABLE OF CONTENTS

ix

TABLE OF CONTENTS

TABLE OF CONTENTS

PETER LAURE.

JOHN AULNEAU.

SEBASTIAN RALE.

ILLUSTRATIONS

AUTHORITIES

RELATIONS—Quebec, 1858.

RELATIONS—Thwaite's Edition. Cleveland, 1897.

JOURNAL DES JESUITES—Quebec, 1871.

ROCHEMONTEIX—Les Jesuites et la Nouvelle France. Litouzey, Paris, 1895.

ARCHIVES MSS.—St. Mary's College, Montreal.

CHARLEVOIX—Hist. de la N. France. Paris, Giffard, 1744.

SPARKS—American Biography. Boston, 1845.

HUTCHISON—History of the Colony of Massachusetts Bay. Richardson, London, 1760.

BANCROFT—History of the United States. London, Routledge, 1854.

CARAYON—Relations Inédites de la N. France. Dounuil, Paris, 1861.

GARNEAU—Hist. de Canada. Beauchemin, Montreal, 1882.

PARKMAN—France and England in North America. Little, Brown & Company, Boston, 1867.

PRAT—Récherches Historiques. Briday, Lyons, 1876.

CHAPOT—Marie de l'Incarnation. Poussielgue, Paris, 1892.

CHAPAIS—Jean Talon. Demiers, Quebec, 1904.

CARAYON—Jésuites de Paris. L Euneux, Paris, 1864.

DANIEL—Histoire de France. Paris, 1756.

GOSSELIN—Jean Nicolet.

DIONNE—Le Père Sebastian Râle. Pamphlet. Hope et Fils, Ottawa, 1903.

LETTRES EDIFIANTES—Bethune, Paris, 1830.

INTRODUCTION

THE name Algonquin is said to mean "the place where they spear fish," *i. e.,* the front of the canoe. Other philologists insist that the proper interpretation of the word is "the men on the other side of the river," namely, the St. Lawrence. As many of the Algonquins did not live on the other side of the river, the latter meaning may be questioned unless it applies to those who, unlike the other branches of the great family, retained for themselves the name Algonquin; those namely who lived north of the St. Lawrence and whose stronghold was on the Allumette Island far up the Ottawa. In the days of the missions, the Ottawa and the St. Lawrence were regarded as the same river.

When the Algonquins were a great nation they claimed as their own almost all the upper regions of the North American continent, and even out in the Atlantic there was no one to dispute Newfoundland with them except an inconsiderable and now forgotten people known as the Beothukcn. Cape Breton and Prince Edward Island and Nova Scotia and all the country from Labrador to Alaska was theirs, except where the Esquimaux lived in the East, the Kitunahans in the far Northwest, and the Hurons, Petuns and Neutrals in the region near Georgian Bay. In what is now the United States, New England was counted as their country, and though their deadly enemy, the Iroquois, had somehow or other seized the greater part of New York, yet the strip along the Hudson belonged to the Algonquins, as did also New Jersey, a part of Virginia and North Carolina, Kentucky, Illinois and Wisconsin.

Generically they were all Algonquins, but each section had assumed a different designation. It is impossible to remember them all, and it will suffice to mention the principal ones; taking the alphabetical order in which they are set down in the ethnological tables. They were classified as Abnakis, Arapahoes, Cheyennes, Crees, Delawares, Foxes, Illinois, Kickapoos, Mohicans, Massachusetts, Menominees, Montagnais, Montauks, Narragansetts, Nipmucs, Ojibways, Ottawas, Powhatans, Sacs, Shawnees, Wampanoags, Wappingers, etc.

Of all these tribes there are only about 95,000 left at the present day, 35,000 of whom are in the United States and the rest in Canada. Their number, of course, must have been considerable in former times, but any exact estimate of their strength can only be a matter of conjecture. As far as we remember, no systematic Indian census was ever attempted, except by Fathers de Brébeuf and Jerome Lalemant, and they were interested only in the Hurons. But the evident power of this great people and the extraordinary way in which they were scattered over a vast extent of territory will easily explain why Champlain had no hesitation about entering into alliance with them against the sixteen or seventeen thousand Iroquois of New York, who could easily have been destroyed if the Algonquins had been united.

It is commonly asserted that the Algonquins were the noblest of the North American Indians, but for those who are familiar with their history it is hard to find any notable difference between them and their fellow savages. When Cartier sailed up the St. Lawrence almost a hundred years before the arrival of the missionaries, he was shocked by the indecency of the Montagnais at Tadoussac. When Le Jeune arrived at the time of the *recouvrance,* the savages near the same place invited him to see them eat their captives. One of the victims was a mere lad, whom they refused to sell to the horrified priest. Even the Hurons told their boys, whom they sent down to Quebec to be educated, not to consort with the Algonquins; and the fiendish and indecent torture which the squaws inflicted on an Iroquois prisoner under the very walls of the city, warranted the ad-

INTRODUCTION

vice. It is true that the Indians north of the St. Lawrence were of a meeker and kindlier disposition than their relatives elsewhere. Thus the Papinachois were well disposed to the missionaries, as were the Whitefish whom Father Buteux was evangelizing at Three Rivers, but that may have been due to the poverty and wretchedness in which they were compelled to live. They were not warriors but wanderers in the woods, and they naturally listened to men like the missionaries, who were interested in their welfare. The trouble was that they had no fixed habitations like the Iroquois or Hurons, and thus, while being always an easy prey to their enemies, they were absolutely shut off from any possibility not only of learning any of the textile arts, but of even acquainting themselves with the most fundamental notions of agriculture. They always remained savage. The same was true for the Algonquins in the West. Although they were not confronted by the hard conditions of climate which made life miserable for their brethren on the St. Lawrence, nevertheless Marquette found some of them at Green Bay too stupid to make a dish or to scoop out a ladle. They were all worshippers of the manitou. Most of them were shameless in their immorality, and were just as cruel as the Iroquois in their treatment of captives, though their hereditary foes are credited with having taught them these practices.

The fact that they were nomads prevented the missionaries in the beginning from attempting to Christianize them. It was simply impossible to follow them in their wanderings. A priest would be needed for every group of Indians. For that reason, when the missionaries were few in number, no systematic effort was made to convert them, and both Recollects and Jesuits concentrated their energies on the Huron tribes who lived in fortified towns and cultivated the fields. Hence it was that de Brébeuf, although he passed his first winter in America among the Algonquins, did so only because he was unsuccessful in reaching the Huron country. Before that, Biard and Massé had endeavored to get in touch with the Souriquois or Micmacs of Acadia, and with the Etchemins of Maine, but without any great result. When the missions were resumed after the restoration of Quebec, Le Jeune went out on the winter hunt with the Algonquins, so as to learn their language and to teach them some of the elements of Christianity, but he found all his efforts useless. It was only when the Reservation at Sillery was begun that some good was effected. Thither the Abnakis of Maine came in great numbers and thus prepared the way for the work on the Kennebec and elsewhere. Father Buteux also, as we have said, had some success with his Whitefish Indians, who willingly flocked around him at Three Rivers, but left him as soon as there was any fear of the Iroquois. Hence it was only in 1649, when there were no more Hurons to evangelize, that the Fathers were, so to say, compelled to direct their efforts to the Indians north of the St. Lawrence. It was almost in spite of themselves that they entered upon one of the most heroic though not perhaps the most brilliant period of their apostolic labors.

The work began with the journey of Dablon and Druillettes up the Saguenay and Aspamouachan as far as Nekouba; then came the heroic Albanel, who was the first to reach Hudson Bay by an overland route. He made the journey twice, but on the second expedition he was seized and sent as a prisoner to England. De Crespieul, Sylvie and Maret then entered upon the scene. The saintly Father Laure underwent eighteen years of terrible suffering on the Saguenay, and descended every winter to the Gulf of St. Lawrence in pursuit of the Betsamites and the Papinachois, striving at the same time, but without success, to establish a post among the degraded Esquimaux.

Meantime, the Western country was opened up by the explorers, and in 1654 Garreau was murdered by the Iroquois when he was endeavoring to reach the Ottawa coun-

INTRODUCTION

try. Claude Allouez succeeded him and founded the
missionary post of St. Esprit at the further end of Lake
Superior. In 1673 Marquette discovered the Mississippi
and thus the Illinois Indians came under the influence of
the missionaries. The priest who had gone furthest in the
western wilderness was John Aulneau, who was killed by
the Sioux on a barren island in the Lake of the Woods. A
short time before, Râle had fallen under the bullets of the
English in the Abnaki village on the Kennebec.

The story of the Algonquin missions is not as tragic as
that of the Hurons; but it is safe to say it is just as heroic.
Especially in the North and East, the work was absolutely
devoid of every natural comfort. It was in a region of almost uninterrupted ice and snow except for a very brief
part of the year. The journeys were over frozen lakes and
down ice-clogged cataracts. The pangs of hunger and starvation were almost an every day experience, and the missionaries frequently made their beds in the snow drifts;
their daily tramp was often waist deep in icy water or in
driving storms, and when they were shivering behind the
wretched bark shelters in the forests or on the slopes of
mountains, it was only to exchange their sufferings outside
with the torturing smoke of the fire and the inconceivable
filth of the people who swarmed into their cabin with them.
It was a life of uninterrupted horror.

There is some relief in the narration in the fact that several of these old missionaries were identified with the great
events of the day. Thus Albanel was sent to find Radisson at the North Sea. Sylvie and Maret and Dalmas
were in the wild raids of Iberville; Marquette was with
Joliet in the discovery of the Mississippi; Druillettes was
the envoy of Quebec to the magnates of Boston, and the
death of Râle was the end of a fight for the possession of
the State of Maine.

Only a few of the heroic men who devoted their lives
to the conversion of the Algonquin Indians have been men-

INTRODUCTION

tioned in this volume. There are many others of whom no records are kept, except that like true soldiers they never flinched in the fierce battle which they had set for themselves to save the souls of those degraded savages. We shall know more of them in heaven.

PAUL LE JEUNE

CHAPTER I.

WINTERING WITH THE SAVAGES.

The distinguished historian of New York, Dr. O'Callaghan, calls Le Jeune "the Father of the Canadian Missions." He was so in fact, and the reasons of this distinction are as follows: (1) When Canada was restored to the French, he was selected as Superior. (2) It was he who rebuilt the dilapidated residence and church of Notre Dame des Anges. He established the first parish of Quebec, that of Notre Dame de Recouvrance. (4) He organized the missions of Miscou, Tadoussac, and Three Rivers. (5) He conceived the idea of Sillery as an Algonquin Reservation. (6) He instituted a native school for Indian boys, and prompted Marie de l'Incarnation to undertake the education of Indian girls. (7) He founded the College of Quebec, and suggested to Cardinal Richelieu's niece, the Duchesse d'Aiguillon, to build the first hospital in Canada, the Hôtel Dieu of Quebec.

As far as we are aware, he was the only one of the early missionaries who was a convert from Protestantism. He was born at Châlons-sur-Marne, in July, 1591, and when still a young man he became a Catholic in spite of the bitter opposition of his family. He entered the Society of Jesus at Rouen, September 22, 1613; studied philosophy at La Flèche, was professor at Rennes, Bourges and Nevers, and then followed the four years' course of theology at Clermont. The famous Louis Lalemant was his spiritual guide in the Tertianship, and after that we find him teaching rhetoric, and preaching at Dieppe, and subsequently presiding over

1   I

the Residence of that place. He was occupying that position when the question began to be mooted about resuscitating the missions of Canada, if ever the colony were restored to France.

At first there was no thought of entrusting the work to the Jesuits. They were already too influential in France to suit Richelieu's taste. He would brook no rival at court, and for that reason was unfriendly to Father Coton, whom he proposed to attach to the French embassy at London. Coton was too near the throne. The scheme was thwarted by the Father General Vitelleschi, who made Coton, Provincial of Paris. A similar apprehension made the Cardinal extremely suspicious of the young king's confessor, Father Suffren, and hence every movement of that very worthy man who, on his part, never dreamed of meddling in State affairs, was carefully watched. It also happened that at the same time two somewhat defamatory pamphlets were published; one the *Mysteria Politica,* and the other *Commendatio ad Christianissimum Regem,* both aimed at Richelieu. They were ascribed to Jesuit authorship. Finally the Cardinal's great friend and advisor at the time was the Capuchin Joseph, *son eminence grise,* as he was called, of whom the Cardinal used to say: *" Aucun ministre ou plénipotentiaire en Europe n'etait capable de faire la barbe à ce Capucin"* (no minister or plenipotentiary in Europe could get the better of that Capuchin).

Naturally, therefore, because of Friar Joseph's influence, the Capuchins were chosen for the work in America; but they declined the offer and suggested the Jesuits or Recollects, who had already labored on those missions. As the authorities, however, had already determined to take only one religious order, so as to keep clear of those little misunderstandings which sometimes occur even among holy men, the Jesuits were selected and letters patent were immediately sent to Fathers Le Jeune, Anne de Noüe, and Brother Gilbert Buret empowering them to take possession of their former establishments, and resume their work of evangelizing the savages.

The Fathers had all along expected that such would be the issue, and were ready when the call came. Indeed, although Le Jeune and his companions were informed of the Cardinal's decision, only at the end of March, they were on board the ship, at Honfleur, on April 18, 1632.

Unfortunately this choice annoyed the Recollects. They admitted that they could not have set out for America with such little time to prepare, but they asked to go later on. They were refused; but what was most exasperating in this arrangement was that it was the Intendant de Lauson himself, though owing his position to their influence, who told them they were not wanted. Some unpleasant things were written by the Recollect historians Le Clercq and Le Tac on the subject, and the Jesuits were accused of working underhand to exclude the Friars; but of course those accusations were only the expression of a temporary irritation. Indeed it is clear, when one examines the documents published at the time, that there was no desire to debar the men who had really been the first missionaries of Canada, and had displayed the greatest heroism during fifteen years of apostolic labor. Fortunately the first missionaries had departed before these charges had been made. The weather was fair when they left Honfleur and " in ten days," says Le Jeune, " we sailed six hundred leagues," which was certainly rapid travelling for a clumsy vessel of those times; but the thirty-three following days made the unfortunate passengers pay for their previous enjoyment.

" I have often beheld the sea in its fury, when I looked out of the window of our little house at Dieppe," writes Le Jeune, " but it is quite another thing to be tossing on the ocean than it is to gaze at it from the shore. We had to go before the wind for a long time and were lifted on the crest of mountainous waves, only to be flung into yawning abysses. Every moment we thought our masts would go by the board, or that the waves would crash through the sides

3

of the vessel. At one time, at least a sailor told us so, we came very near going to the bottom. We found then how easy it is to meditate on death in one's room while kneeling before the crucifix, but how hard when one is at close quarters with it. But I must confess that I was indifferent; and perhaps I had a slight desire to die. It may be if the actual moment arrived I might have thought differently, but in any case I concluded that the best I could do was to offer my life for the crew.

" It was then the end of the month of May, but the wind and the fog made us shiver with cold. Father Nouë's feet were frozen, and for a whole month I was troubled with pains of the heart and head. There was no fresh water on board, and in our little cabins, where we could neither stand, nor sit, nor kneel, the sea sometimes poured down on our faces when we stretched ourselves out for a rest.

" On Pentecost Sunday I was just about to preach when a sailor cried out *morue! morue!* codfish! codfish! Every one hurried to the sides of the vessel and without difficulty hauled in all they wanted. It was a pleasure to see such a slaughter and so much blood bespattering our deck. We needed this change of diet after the terrible squalls we had encountered."

He saw Newfoundland on the 18th of May. The icebergs glittering in the sun seemed like churches or rather like mountains of crystal. "You could not believe it," he says, "unless you saw it." Bird Island was sighted on June 3. The whales, the seals, and the white porpoises all passed before his delighted eyes, and at last the ship cast anchor in Gaspé Bay, where they met two other French vessels. Mass was celebrated in the cabin of one of them, and a sermon was preached. Very appropriately the Gospel of the day was " Go forth and teach all nations."

On June 14th they arrived at Tadoussac, and a Sagamo and ten Indians came to meet them. The natives had put on their paint for the occasion, and the priest wondered as he looked at them. Some of them had made their noses blue, and the eyes and cheeks black, while the rest of the face was vermillion; others had glittering streaks of red, from the

MODERN TADOUSSAC.

ears to the mouth; others again appeared with the face all black except the ears and the chin; or there would be some with bands of color across the eyes and running from ear to ear. The natural hue of their skin he thought was like that of the sunburned beggars in France, and he ventured the opinion that if their bodies were clothed, they would be white. The men, he said, were dressed like St. John the Baptist, though the leathern girdle was usually the entrail of some animal. Like the ancient philosopher they wore nothing that they did not make, but as it was all very simple he suggests that it would not take many years to become an accomplished native tailor.

While at Tadoussac he was treated to the horrid spectacle of the torture of three Iroquois captives, one a lad of only fifteen or sixteen years of age. In vain he begged them to cease, and offered to buy the boy, but they refused, and he noted that the women were the most fiendish and the most indecent in the means they employed to make the victims suffer. The captives were to be eaten, and he was asked to stay for the feast.

Of course he did not accept the invitation, but started up the river with his companions. They were not far on their way when a frightful squall nearly sent them to the bottom. Within four leagues of Quebec another tempest compelled them to drop their anchor, but the cable parted, and they came near being driven on shore, especially when a second anchor shared the same fate. At last the storm ceased when they were within three quarters of a league of Quebec.

The city was in a deplorable condition. Champlain's "habitation" near the fort had been burned, and the stone work that had once supported the timbers was in ruins. The Jesuits' house on the St. Charles was uninhabitable, as was the old Recollect convent near by. Only one family had remained in the city—the Héberts, who were just on the point of abandoning their possessions and returning to

France. Mass was celebrated in their house, and a *Te Deum* was sung in thanksgiving for the *recouvrance*. The next day, Thomas Kerk, the English-Frenchman who had remained in charge of the fort since its capture, was formally visited and shown the treaty between France and England. He agreed to withdraw within a week, which he did to the delight of everyone, as even his own retainers complained of his brutality.

When the English had departed, Le Jeune betook himself to the dilapidated dwelling on the St. Charles, and did what he could to patch it up. Being a very observant man he naturally began to make careful notes of everything he saw. Sometimes he appears to be talking about mere trifles, but no doubt they were invested with much importance for him, as well as for the people in France for whom they were intended. If nothing else they are at least an excellent mirror of his impressions, and help us to know the man. They are also a valuable picture of conditions that prevailed among the savages along the St. Lawrence at that time. Their religious ideas, their superstitions, their belief in dreams, their dress, their marriage, their domestic habits, etc., are all carefully set down. While being very precious from an ethnological point of view, they also help us to understand the religious difficulty that confronted the missionaries.

His first care was to study the language. He had already made an offer at it, on the way over, by poring over a book, but he complains that it was full of blunders. He appealed to the interpreter Marsolet to assist him, but that worthy assured him that he had taken an oath not to reveal the secrets of the Indian language to any one. This singularly scrupulous individual was the same man who had been found by Champlain among Kerk's soldiers at the capture of Quebec, though he protested that he had been made a prisoner by the English and was on the wrong side in spite of himself.

PAUL LE JEUNE

Thus thwarted, Le Jeune had recourse to the children as teachers. To his amazement he found among them a little negro who had come from Madagascar, and had been sold to a colonist by one of the English traders. He was the first of his color to appear among the snows of Canada, and of course Le Jeune soon made him spiritually white by baptizing him.

He learned very little from his youthful instructors, and was at his wits' end, when hope came at last. An educated Indian who spoke French appeared on the scene. He was an Algonquin who had been sent to France and had been baptized there with great ceremony, having had most distinguished people for his sponsors. But Pierre, as he was called, is an early and notable example of the futility of endeavoring to make a European out of an Indian. The leopard had not changed his spots.

Unfortunately Pierre had remained at Quebec while it was in the possession of the English. They quickly dissipated what Catholic faith there was in him, and taught him everything evil. He soon became a hard drinker and by the time the French returned he was again a savage. Being a clever fellow, however, he immediately made court to his former friends, and was established in the household of de Caen, who in the interval between the restoration and Champlain's arrival was in charge of the colony. Indeed, so well educated was Pierre, that de Caen admitted him to his table, and used him as intermediary in all important transactions with the Indians. He soon quarrelled with his benefactor, however, and was dismissed, whereupon he addressed himself to du Plessis, the commander of the Fleet.

But du Plessis would have nothing to do with him, for Pierre's moral record was now known, and so Father Le Jeune gladly took him in, hoping to bring about the poor wretch's reformation while using him as a teacher in the Indian language. But it was all in vain. Pierre would never teach the priest a single word without a corresponding compensation in tobacco, although he was being lodged and fed in the house. Soon he began to give false meanings to certain words, in order to make the instructions to the children ridiculous. It was clear now that he had lost all belief in Christianity, and, that fact, along with his drunkenness and immorality made his dismissal imperative. We shall find him again as the evil genius of the missionary during a winter's experience which Le Jeune was soon to have among the Indians.

Later on, another native appeared who it was hoped would be useful in many ways, but, unfortunately, he was not available as an interpreter, for he was a Huron. He also had been sent abroad and had been very well instructed, but, like the Algonquin, he had become a moral wreck during the English occupation. However, he had not lost his faith. He was known as Amantancha, or Louis de Ste. Foy. After some time, Father Le Jeune induced him to resume the practices of Christianity, and, with the exception of a few lapses, Amantancha continued to be a great help to de Brébeuf and the other missionaries in the Huron country. He was captured at one time by the Iroquois, but succeeded in returning to his own people, and, thanks to his good example and instructions, he brought his whole family to the Faith.

Besides laboring with the Indian children Le Jeune had the white people of the colony to look after, and this branch of his ministry came near putting an end to his career. Some one fell sick on the ship, which was anchored out in the river. Le Jeune hurried to bring him the ministrations of religion, but in leaving the vessel the canoe in which he was returning upset, and he and his man found themselves floundering in the waves of the St. Lawrence. "It was twenty-four years since I had my last swim," he wrote afterwards, "and I never was very much at it, but as the canoe was going down, I determined to strike out. I had only gone a short distance when my cassock got around my head, and I sunk. The sailors were shouting 'Help! help!' but no boat on the vessel could be lowered to my assistance. Fortunately some one on shore heard me screaming and started out in a shallop. It arrived just in time. A part of my cassock was yet visible, and my rescuer seized it and hauled me out. Another 'Our Father' and I was gone. As it was, they had a great deal of trouble in bringing me to."

In May, 1633, Champlain arrived. Everyone was happy, for it was feared that de Caen, who was a Huguenot, might be assigned to the post. With Champlain were de Brébeuf, de Noüe, Davost, and Daniel. No one felt happier than Le Jeune at the splendid reinforcement. He was now determined to make an effort to pass a winter among his Montagnais, for he saw it was unavoidable, if ever he was to learn their language. The Hurons had come in from the west, but in spite of the efforts of Champlain and the eloquence of de Brébeuf they refused to take the missionaries back with them on the journey home. So, leaving the four Jesuits to look after things in Quebec, Le Jeune set out with his Montagnais to pass the winter in the forest.

He was not acting blindly. He knew perfectly well all the horrors of an Indian wigwam: its filth; its indecency; its sufferings; its dangers. There was even a very great likelihood of his never returning alive, but the attempt had to be made, otherwise he would be forever dumb among the neophytes. Fortunately he kept a fairly exact diary of what occurred, though it is surprising how he did it. It presents us with a tableau of the Indian life in one of its worst aspects. Some idea of it may be of service in helping us to estimate the character of the man who dared to face its horrors and privations.

He was very much annoyed at that time by a disreputable savage, a handsome and intelligent fellow, but who had completely wrecked his health by his immorality, and who moreover pretended to be a sorcerer. He had done all he

9

could to discredit Le Jeune in the eyes of the Indians, and hearing of the proposed winter expedition he determined to be one of the party, but Le Jeune stubbornly persisted that he was not to be accepted, and exacted a promise to that effect, which, of course, the Indians did not keep. A lie never troubled the red man.

The day of the departure arrived. Le Jeune loaded into the canoe a barrel of bread, a sack of meal, some ears of corn, and a supply of prunes and turnips. That was to serve through the winter with what ever else could be picked up. He was urged very strongly to take with him a small cask of wine, but he stoutly refused, for he was afraid that some one would get drunk, but as they all solemnly promised not to touch it without his permission he consented; but he regretted it afterwards. Finally, on October 18, he bade good-bye to Champlain, who strongly recommended the Indians to take care of him. The chief in command of the expedition promised that if the Father died, he himself would never be seen in his tribe again. There was some comfort in that, though the Frenchmen who had come down to the river bank to see them off were full of gloomy forebodings, as the shallop and canoe left the shore. Le Jeune was the only white man among twenty Indians—men, women, and children.

It was ten o'clock in the morning; the wind and tide were favorable, and they passed the Isle d'Orleans, and reached a place which the enthusiastic missionary found to be wonderfully beautiful. There the camp was pitched, and while Mestigoit, the Indian who was responsible for Le Jeune, took his gun and started out to shoot something for supper, the squaws busied themselves in putting up the hut. Everybody was working except Pierre, the Gallicized Indian, whom Le Jeune from that out designates as the apostate. He was watching, and saw his chance. He made for the cask of wine in the boat and drank and drank till he was stupidly drunk. Then, after first tumbling into the river and nearly drowning himself, he staggered into the camp howling like a demon and proceeded to tear down the hut. The squaws in alarm fled to the woods. Mestigoit had returned meantime with some birds and was boiling them in the pot over the fire, when Pierre rolled up towards him, threw down the pole on which the pot was hanging, and upset the contents in the ashes.

Mestigoit, however, showed no sign of anger, but quietly picked up the birds, and proceeded to wash them in the river, while Pierre, now foaming at the mouth, made after the women who had returned to gather up some of their traps. They decamped again and he pursued them into the woods. It was now dark night, and after a while the furious man returned, attracted by the glare of the fire, and tried to upset the pot again, but his loving brother Mestigoit anticipated him and flung the scalding water in his face. That did not altogether sober him, but at least it diverted his fury for a moment from the pot and he made another assault on the hut, which he now completely demolished. At this stage Le Jeune approached to calm him, although the Indian was looking for an axe to kill somebody. "Don't be afraid," he stammered out; "it is not for you, but for somebody else. You and I ought to go home; you don't know these people. They don't care for you at all. They only want to feed on you."

The advice was not taken, of course, and, leaving the unfortunate wretch to himself, for it was useless to talk to him, the priest went off to the woods to sleep, stretching himself on a pile of leaves far enough away not to hear the drunken man's shouts.

"Such," he said, "was my first lodging; under the light of the moon; and in this wise was I inducted into this savage academy for the study of their language. Rain came on after a while, but it did not last long, and next morning I found that my bed, which had not been made since the creation of the world, was not as hard as I fancied it would be."

The first thing he did on awakening was to empty the barrel of wine in the river, in spite of the protests of the Indians.

" Pierre has no sense," they said, " we will not touch it "; " but I stuck to my resolution," says Le Jeune, " of making this contribution to the river, lest a little wine might make us drink a good deal of water; for if they all got drunk the St. Lawrence would swallow us up.

"That night, under the brilliant moonlight," he continues, " we reached White Duck Island. It was well named. I saw a thousand of these fowl in a single flock. There was no one living there. It was only a stopping place for our roaming savages; but a painter would have been delighted to be seated on its high and jagged rocks, crowned with cedars and pines and a variety of other kinds of trees with which art seemed to have had something to do in planting them on the edges of those gloomy and beetling crags which towered above the bays and swamps, that were swarming with game."

Another day's journey brought them to a barren rock, where they could scarcely find saplings big enough to build their hut. They had had nothing to eat all day, except a biscuit, and there was no water to drink, for the St. Lawrence is brackish there. Wind and rain penetrated the miserable shelter, and during the night the storm carried off their shallop and then their little bark canoe. The travellers were thus left on a barren island. Instead of getting angry, however, the Indians began to laugh, and when the priest showed some annoyance the chief said: "Don't worry, Nicanis, my beloved, worry brings sadness, and sadness sickness." The missionary remembered the lesson forever afterwards.

When morning dawned, they saw the boats a long distance off on the rocks, and when the tide was out, they were able to recover them. Though they expected to find them badly shattered they were, on the contrary, comparatively uninjured. But it was impossible to leave the rock on account of the storm, and one night while they were there, and all the men but one were away, a squaw ran into the wigwam screaming that she had seen the devil and that he was outside. Le Jeune went out to interview his Satanic Majesty, but he saw nothing and though he shouted at the top of his voice defying him to put in an appearance, nothing occurred, and the terrified squaws were tranquillized. When the braves returned, they heard with amazement of the audacity of the white man. His influence was supreme after that, but the sorcerer, who was to ruin all his work, had not yet arrived.

"On the 30th of October," says Le Jeune, "we reached an island with a name larger than itself. Indeed I think that the savages coin these appellations on the spur of the moment." There was not a tree of any size on it, and that night, the few pine branches they could gather scarcely covered the snow on which they had to stretch themselves. It was on that barren rock that the evil genius of the expedition, the sorcerer, found them. "To think of it," says Le Jeune ruefully, "he came on the Feast of All Saints."

His arrival inaugurated a succession of feasts which were celebrated with as much assurance of the future as "if all the beasts that had to be hunted for in the woods were safely housed in stalls near by." Le Jeune attempted a speech at one of the banquets, and was laughed at uproariously, for his knowledge of the language was as yet very elementary. "Wait till I can speak," he said, "and I shall tell you plenty of things that will make you listen," and he contrived somehow or other to put questions to them about the natural phenomena, which they confessed they could not answer.

At another revel there was a theological battle with the sorcerer and it is curious how that wild man of the woods was puzzling over the same objections against the existence of God and the necessity of belief as the learned philosophers of civilized countries. Le Jeune begged the apostate Algonquin Pierre to help him out with his explanations and proofs, but the surly wretch, who could have been of great assistance, refused to open his mouth.

It was now the 12th of November, and leaving their two boats on the little island, the party struck out into the woods in search of game. There they remained till April 22nd, camping in twenty-three different places, on high mountains and deep valleys, in woods and in swamps, but always in the snow. There were lakes, and ponds, and rivers to cross; all of them, however, were solid ice. Some other Indians had meantime joined them, making forty-two persons all told, who found shelter in the three wigwams. In Le Jeune's there were nineteen inmates. Camp was shifted as soon as the game was exhausted, and the party started on its journey with a mouthful to eat if there was anything to be had, but often passing whole days with nothing at all.

Men, women, and children put their packs on their backs, and with their long toboggans tramped from morning to night in the snow. If there was a thaw they were often up to their waists in icy water. Le Jeune tried to build the huts with the others, but he was so stiff with cold that he could scarcely move, and had to wait till the fire was made. The savages who were sweating at their work could not understand why he suffered, nor why he was unable to carry a heavy load on the trail. Even he felt ashamed of himself when he saw a poor sick squaw, carried on a stretcher, wait patiently in the snow for hours until the wigwam was made, without ever showing a sign of impatience.

At one of these stations, while supper was being prepared, the sorcerer suddenly sprung to his feet and announced with a loud shout that his senses had left him. At times he yelled with all the power of his lungs, and stopped short as if frightened; he laughed, and cried, and sang without measure or meaning; he hissed like a serpent and howled like a wolf; he was an owl and a wildcat; his eyes rolled in his head, and he groped around him as if he wanted to seize something. Le Jeune expected to be struck at any moment, but he kept his eyes on the maniac, or sometimes quietly read his book or wrote while these antics were going on. He even stretched himself out on the ground and pretended to sleep.

The next night the same performance was repeated. " I thought perhaps," says the priest, " that it was the delirium of a fever, and I went over and felt his pulse. He glared at me astounded, and began to roll his eyes wildly. I then passed my hand over his forehead and found him as cold as a fish, and as far from a fever as I was from France. He was shamming. It was all put on to get his staring companions to give him out of pity the best food they had."

The poor missionary tried his best from time to time to talk to the sick squaw, who was sinking rapidly. No doubt he would have put some good thoughts in her mind, but whatever he said or did was thwarted by his enemy the sorcerer. Finally the poor woman was either killed or abandoned in the woods. She disappeared mysteriously in the night and Le Jeune never saw her again. He tried to bring the magician himself to a sense of better things, and the miserable fellow agreed to throw away his conjuror's drum and the other implements of his profession, if Le Jeune would cure him of the disease that was hurrying him to the grave; but his desire of Christianity went no further, and entreaties, expostulations, and explanations were lost on him.

By this time they were opposite Tadoussac, and as there was nothing to eat, the savages invited each other to a feast of tobacco. They were so addicted to the weed that not only was the pipe in their mouth the first thing in the morning, and the last at night, but if they awoke from their sleep their hand went out instinctively to their tobacco pouch. The missionary had a supply of tobacco with him, but not for himself. It was a tuition fee to his professors for helping him in his study of the native speech.

About this time he lost himself in the woods, which was bad enough, but he barely escaped being killed by the savages because a little boy who had followed him on a false trail failed to reach the camp along with him. Fortunately the child was discovered in time by two squaws who went out to look for him.

It was Christmas Day and the savages, now on the verge of starvation, implored him to do something. By dint of persuasion he induced the apostate Indian to translate a little prayer into the language of the people, and the next morning he built an altar in the cabin, decorated it as best he could with a crucifix, a reliquary, and picture he had in his breviary. He then, with the help of his interpreter, explained to the Indians that he wanted them to ask God to assist them. Kneeling down, he made them all repeat the prayer after him. Only the sorcerer refused. But all were astonished when they heard the priest make the offering of his own life to God if He would deign to come to the aid of the suffering people. "No, don't say that," they cried; "we all love you." At last even the sorcerer joined in the prayer. When the prayer was over all the men started out on the hunt, and at evening came back loaded with game. Only the apostate was unsuccessful, and he disgusted the priest by saying that there was no need of prayer after all, for the animals were there if the people had known enough to go out to hunt for them.

Le Jeune had passed triumphantly through the period of famine with unimpaired health. Nor did the fresh meat of the moose and elk disagree with him; but the filthy dried beef he had to subsist on at one time brought on a sickness that did not leave him for three weeks after he had returned to civilization. The sorcerer was delighted to see him fall ill. "It is the manitou that is afflicting you," he said, "for mocking at him." Over and over again the taunt was repeated till the people began to believe it. The priest could bear it no longer and starting up from his miserable couch, he cried out: "Come, manitou! Come, devil! Kill me if you have the power. I defy you. I scorn you and do not fear you. You have no power over those who believe and love God. Come, kill me if your hands are free, but you have more fear of me than I have of you."

The sorcerer stood aghast. "Why do you call him—do you want him to kill you?" "No, but I want to let you know that he has no power over those who adore the true God, and to let you see he is not the cause of this sickness. It is the meat and nothing else." The medicine man held his peace after that and soon left the party. But poor Le Jeune felt his limbs becoming paralyzed from lying on the icy ground. He finally succeeded in purchasing a small piece of elkskin from a squaw. It was only half long enough, but it kept off the chill to some extent.

On the 4th of April they were back again on the little island where they had left their boat, and on the 5th Le Jeune and Mestigoit started up the river for Quebec. It had to be done, for the priest's strength had given out, and it would never do to return to the city with the news that he was dead. With him was the unfortunate apostate. That journey was a fitting climax of the winter's expedition.

The weather was still very cold, and a little up the stream they found a thin coat of ice on the river, but Mestigoit broke it with his paddle as they went along. They had, however, miscalculated its thickness or forgot the condition of their bark canoe. A cake of ice cut through the bow and " the water poured into the boat and fear into our hearts," says Le Jeune. "We made for an island which was fortunately near by, I bailing and the Indians paddling. We reached the shore; the red men lifted their boat out of the water, turned it upside down, struck fire with their flint, and very deftly mended the break in the bark with some gum which they found on the trees, and in a very short time the canoe was afloat again and we were on our way as if nothing had happened. 'If the break had been a little bigger we were lost,' said the Indian. 'Well, why not remain on shore till the river is clear?' he was asked. 'Oh, that thin ice is nothing,' was the answer."

About three in the afternoon there was plenty of ice thick enough to satisfy the most confident Indian. It stretched clean across the river for three or four leagues, but there was a break in it and thither the canoe was directed. It was a perilous trick, for the boat had to wriggle to the right and the left, to avoid the huge pieces which a gust of wind might at any moment hurl against the frail bark, and crush it like corn under a mill-stone. Finally, aware of the danger, the Indians jumped from cake to cake, like squirrels on the trees, and pushed the boat away from them. Le Jeune remained in the canoe. He was too weak to move. They thus kept up the battle till five o'clock and then went ashore, where they ate a little dried beef, lighted a fire, and lay down at the foot of a tree and went to sleep.

Early next morning they started out again. The tide had carried off the heavy ice to the other side of the river, but the wind arose and as the canoe began to dance too recklessly on the waves the travellers had to land again. There was another night of cold and exposure on the bleak shore under the canoe, and the next night the same thing was repeated. Meantime the provisions were giving out, and the two Indians started out to hunt for food. Mestigoit shot a partridge, and that served as breakfast, dinner, and supper for all three. The fierce winds kept them prisoners there for another day and a night. Their bed was the bare ground, but it was better than being caught on some barren island without even wood to make a fire. There was some comfort in that thought.

While the two Indians were out hunting, and the Father was alone on the rocks, the sun suddenly came from behind the clouds, the wind subsided, and the river became smooth. Now was the time to make head up the stream. As he lifted

PAUL LE JEUNE

his eyes he saw the two redskins making like deer for the river. Le Jeune knew what it meant and he hurried down with his traps to the canoe, and in a few minutes the boat was skimming like a bird over the surface of the St. Lawrence. At ten o'clock that night they were at the end of the Isle d'Orleans, only six miles from home. They had not eaten a bite that day, but it was impossible to go any farther, for the tide was running out, and they could not cross the river to the St. Charles, so they ran into a little cove, lighted a fire on the beach, and went to sleep. At midnight the tide changed, and there was a bright moonlight. Both wind and tide made the canoe scud rapidly on its way, but when they reached the St. Charles they found ice everywhere; huge blocks of it were piled upon the shore and battering against each other, threatening to crush the canoe if it ventured near. So they had to put about and face the incoming tide. It is in such circumstances that the skill of the savage displays itself. Mestigoit stood in the bow.

"I could see him in the obscurity (for the moon had gone down) as he stiffened his sinews in the struggle with death," says Le Jeune. "He steadied the frail bark in the midst of waves that might have swamped a ship. 'Make for Quebec, Nicanis,' I cried. When we doubled Sailors' Point, around which the St. Charles emptied into the St. Lawrence, you could have seen him yield before one wave, then cut another midway, dodge one cake of ice, shove another aside, all the while fighting steadily against the furious north wind that was driving in his face.

"We were out of the stream at last, but the ice floes tossed and tumbled about by the fury of the winds shut us off from the shore. We were in front of the fort, keeping as close as we could to the beach, and seeking some inlet or a part of the ice which was sheltered from the wind, but without success. Quick as a flash the Indian thrust aside with his paddle three or four blocks that were bearing down on us, and then made a leap from the canoe, crying, 'Ashore! ashore!' But the ice was so high and thick that I could not reach the top with my hands; so I seized the Indian's ankle with one hand and a projecting piece of ice with another,

19

and eventually reached the top. Even a heavy man becomes agile in such circumstances. We were out of the canoe, which we pulled up after us, and then gazed at each other breathless. 'Nicanis,' he said, 'we were nearly lost.' Even he had still the horror of death depicted on his face. Indeed, had he not been the giant that he was, and a man of more than usual skill, we should have been capsized by the gale, or a cake of ice would have crushed us. Or, rather, had not God been our pilot, the waves that dashed against the shores where our little dwelling was built would have been our sepulchre."

Singularly enough they did not seek shelter in Quebec that night, but travelled further up the St. Charles where the ice was solid and at three o'clock on the morning of Easter Sunday, April the 9th, Le Jeune awoke the occupants of Notre Dame des Neiges, who welcomed him with wonder and delight. Next day, Champlain sent two of the chief men of Quebec to inquire about the missionary's health, and the great Indian chief of the country came to visit him. There was much rejoicing and weeping among them as he told the tale of the journey. The rest of Le Jeune's party came up the St. Lawrence later.

FATHER LE JEUNE.

CHAPTER II.

FOUNDATIONS.

Shortly after Le Jeune's return to Quebec missionaries began to arrive, and he saw the possibility of doing something for the nomadic tribes north of the St. Lawrence. They could not be reached like the Hurons, who had fixed habitations, and the only solution of the problem was to establish stations at the places where they were accustomed to meet at certain periods of the year for trade. The savages, who might possibly be instructed during their short sojourn in such places, would exert some influence on their tribes later on, and thus be a means of introducing the missionaries into the interior of the country, which so far had never been visited.

The first of the outposts was at Three Rivers, where some enterprising French colonists had built their huts and erected a fort. Thither Le Jeune repaired with Buteux, who became afterwards the great apostle of the Indians in that section.

Tadoussac, one hundred and twenty miles down the river, was another important position, known even long before Cartier's time as a trading post. The Recollects had already been there, but had left no permanent establishment. Hence, in 1648 Le Jeune went thither with de Quen, and founded a mission post among the Indians, which the Jesuits attended long after the suppression of their society.

A third mission was that of Miscou, on a little island on the Baie des Chaleurs. It never figured to any great extent in the history of the Canadian missions, although the heroic men who were sent thither underwent awful sufferings. Their journeys led them as far as Richibouctou, Miramachi, Nipisiguit, Chedabouctou and Gaspé. They even descended to Acadia and Cape Breton.

Sillery, near Quebec, which was also one of Le Jeune's foundations, was projected on a more ambitious scale. It was intended for educational and hospital work among the Indians, and it was hoped that by inducing a certain number of families to settle there they could be taught the elements of agriculture. For that purpose more money was needed than the miserable one hundred dollars doled out to the missionary at Tadoussac. "It was a delusion," Le Jeune wrote to his friends in France, "to imagine that the savage would be so charmed by the sight of the French colonists sowing the fields and reaping a rich harvest and living in comfort, as to be quickly induced to do the same. Even if an Indian were seized with a desire to work, where would he get his tools?" asks Le Jeune, "and supposing he did succeed in gathering his crop, where would he store it? Not in his miserable bark hut. Besides, where would he live while his crop was ripening? In brief, a good deal of money would be needed to build houses for them to begin with." The trading company was willing to give land, but would do no more, and the difficulty arose as to how the poor savage would fell the trees and clear his farm? Evidently he had to be helped.

Year after year Le Jeune kept urging these needs upon the wealthy people in France, who were supposed to take some interest in the colony. At last he found a friend in the person of Noël Brulard de Sillery, a nobleman of the court of Henry IV. Sillery had been entrusted with offices of the greatest distinction, was very rich, and indeed was known as "The Magnificent" because of the sumptuousness of his many establishments.

Urged by his sister, he withdrew from the world and betook himself to a life of good works. He heard of Le Jeune's appeal, and forthwith made over a generous supply of money and sent twenty men to build the houses and clear the land. The result was that, in 1637, at a place called Kamiskoua Ouangachit, Le Jeune laid the foundation of a house for the missionaries, a school for the neophytes, and a hospital and church. He called the establishment after the founder, Sillery. Two Algonquin families, consisting of twenty persons, were the first to be admitted to it. In 1641 there were thirty families, and in 1641 it could boast of a number of Christian Indians who astounded the people of Quebec by the holiness of their lives. Le Jeune was constantly among them, and not only preaching and instructing, but teaching them the arts of civilization. For the Indians he was a man of miracles. Marie de l'Incarnation wrote of the red men of the reservation that you could not find anywhere purer or simpler souls, or people more eager to observe the laws of God. "We are used to them here," she said, "but the French who arrive from Europe regard them with wonder and amazement. You cannot go to the chapel any time in the day without finding an Indian there praying, and if any one in the settlement misbehaves himself he disappears immediately, being well aware that he would have to undergo a rude penance. If he refused, his presence would not be tolerated."

Meantime Le Jeune had built Notre Dame de Recouvrance in Quebec, and assigned Fathers Charles Lalemant and de Noüe to it. The transformation effected in the city by the pious exercises that were practised, the fervor with which the offices of the Church were followed, seem to be almost incredible as we read the account. But we have this solid fact to build on, which redounds greatly to the credit of Quebec, namely: that, up to 1667, that is, for a period of more than thirty years, although there had been 674 baptisms, the official register shows only one illegitimate birth. This is most remarkable when we reflect that the population, besides the colonists, had in it a large contingent of soldiers, sailors and *voyageurs*.

Another scheme which Le Jeune had been elaborating was that of the education of Indian boys. He had decided to begin with the Hurons, who were more stable than the other tribes, and he resolved to start the work at Quebec. A school in the Indian country would never succeed, for no Indian father would ever permit his young hopeful to be punished, and in all likelihood that aid to scholarship would have to be invoked. When Father Daniel, who had promised to procure twelve Huron lads, appeared with only two, Le Jeune had to give up the plan of restricting it to Hurons, and he took those he could pick up anywhere. Not that there was any uncertainty or vacillation in his proceeding; he was doing the best he could under the circumstances.

But when the scholars arrived he had not only no place to lodge them, but no means to support them. No interest in the plan had been aroused, and the best he could do was to install them in Notre Dame des Anges, an arrangement as inconvenient for the boys as it was for the Fathers. It did not take long to show the hopelessness of it all. Besides draining all of Le Jeune's slender resources, "the young savages were as hard to manage as wild asses," he wrote gloomily. One after the other broke away and made for the woods, or were so deplorably wicked that they had to be dismissed. Only one turned out well, a boy who was named after Richelieu, Armand-Jean. He was true to his training till the end of his life. It would have been worth building half a dozen schools to have formed him. We have told the story of this lad elsewhere. This first Indian seminary lasted scarcely five years.

The failure of the undertaking was very gratifying to a certain number of people who had never left France, but who fancied they knew all about America. They were sure that such would be the result, and that the Jesuits were all along on the wrong track. The proper way to train the Indian was to make him a Frenchman in language, dress, manners, etc. Indeed there was a party formed at court which demanded what they called the Francization of the savages. Even the great Colbert insisted on it. Later on, when Mgr. Laval came to Quebec, positive orders were given to effect this transformation, and Talon was instructed to see that they were carried out. Hence, a short time afterwards, Laval informed the Home Government that he had establishd a seminary for that purpose, and to hasten the work he had put several little French boys on the benches with the savages. The effect on the white children may be imagined. The institution was closed, or rather the six little Hurons who had to be checked in the evil things they were teaching their white companions in the Seminary of the Infant Jesus took to the woods and disappeared. Like Father Le Jeune's, that institution also lasted only five years.

The Sulpicians at Montreal, under de Queylus, made an effort in the same direction in 1668, and were warmly felicitated by Colbert, who did all he could to ensure its success. In a few years the king " complained that the priests of the seminary did not apply themselves to the work." The king was mistaken. The Sulpicians did their best, but you cannot change a race in a single generation. The French government, however, has persisted in this policy whenever it has established a colony. The zeal with which the French missionaries all over the world at the present time endeavor to Frenchify their neophytes is very remarkable. But the wisdom of it may be questioned.

Very naturally, while dreaming of a school for Indian boys, Le Jeune saw the necessity of a similar institution for girls. He wrote to the Provincial about it in 1633, but without any practical result. In 1635 he reported that a great many nuns in France had written to him about the desire to devote themselves to the American missions. " There are so many inquiries," he said, " from such different kinds of convents, even the strictest, that you would imagine they were laughing at the difficulties of the journey, the storms of the ocean, and the savagery of the country."

In that year Marie de l'Incarnation was telling her spiritual director about her wishes in this regard, and among other things, she spoke of a vision she had had. The director was Father Dinet, the rector of the Jesuit College of Tours. "Your dream," he said [he refused to call it a vision], "can be realized by going to Canada."

But the wise Le Jeune had written:

"Do not let them hurry. If they come they must have a good and a well built house, with ample revenues, otherwise they would be a burden on our hands. Men can put up with difficulties, but a convent calls for a house, cleared lands and money, so as to help and to comfort the wretched Indian girls and women in their poverty. My God," he added, "if the extravagances and superfluities of some of the ladies of France were employed in the holy work what a blessing it would bring upon their families. Here are tender and delicate virgins ready to risk their lives on the waves of the ocean, to come to seek a few poor souls in a country much colder than that of France. They are willing to undertake work at which even men balk, and we cannot find any valiant woman who will give these Amazons of the Great God a chance to attempt the work by endowing a house where the Divine Majesty will be praised and served in this distant world. I cannot imagine that Our Lord will not inspire some one in this matter."

This eloquent appeal fell under the eyes of Mme. de la Peltrie, and the effect was immediate. She went to see Marie de l'Incarnation, and the arrangement was made to establish the Ursulines at Quebec. That splendid house of education, which is still one of the glories of Canada, thus owes its origin to Father Le Jeune.

He had succeeded in getting only a partial foundation for a hospital at Sillery. Munificent as the gift was, it was far from satisfactory. Besides, there were no nuns to take charge of it. But the apostolic utterance in the "Relation" of 1635, which had so deeply impressed Mme. de la Peltrie, produced a similar effect in the heart of a still greater personage, the Duchesse d'Aiguillon, the niece of the great Richelieu.

PAUL LE JEUNE

She was interested in charitable works, and naturally thought of the Hospital Nuns at Dieppe. She inquired if they would think of going to America. Whereupon she wrote to Le Jeune: "After having read the 'Relation' which you wrote, God inspired me with the desire of establishing the Hospital Nuns in New France, and for that purpose to send over six workmen to clear the ground and begin a house for those excellent religious."

Le Jeune could not have received more delightful intelligence. Dieppe was the place where he had last labored in France, and these were the very nuns whose Constitution he had drawn up. He borrowed the methods, spirit and name from that of the Daughters of Mercy, and created the new Congregation of the Religious of the Mercy of Jesus.

Richelieu united with his niece in establishing this new foundation. He assured it a revenue of 22,400 livres, besides procuring for it a grant of seven acres in the City of Quebec and sixty more between Cape Rouge and the Coteau Sainte-Geneviève. The only condition imposed was that prayers should be offered for the Cardinal Duc de Richelieu and Madame la Duchesse d'Aiguillon, and also for the Indians. By a fortunate coincidence the three nuns of Dieppe were to embark on the same ship as Mme. de la Peltrie and Marie de l'Incarnation. The Duchesse d'Aiguillon, writing to her beneficiaries, expressed herself as sure that the two communities would get on well together.

They set out on May 4, 1639, and had a perilous voyage. On July 31st, which no doubt Le Jeune thought auspicious, the ship doubled Cape Tourmente, and as the sun was setting they passed the upper end of the Isle d'Orleans and saw the white cascade of Montmorency. The next morning their eyes rested on the rock of Quebec, whose scattered houses were but half revealed amidst the trees which crowned its summit. Their arrival was a great event for the colony, and in good French fashion the holy women knelt down and kissed the ground which they were going to consecrate by their labor. Montmagny met them at the landing place and led them, with great pomp and ceremony, to the temporary quarters they were to occupy.

The happiest man that day was Le Jeune. "Am I dreaming?" he asked, as the news came of their arrival. "Here on one ship are an Ursuline convent, a hospital directed by nuns, and a Jesuit college." The foundation of that college was also partially his work.

René Rohault, the eldest son of the Marquis de Gamache, had been received into the Society of Jesus by Father Coton, and was assigned to the Canadian missions. When bidding farewell to his father in 1626 he asked that his patrimony should be devoted to the establishment of a college at Quebec. The aged Marquis consented, and made over to Father Coton the sum of 16,000 livres d'or for the purpose designated by his son, and added as his own gift a yearly revenue of 3,000 livres while he lived.

The occupation of Quebec by the English interfered with the plan, but as soon as Le Jeune reached Canada he laid the foundation of the college near Fort St. Louis, on a piece of land twelve acres in extent, which was granted in perpetuity for that purpose by the Company of the One Hundred Associates. In the concession of this property de Luson, the Governor, gave it to the Fathers in mortmain, without obligation or condition, and " in recognition of the services rendered by the said Fathers both to the savages and the French, they having been engaged, at the peril of their lives, in the conversion of the savages, and having ever contributed mightily to the establishment of the colony."

The only stipulation in Rohault's gift was that the college should be established for the spiritual aid and education of Canadians. The spiritual part of it was, of course, sure to be attended to; but in 1637 Le Jeune was able to write to the Father General: "The college, which began with one class and a few pupils, is growing every day on account of the arrival of new colonists from France. We are now teaching Latin, French, Montagnais and Huron." In Ragueneau's letter to the General in 1651 we find that there were then two regular classes, one of grammar and the other of mathematics, and a third was about to be formed. In 1655 it had four professors, one of whom taught philosophy, another humanities and rhetoric, and a third grammar. The fourth class was for the elements. In that year Louis XIV added to the foundation a grant of 400 livres. In 1665 it could boast of a professor of theology, and a little later, at the request of Governor Beauharnais and of the Intendant Noquart, the Ministre de la Marine Maurepas sent over 300 livres to support another professor. In 1671 there was a course of higher mathematics and hydrography. This branch was strongly encouraged by Talon, who saw in it a means of preparing a large contingent of navigators and handicraftsmen who would be extremely useful to the colonial government. The popular drift at that time was in the direction of the positive sciences— physics, astronomy, geography and navigation—and the common demand had to be heeded. In a work published in 1671 and entitled *Description du Canada,* the author advocates rather ambitiously the establishment of an *Académie de Marine* for the training of pilots and explorers. The king even sent a set of mathematical instruments to encourage the work. The study of Latin was for a time in disfavor, though we find that regular monthly disputations in philosophy were held, and that such men as Joliet defended the theses, and even distinguished officials like Talon condescended to appear as objectors. In furthering this collegiate development, however, the colonial authorities counted for nothing. It bent all its energies to the increase of trade, and let the Jesuits bear the whole burden of providing money for the enlargement of their institution.

As early as 1661 the Bishop, Mgr. Laval, writes that the education given in the school was on the same footing as in Europe. Music was taught and public literary exhibitions were given. In 1658 the new Governor d'Argenson presided at a dramatic representation written for the occasion. Fifty years later Father Germain could report to his superiors in France that everything went on in Quebec as in the colleges of Europe, and perhaps with more regularity and exactness. The students were industrious, eager and capable. In 1712 there was a two years' course of philosophy, and another two of theology. Such was the result of what Le Jeune had begun in 1637.

It will be of interest to add here that the first college which was built in 1635 was only a wooden structure and did not last more than five years. It went up in the same fire that consumed Champlain's votive church of the Recouvrance. Another building was erected in 1648 by Brother Liègois, and had the distinction of being, at that time, the only stone building in Quebec besides the fort. It could accommodate fifty or sixty boarders. It was there that Joliet studied. While it was being built classes were held on the ground floor of the warehouse of the One Hundred Associates, which was probably on the northwest corner of the property of the present Anglican cathedral.

There is a common impression that the great building known in Quebec as the *Caserne des Jesuites*, which was demolished in 1878, was the edifice built by Brother Liègois. Indeed, one of the literary celebrities of Canada has, in perfect good faith, written some very eloquent pages on that theme. But, as a matter of fact, that particular structure was erected somewhere between 1725 and 1730. In Charlevoix's *Journal d'un voyage fait par ordre du Roy, dans l'Amérique Septentrionale, addressé à Madame la Duchesse de Lestiguières*, he says:

"You have, no doubt, seen, Madame, in some accounts that the Jesuit College is a beautiful edifice. It is certain that when Quebec was a shapeless jumble of French barracks and Indian huts, it and the fort cut something of a figure because they were in stone. The first travellers, speaking comparatively, represented it as a fine building. Those who came after, and who, as usual, copied the first accounts, made use of the same language. But since then the cabins have disappeared and the barracks have been replaced by houses, most of them fairly well built, while the college now disgraces the city and is falling into ruin."

These lines were written in 1720, but were published only in 1744, and in that edition there is a note appended to the description, which was then twenty-four years old: "They have since rebuilt the college, which is now very beautiful." As every one knows, the site of that college is at present occupied by the City Hall.

It is somewhat amusing to read that when Bishop Fenwick, of Boston, who was a Jesuit, went to Quebec and saw the I. H. S. over the main entrance, he asked what the building was, and being told that it was the old Jesuit College and that it was then being used as a barracks, he grew very angry and refused to enter a building which, he said, "was the home of martyrs like Jogues, de Brébeuf and others, and was now polluted by men of blood."

The sentiment was indeed correct, but unfortunately the historical basis for it was not altogether solid. Jogues, de Brébeuf and others of their time were never inside of it. They had died a hundred years before, for it had been used as a college only about thirty or forty years, as the Society of Jesus was suppressed in 1773.

Champlain saw the first college opened. He died on Christmas Day, 1635. His demise was a great blow to the colony, but it had been expected for some time. Le Jeune pronounced the funeral oration. "I did not lack material," he said, with which sentiment all will agree. It was regarded as a remarkable discourse, but it is to be regretted that he did not leave us a sketch of what he said on that occasion. It would have been an historical document. But he was the Superior in Quebec, and had no one to order him to do things. He was a sort of Government official also, and it was he who was delegated by the Company of the One Hundred Associates to announce to the colonists the temporary appointment of Chateaufort as Governor.

Montmagny, who arrived soon after, was a worthy successor of Champlain. He was Le Jeune's devoted friend. They were often together, and on one occasion we find them on the St. Lawrence as far up as the end of Lake St. Peter, and entering the Iroquois or Richelieu River. On this visit he gave the name of St. Ignatius to the largest of the beautiful islands at the mouth of the river. They travelled up to Montreal, and on the way back they entered the Rivière des Prairies, which flows behind the Island of Montreal, and went ashore on the Isle Jesus, to which they gave the name Montmagny, in honor of the Governor. On that occasion Le Jeune offered the Holy Sacrifice "the first time, as far as I know," he writes, "that mass was ever celebrated on that island." Unfortunately, he does not give us any information which would enable us to identify the place, nor does he tell us the exact date of the visit. We only know that after leaving the island they sailed down to Three Rivers, which they left on October 4th, and that it was the year 1636. He informs us in passing that the river north of the Isle of Jesus, which is now known as Mille Isles, then went by the name of St. Jean, in honor of Jean Nicolet, " who had frequently passed there," and who is described as "an interpreter and clerk in the store at Three Rivers." The present name of Rivière des Prairies was given because a certain man named des Prairies lost his way among the islands there, instead of keeping up the St. Lawrence, where his friends were waiting for him.

At Three Rivers Le Jeune had witnessed a hideous scene of torture of an Iroquois prisoner which had filled them with horror, and he refers to it briefly. But he recounts with relief, if not with pleasure, a little hunting adventure which took place as his boat was sailing down the St. Lawrence to Quebec. They were then about four or five leagues

below Three Rivers. He writes rather poetically about it,
and says:

"We were sailing peacefully along in the glory of a
golden day when we perceived a great elk browsing on the
shore. The Governor ordered the sails to be lowered and
bidding every one to be silent sent two or three Frenchmen
in a little canoe to drive the animal into the river, or shoot
it if it made for the woods. The hunters landed and drew
near, but hearing the noise the elk took to the river. Immediately the shallop was launched and the strong arms of the
rowers drove it swiftly over the waters in pursuit. Poor
beast," says Le Jeune, "it did not know where to turn; it
saw the hunters on shore with their arquebuses, and on the
water the shallop was speeding toward it. It was the men
in the boat who finally killed it and hoisted it on the deck.
If all the journeys in New France," he continues, "could
be as peaceful as that, the country would be more attractive,
and perhaps the body would gain more than the soul; for elk
and beaver and fish are not lacking in their season. May
God be praised by all his angels for the blessings he bestows
on men. We reached Quebec on the 7th of October."

Arriving in the city, he was immediately engrossed in
the ceaseless work of instructing the Indians. It was a
wearisome task, but those old Frenchmen had the knack of
lightening labors with good humor. We find in his diary
a question of woman's rights. "One day," he says, "a
squaw came to me and wanted to know if woman could
not go to heaven as well as men and children. 'Certainly,'
I replied, 'Then why don't you instruct us as well as
the men and children?' I assured her that her protest
was well founded, and appointed a time for catechism class
for women, but I had to give it up, for they all brought
their babies, and the noise was so great that we could not
get on at all."

Some students of Indian characteristics have said that
Indian babies did not cry. This incident would seem to suggest the contrary, unless the little heathens were in that
instance protesting against Christianity.

On the 10th of January Le Jeune had to solve some problems in astronomy and physics for an old Indian whose name is a philological and almost a physical problem. It was Makheabichtichiou. He was troubled about the lunar eclipses. When he was told that they were caused by the earth coming between the moon and the sun, he said "that it couldn't be so, for the earth often got between the sun and the moon without any eclipse coming." "I told him," said Le Jeune, "that as the heavens were so vast and the earth so small, such interventions did not occur as often as he thought, and when I illustrated it by passing a torch around a ball, he was satisfied."

"But the red man had another difficulty. 'Why was the sky sometimes red and sometimes another color?' I said it was due to the vapors of the clouds varying in density. I took a triangular prism. 'There,' said I, holding it off from him, 'it looks white, does it not?' 'Yes.' 'Now put it to your eye and you will see all sorts of colors.' 'You French are manitous,' he exclaimed; 'you know all about heaven and earth.'"

But these troubles were slight compared with Makheabichtichiou's theological difficulties. He wanted to be a Christian, and took upon himself to explain some of the doctrines of the Faith to his people. But when he made the announcement that Father Le Jeune wished the men to have only one wife, singularly enough he fell into great disfavor with the women. They were more numerous than the men, and hence many of them would be obliged to live in single blessedness. A great tumult ensued, and Makheabichtichiou's life was made miserable for him ever afterwards. He had three wives of his own. "Oh," exclaimed poor Father Le Jeune, "what trouble flesh and blood have to know the sweetness of God."

CHAPTER III.

In the Ranks.

Le Jeune was thus laboring in the humblest works of the ministry, and at the same time directing the energies of all the missionaries from Miscou to Lake Huron; but a change came in 1638. It is announced in the following delightful fashion in the first paragraph of the "Relation" of 1639:

"The birth of a Dauphin, the love and benefaction bestowed by our great king on the savages, the solicitude of M. le Cardinal for this country and his pecuniary aid for the Huron Missions; the assistance given to the neophytes by the gentlemen of New France, the continuation of the government of M. de Montmagny, the arrival of the nuns, the help of many persons of merit and social condition, the prayers and vows of pious souls, the holy Associations which have been formed to draw God's blessing on our Indians, have been the subjects of our conversations on board the ship, not only in our intercourse with the world, but in our personal communication with God. All this joy was so much the more profound, because at the same time I at last enjoyed the sweet liberty for which I have been so eagerly longing, and also because your Reverence has at last accorded it by sending to us the Rev. Father Vimont whose virtues will repair the faults which I have committed in the charge which I have now given into his hands."

In other words, he was no longer Superior. He had descended into the ranks and was free. He left office when every one was happy. After that he is undistinguishable in the throng, and there is nothing noteworthy except that the Provincial in France assigned to him the work of continuing the writing of the "Relations." It was a wise appointment, because of the valuable information which he has given us about early American history. In doing so he was incidentally compelled to describe an occurrence which happened shortly after, and which came near ending his career in America.

"Although we are living here at present in a time of peace," he says, "misfortunes sometimes penetrate into our great forests as into your great cities. Father Vimont our Superior took Father Raimbault and myself on a journey up to Three Rivers. Our boat began its mishaps by being nearly smashed to pieces just off Quebec. Next night, as we were sailing happily along, we ran on a rock. Before we could get off, the tide left us high and dry, and our bark went over on its side. At high tide it straightened up again, but was so battered that it immediately began to fill. We made for the other side of the river, to calk it, and reached the shore just in time. Another quarter of an hour and we should have all gone to the bottom. When the tide rose the boat sunk, but contrary to our expectation it came to the surface again and we hauled it on shore and began to patch it up. While we were at work a gale arose and flung it against the rocks where we thought it would be dashed to pieces; but we secured it again and mended it so that it could float. But the water had spoiled all the provisions we were bringing to the poor Indians. That night we lodged on shore at the sign of the Moon and the Cold and the Rain. Such was the first trip attempted by our Rev. Father Superior. He gave it up and went back to Quebec."

In 1640 Le Jeune was sent to France, and when he arrived he sent a characteristically joyous letter to his Provincial. It is prefixed to the "Relation" of 1641, which he brought with him:

"Reverend Father:
"I am like a man who wrote a letter and then carried it himself. I indited the following chapters in New France and I am going to hand them myself to your Reverence.
"The fleet which carried these few lines over the ocean carried also three of our Society: Father Nicholas Adam, who was recalled by your Reverence because of his shattered health; Father Claude Quentin, who was sent on business of the mission, and your humble servant, who appears without being expected, but not without being sent. For

M. de Montmagny, our Governor, the principal men of the colony, Father Vimont, our Superior, and all our Fathers and the savages themselves have condemned me to undertake the voyage for the public welfare.

"Our fleet of four ships, commanded by the Sieur de Courpon, a brave man and an excellent navigator, was scattered by a tempest at the entrance of the Gulf of St. Lawrence, and we never caught sight of each other on the ocean afterwards. Father Quentin's ship having mistaken St. George's Channel for that which separates France and England, was a long time without making its appearance, but at last God conducted it to port. As we came near land we saw the main mast of a vessel, and other portions of wrecked ships which had gone down on the coast of France. It made one think that there is only one good thing about the sea. It is that you are at every moment in a greater and more immediate and consequently more delightful dependence on God than when you are on land."

He then goes on to tell the Provincial the general drift of what his "Relation" of 1641 contains, and adds:

"I shall console your Reverence by assuring you that you have subjects in the New World who run with great strides in the path of holiness. God gives them favors in abundance. Difficulties awaken courage; want is their treasure; dangers their trust; sufferings their delight; death and the cross their expectation, and the God of the living their exceeding great reward. I hope that as soon as I have acquitted myself of my commission, that your Reverence will hand me my passport for the New World, to die among my neophytes who by their piety and devotion have won the affection of my heart."

"The Relation" of the following year, which was written by Father Vimont after Le Jeune's return to America, begins by saying that the condition of things in Canada had compelled him to send one of the Fathers to France to explain to what a state the incursions of the Iroquois had reduced the infant Church of the colony, and that he could find no one better than the one who had labored so hard to establish it—namely, Father Le Jeune. "Nor was I deceived," he continues, "for during the short time he remained in France he saw many persons of distinction whom he acquainted with the great spiritual riches that could be hoped for here. Among others he induced the Duchesse d'Aiguillon, who had founded a House of Mercy for sick Indians, to obtain from her uncle, the Cardinal, the greatest help against our enemies, the Iroquois. The Father's arrival here revived the sinking spirits of the colonists. They now hold their heads erect with as much assurance as if the fort was already built."

The next six years he was engaged in the routine work of the missions, and in 1649, after the death of de Brébeuf, he departed for France again, never to return. On this journey over the ocean he had with him the remarkable Iroquois who had endeavored to save the life of Father Jogues. We have told his story in the sketch of Father Daniel in Vol. II.

In France he was engaged as Procurator of the Canadian missions, and was so wonderfully successful in interesting the world at large in the work that, when there was a question of changing him from the office, eager entreaties were made by the Fathers in America to leave him at the post.

Later on, when there was need of naming a bishop of Quebec, Le Jeune was the choice of the Queen Regent. Ragueneau and Charles Lalemant were also mentioned, but the Father General forbade the consideration of any Jesuit for that post.

In 1661 Le Jeune made a touching appeal to Louis XIV himself for the perishing colony. It is worth reproducing here. It runs as follows:

" Sire:

" Behold your colony of New France at the feet of Your Majesty. As you will see in this account a small band of savages has reduced it to the last extremity. Listen, Sire, if it so pleases you, to her languishing voice, nay, to her dying words: ' Save me,' she cries, ' I am going to be bereft of the Catholic Faith; they are tearing from my hands the fleur-de-lis; I shall be no longer French; they are taking

from me the beautiful name with which I have so long been
honored; I shall fall into the hands of the strangers, when
the Iroquois shall have drained all my blood which has now
almost ceased to flow; I shall soon be consumed in their
fires,' and, Sire, the demons will bear away a great number
of nations who expect salvation from your piety, your power
and your generosity. Sire, listen to the sighs and the sobs
of your afflicted one. It is almost a year that your children
and your subjects, the dwellers in the New World, made
you know the extremity of the peril in which they were; but
alas! the misfortunes of the time did not permit you to send
them help. But since that time by the prodigies which have
occurred the heavens and the earth have proclaimed to you
the cruelties and the fiery tortures which the enemies of God
and of Your Majesty have made us suffer. These perfidious
foes will tear a gem from your crown if the acts of your
powerful hand do not correspond with the words that fall
from your lips. If you turn towards heaven, it will tell you
that perhaps your very salvation is bound up with the salvation of so many people, who will be lost if they are not
helped by the care and solicitude of Your Majesty. If you
consider the name of Frenchman, you will remember, Sire,
that the great king who has made Europe tremble should
not be mocked at in America. If you regard the good of
your States, your gaze which at the age of 24 discerned what
so many great princes do not see at 50 will now recognize
how the loss of this great country will work to the detriment
of your kingdom. But a heart so royal, a virtue so heroic, a
generosity so magnanimous, can have no need of my words.
The Queen, your most honored mother, whose goodness is
known beyond the seas, has thus far prevented the entire
ruin of New France; but she has not given it freedom. She
delayed its death, but she did not give it health or strength.
This achievement is reserved for Your Majesty, who by saving the lives and the possessions of your French Colony, and
the souls of a great number of the aborigines, will compel
them all to pray that, like your great ancestor, whose zeal
you imitate, you may merit the name of saint by undertaking this holy war. Such are the desires, and the wishes, and
the trust of one who by permission of your bounty calls himself not in the language of the court but of the heart,

"Your Majesty's most humble and most obedient subject, and most faithful servant,
"Paul Le Jeune,
"Procurator of the Missions of the Society
of Jesus in New France."

It may be questioned if Louis XIV. was ever spoken to
so pointedly even by the greatest of his preachers. To tell
him that his actions should correspond with his words, and
that his salvation, perhaps, depended on the course he
adopted in Canada, required more than usual courage, but
Le Jeune was equal to it; and if the King read the "Relation" of 1642, as no doubt he did, he must have been
appalled at the deplorable state of his colony.

A terrible earthquake had struck consternation into the
hearts of the miserable colonists, and the bloodthirsty Iroquois were more than ever bent upon the extermination
of the whites. Fierce battles had been fought in Montreal;
men, women and children had been slaughtered or carried
off to captivity and torture; and at Three Rivers thirty-two
men maintained a fight for forty-eight hours against eighty
Iroquois; even women mingled in the fray. Quebec had
also its fill of horrors, and the young Seneschal de Lauson,
on whom the colony had founded its highest hopes, trag-
ically ended his career. He had gone over in a shallop with
seven men to attack a band of Iroquois who were en-
trenched on the Isle d'Orleans. He met them near a rock
on the shore—the place he himself had chosen for the fight,
but the enemy had reached it before him. As he approached
his shallop capsized, and he and his men saw that they were
doomed. They were no longer to be defenders, but assailants, and the effort to take the post seemed futile. However, there was nothing else to be done, and before they
made the attack they knelt down and prayed, and then
rushed at the foe. Only one of the eight was left alive, and
he was badly wounded and carried into captivity.

It was at that time, also, that the Sulpician Le Maistre

was killed near Montreal. He was in the field with eight Frenchmen who were gathering the harvest, when fifty Iroquois rushed upon them. They cut off the head of the priest and one of the savages later on came strutting past the palisades, dressed in the soutane which they had torn from his body. Six of the Frenchmen cut their way through the crowd of Indians and succeeded in reaching the palisades.

These were only a few of the gruesome things that Father Le Jeune presented to the consideration of his majesty Louis XIV. The "Relation" of 1661 teems with horrors. Meantime Dablon was striving to reach the North Sea, and Le Moyne was suffering the ill-treatment of the Iroquois in far-away Onondaga. But very likely the Great Monarch did not appreciate how widely his realms were being extended by these efforts of the missionaries, nor what it meant for the future. It was only in 1666, two years after Le Jeune was dead, that any assistance was sent to the colony. With a handful of troops, de Tracy and de Courcelles had no trouble in frightening the Iroquois into a peace of fifteen years' duration. That result was achieved without killing a single Indian.

Father Le Jeune died at Paris, August 7, 1664. The veneration with which he was regarded will be sufficiently understood by an extract from the "Relation" of 1666. With it we close this brief sketch of his splendid life.

"An Algonquin named Apicanis was dying of an epidemic which was ravaging an Indian village. He was at his last gasp. The priest had already administered the Sacraments when he heard the sufferer invoking the intercession of Father Paul Le Jeune, who was venerated by the Indians, because it was he who had first preached the Gospel among them, and had undergone such hardships for their conversion. They had heard also of the great esteem in which he was held in Europe, for his holy life. The priest was delighted and made every one in the cabin kneel down and join in prayer with the sick man, to whom at the same time he gave some of the Montagnais manuscript of Father

Le Jeune, and a book which used to belong to him. Suddenly the violence of the sickness ceased, followed by a sweet sleep which lasted till the following morning, and the patient awoke in perfect health, and then amazed everyone by walking into the chapel. He wanted to thank God, and the one whom after God he regarded as the author of the miracle. The same thing occurred to one of the children of the family later. It was the same sickness, and there was an absolutely certain proximity of death, but the same prayer to the beloved priest brought a perfect restoration to health and vigor."

Father Le Jeune was still watching from heaven over his beloved Algonquins.

JAMES BUTEUX

CHAPTER I.

AT THREE RIVERS.

In the " Relation " of 1635 we find a description of a journey made by Father Buteux to Three Rivers. It was the first time he had seen that part of the St. Lawrence, and the beauty of the landscape must have filled him with delight. Another less heroic soul, however, might have been gloomy and depressed, for he was going to begin a mission among the Indians at a new trading post, and his Superior, Father Le Jeune, had informed him that the one who first undertook such a task usually died from hardship and exposure. But Buteux did not give that a second thought. He was a soldier on the field of battle; and as a matter of fact he did not die of hardship and exposure, though his sufferings in that respect were terrible, but fifteen or sixteen years later he fell riddled with bullets on the banks of the St. Maurice, far up in the mountains.

" It was the 3d of September," writes the chronicler, " when Father Buteux and I got into our boat to go to the assistance of some of our French people in the settlement at Three Rivers. We passed close to the little island of Richelieu, on which Champlain had planted a cannon to command the river. For a good part of the way up the channel is narrow and dangerous. Once we ran into the mud; then we upset our canoe, and later on when a stiff gale was sweeping down the river, we just grazed a rock that made us all shudder when we saw it; but," says the good man, piously and patriotically, " God seems to have defended the passage in that way, so as to keep it in the hands of the French, who own it." He did not know what the future had in store for the control of that channel.

43

"On the 8th," he continues, "we arrived at Three Rivers. It is a pleasant place to live in. The soil is sandy and the rivers abound in fish. It is common enough to see an Indian with a dozen or so of sturgeon in his boat, the smallest of them as big as a man; and there are plenty of other kinds besides. The French call the place Three Rivers because a beautiful stream, which empties into the St. Lawrence, is divided at its mouth by several little islands into three branches. The Indian name of the river is Metaberoutin. I would describe its beauty for you but it would carry me too far. Indeed, the whole country between Quebec and the new settlement, which we have named the Residence of the Conception, is very fair to look upon. It is intersected everywhere by streams and rivulets, and as you journey onward you see them pouring their waters into the King of Rivers, the St. Lawrence, which here, ninety miles above Quebec, is two or three miles wide."

Such was the place which Father Buteux was to illustrate by his life and death.

There is a common impression among those who have not carefully read the story of those wonderful efforts of three centuries ago that Providence had furnished these old missionaries with unusual strength of body to resist the hardships which they were called upon to undergo. Father Buteux is an example of the incorrectness of that view. Thus, when on his way from France, in 1634, he nearly died, so weak and exhausted had he become. He was tenderly cared for by no less a personage than the commander of the expedition, du Plessis, and it is quite touching to see how shamefaced the young priest was about being the object of such solicitude.

He was then thirty-four years of age, and had only been fourteen years a Jesuit. He was born at Abbeville on April 11, 1600, and entered the Society at Rouen on October the 20th or 22d, 1620; we do not know which, for there is a doubt about the dates. His health was very frail, but he set out for America as soon as he could after the colony was restored to the French. On the same ship with him was

Brother Liègois, who was also to win the crown of martyrdom.

Buteux had a very hard time of it for some years, but the hardships did not worry him; it was the difficulty of making these wild people understand him. Besides, although the Algonquins are counted as the noblest of the sons of the forest, they were in many ways as wicked as the rest of the red men. We can glean a few instances of it from Buteux's letters to Le Jeune.

He tells of one unfortunate wretch who was baptized at Quebec, but had lapsed into his former savagery. Returning to Three Rivers, he fell sick and was thrown out of his cabin by his relatives. The Fathers could give him no shelter, for their own hut was only twelve feet long, so the sufferer was carried back again to Quebec and nursed all through the winter; but when he was able to stagger about, he insisted on going back to his old haunts. Buteux found him at Three Rivers, naked as when he was born, stretched on the bare ground, and trying to keep life in his wretched body by a morsel of fish which was flung at him from time to time by his devoted relatives. Finally one of them struck him on the head with a tomahawk and put an end to his miserable life.

Another instance is cited which is still more atrocious. We repeat it here, not to add to our mutoscope of horrors, but to show the heroism of the missionaries who could make up their mind to live with such monsters.

An Indian at the point of death had been baptized, but recovered. Unfortunately he was madly in love with a squaw, and without waiting to marry her in Christian fashion, simply took her to his cabin. It happened that he and his family went off to hunt and every one of them perished except the man and two of his children, who made their way back to Three Rivers. He was exhausted and at the point of death, and naturally might have expected some help from his sister, who lived there with a sick boy. But, not wanting to be troubled with the care of another invalid, she brained her brother in the presence of his two sick and starving children, a boy and a girl, and then, heedless of their clamors for food, she put her own hopeful in a canoe and started down the river to Quebec. The children followed her all day along the shore, begging to be taken on board. At nightfall the fierce hag beached the canoe and told the boy: "I can't carry both of you with me; kill your sister, and I will take you." Horrible to relate, the young brute seized a string and tied it around the throat of the girl. Then, holding one end with his foot, he choked her to death. "Did she struggle with you?' asked the priest, when the story was told at Quebec. "No; she did not even try to run away, but only looked at me, and let me do it."

The sequel to this crime is one of the mysteries of God's Providence. The trio arrived at Quebec and the sick man, whose disease made him too loathsome for any one but his mother and the priest to approach, was taken care of, and we are told died in good dispositions. Of course, they tried to do something with the young fratricide, also, but of the squaw nothing is said.

Everything, however, was not so hideous in those first days at Three Rivers. Many of the women were well behaved. One group of them, for instance, took care of a number of fatherless children, and begged Buteux for food to keep the life in their little bodies. "I do not know how we did it," he writes. "I had nothing to give, but somehow or other God, who feeds the birds, provided for them; and when the dreary winter was over, the children were as plump and as merry as if they had been plentifully fed during all that dreadful season."

One of the squaws who was a great comfort to him had a curious story to tell. She had been captured by the Iroquois, when she was young, and on one occasion when Champlain, with some Algonquins, was attacking an Iroquois village and killing every one, she kept shouting out

46

an Algonquin word: *"Nir, nir, nir!"* (Me, me, me!).
It was all she remembered. A warrior heard her and recognized her as belonging to his tribe. She returned with the victors and became an Algonquin again. It was a romantic story, but genuine history says nothing of Champlain carrying off prisoners from an Iroquois village.

In 1641 we find Fathers de Quen and Poncet working with Buteux at Three Rivers.

" I think," writes Le Jeune, " that poor church was more battered by all sorts of tempests than ever a vessel on the high seas. There was a motley crowd of all kinds of Indian wretches, who gave no end of trouble to the Fathers. There were savages from Allumettes, from the little nation of Attikamegues, from the Montagnais, and Oukotocmis, and Ounatchatsonons, and others besides, sometimes at peace and often at war, but always with their little jealousies and spites against each other. The bad were spoiling the good, and the devil renewed all the old superstitions, which had been banished from Sillery and which we thought were forgotten at Three Rivers. Father Buteux tells me that the Sillery Indians who are at Three Rivers, do their best, but that the conditions are awful. You hear nothing but the drum of the sorcerer, and see only the abominations of the dream superstition.

" Those who have come down from the land of the Hurons have introduced a diabolical dance which fills us with horror. Though they are all starving, they are still as proud as the devil. The terror they have of the enemy prevents them from going out to hunt to get something to eat ; but all day and all night they have visions. They fancy the Iroquois are lurking in the corn fields, they see them hiding in the woods, in the canoes on the river and the canoes on the shore ; they are pursued by them ; they discover their trails ; they find the place where they camped, the trees where they plucked the fruit ; they hear them howling in the forests and they keep the French on the jump, with a thousand false alarms. Unfortunately these phantoms of the imagination turn them from the fear they ought to have of offending God. It is a case of the wicked fleeing when no man pursueth."

On one occasion a very indecent dance was to be performed; men and women were to join in a wild orgy, and the juggler in chief was to walk through fire. Father Buteux determined to stop it, and he and Father Poncet burst into the wigwam at 10 o'clock at night and fiercely harangued the multitude. It was too much for the sorcerer, who appears to have been the famous One Eye from Allumettes, the wily individual who figures so frequently in the " Relations."

One Eye was usually as cold as ice, but this interference made him blaze up in a wild fury. Seizing some of the firebrands in his hands, he flung them straight into the eyes of Buteux, ordering him to be off, and shouting out that the Christian baptism was killing the Indians. But Buteux could not be stopped. " It is your sins that are doing it," he replied. The excitement spread and the savages came running in from all directions. The Christians, being very few in number, kept quiet, while the pagans were yelling like demons. Growing wilder than ever, One Eye seized a rope and attempted to strangle the priest who, quite coolly, held out his neck to facilitate the operation. At last some one begged Buteux to withdraw, which he did; but there was no dance that night.

When the French heard of the affront they demanded satisfaction. Champfort, the Governor, summoned One Eye, but the cunning old wretch humbly admitted that he threw the fire into Buteux's eyes, and offered to let the priest do the same to him. He knew very well that retaliation of that kind would not be resorted to. As for the strangling episode, he said: " Why, no, that was far from my thoughts. I merely seized the cord to show that both of us could not be right, and the one who lied deserved to be choked." Nothing was done to this excellent lawyer, but the victim of his efforts in medicine died during the tumult.

In spite of all this, however, the little church of Three Rivers began to thrive. There were eighty neophytes there in 1641. Notwithstanding the threats of their tribesmen, they came every day to the chapel to hear Mass, which was celebrated at daybreak, even in mid-winter; they frequented the sacraments and suffered no harm from the horrible examples around them. On the feast of SS. Peter and Paul there were thirty-two at the altar-railing, " which wasn't bad," writes Buteux, " for a church that had to eat its spiritual bread soaked with tears." After a while there had to be a separate Mass for the French, the chapel being too small for both the Indians and the white men at the same time. The pagans also relented somewhat in their antagonism.

Among the red men who were in the habit of visiting Three Rivers were the Attikamegues or the White Fish Tribe. Like their namesakes of the sea, these Indians had the habit of disappearing like a flash at the first approach of a foe. It is from Buteux we get the first account of them, and he tells us incidentally that the fish from which they took their name are plentiful in this country, have an excellent flavor, and as far as he is aware, are unknown in France. Whitefish is still a favorite in America.

The White Fish Indians lived north of Three Rivers, and travelled down what is now the St. Maurice, to trade with the French. At these assemblies the missionaries did what they could to get some notion of Christianity into their heads. However, they were not difficult to deal with, and had even promised to settle in the neighborhood, so as to be better instructed; but the ever-present fear of the Iroquois made them always give up the project. "You see," they told Buteux, " we are not warriors. We know how to handle a paddle, but not to wield a tomahawk. We love peace, and that is the reason we live far away, so as to avoid the occasions of war. If you could only conquer these people who want to massacre us we should very soon come and settle here." " Indeed," writes the priest, " when they do come to the post they are more frequently in the church than in the store."

There was one of them who was especially eager to know all about the Faith. He had already received a good deal of instruction, and when about to return to his country he asked for a rosary and a picture, so that he might say his prayers more easily; in addition, he begged for a piece of paper on which the prayers were to be written. Of course, he did not know how to read, but he used to hold up the scrap of writing, and tell the Lord that it contained what he wanted to say.

Some months passed by, and he returned to Three Rivers. Immediately he pulled his picture out of a bag and said: "There it is, Father. It is pretty black, but the smoke of the wigwam did it. However, we all used to kneel down before it, night and morning. Now read the prayers you wrote for me, so as to see if I have learned them correctly;" and he produced the crumpled piece of paper. The Father was nonplussed. He had simply scrawled some capitals, here and there, and added an occasional word, but it was impossible to remember what he had put down. He could not betray himself to the Indian, however, so he said: "You begin first." To his amazement this son of the forest not only remembered what had been indicated on the paper, but everything else that he had been taught. He was a likely candidate for baptism. Indeed, the time had been fixed; but one day a shout was heard: "The Iroquois are coming!" and he, with the rest, vanished from the scene, "dreading the Iroquois," moans the missionary, "more than he did the devil."

In 1642 there were very few Indians of any kind at Three Rivers, and we discover Father Buteux down at Sillery. What was he doing there? Gratifying his thirst for hardships, in the first place, and secondly, availing himself of the opportunity to see a party of his beloved White Fish. The Sillery chief had invited them down to pass the winter near the Reservation, and had promised to provide for them during the winter. About sixty of them had accepted the invitation and, after paying their respects to the Governor at Quebec, were assigned a place some distance away from the Christians. Buteux hurried from Three Rivers to look after them, and his ministry there gave him no end of suffering. We find him, for instance, one night nine miles away from the mission, hunting up a sick squaw who was clamoring for the priest. This particular visit is worth noting, because with him on this occasion was a young physician who was very likely none other than René Goupil, Father Jogues' future companion in martyrdom. He was the only medical man anywhere near Quebec in those days.

Night journeys like that were, of course, common, but even his ordinary work among his people constantly called for unusual heroism. " I have often seen him," says de Quen, " tramping in the dark through three or four feet of snow, groping along by the light of a lantern which the howling wind would often tear from his hand or extinguish, while he himself would perhaps be flung by the violence of the storm down some icy hill into the snowdrift below. This will be surprising news," continues the writer, "for those who remember him in France, frail to the last degree, and almost always a valetudinarian. His zeal for his Indian flock was always rewarded, however, for no matter how bad the weather, all the tribe trooped over every morning to hear Mass in the Ursuline chapel and to receive instructions from the priest and the nuns. You could not give that eager throng too much piety. A hundred Indians, White Fish and others, were baptized that winter; the Sillery Indians contributing mightily to the result by their advice and good example.

A curious fact is brought out in connection with this visit of the White Fish to Sillery. In addition to the usual Indian superstitions of dreams, sweatings, indecent dances, and the rest, every White Fish seemed to have a drum, which he regarded as his most cherished spiritual treasure. Although in the other tribes only the magicians banged this musical implement, its use was universal among the Attikamegues. One would think that the less noise such timid people made the safer they would be; but error, religious or otherwise, is rarely logical. For them the drum was everything, and to give it to the priest was considered to be unconditional surrender to the Faith. Hence Father Buteux was busy that winter making bonfires of these precious instruments, which it cost the red man many heartburnings to abandon. But they yielded and were uncompromising converts when baptized. Thus, one day a zealous convert found a French drum in his cabin, and he immediately proceeded with great fervor to kick it to pieces. It looked too much like the sorcerers' "medicine," and he did not want to have it near him.

It may be of interest to theologians to know that these poor people who had been just dragged from the mire of pagan immorality could easily compound what are called cases of conscience, as well as the rest of us. One scrupulous squaw, for instance, inquired of the confessor: "What am I to do about preparing the cauldron when my husband is going to have a banquet in honor of the devil?" "It would be best if you had nothing to do with it," was the reply. "But suppose he insists upon it?" she urged. "In that case you can get it ready, as you would any other potful of meat you might give him for his supper, and then you can disappear from the scene." "I won't touch it at all," she answered indignantly. She did not believe in the doctrine of material cooperation.

During that winter Buteux was sent down to Tadoussac, for some reason or other, and he had the usual report to make, that everything would be perfection if it weren't for the savage's fondness for liquor. Probably it was he who, on his return to Quebec on August 15, brought a letter from the missionary at Miscou, Father Richard, which conveyed the interesting bit of news that a pious old squaw had just died at that place who had been baptized by Father Biard, at Port Royal, in Nova Scotia, as far back as 1612, viz.: thirty years before. The fact has nothing to do with the present narrative, but it is only given as an example of how the work of those heroic old apostles of Acadia continued after they had gone to heaven.

Those were stormy days on the St. Lawrence. The Iroquois were swarming over it, and Buteux, of course, comes in for his share of the danger. The enemies, however, had changed their tactics. They had been accustomed to come in great numbers, and after the usual ravages of a summer campaign, would withdraw, leaving the river free. But in 1643 they were divided into groups of thirty, forty, fifty, or at most a hundred, and thus covered the whole country. When one band went back to the Mohawk another took its place. They were provided with firearms, which was a tremendous advantage over their enemies, for it often happened that three or four hundred Hurons would come down the river with immense stores of pelts, but with no means of defence, the result being that they were either killed or put to flight.

The first capture by the Iroquois in that year occurred on the 9th of May, within four leagues of Three Rivers. Eight Algonquins who were coming from the Huron country and had been paddling all night so as to avoid the enemy, went ashore in the morning to light a fire to warm themselves, for it was bitter cold. They fancied they were out of danger, when nineteen Iroquois suddenly started out of the woods, murdered a couple of the Algonquins, and hurried off with a number of prisoners and all of their precious possessions.

This encounter is memorable because on that occasion the Iroquois seized some of the letters which were sent down from Huronia, and also the " Relation " of what had occurred there in 1642, a loss which explains the scant account about that mission for that particular year, but singularly enough Jogues, who was then a prisoner at Ossernenon, contrived to send a letter up to the St. Lawrence by an Indian messenger, and among other things he said that the "Relation" had fallen into his hands, but it was never seen afterwards. He evidently lost it.

Montreal suffered much in these raids. Thus, on June 19th, forty Iroquois hid themselves in ambush, half a league from the stockade. On that very day they fell upon sixty Hurons with thirteen canoe-loads of furs, captured twenty-three, most of whom they butchered, and immediately afterwards, while making a feigned attack on the French fort, seized five white men who were building a house two hundred feet away. The men in the fort saw the Iroquois carrying off the prisoners and furs, but did not dare to give chase, for they did not know how many savages would start out of the ground to meet them. Maisonneuve was now realizing what his declaration meant when he said that he would stay in Montreal if every tree were an Iroquois.

Things were worse up the river. The Christian Indians from Sillery were the best friends the French had in those perilous times. They were superb fighters, never skulked like other Indians, but went straight into danger. Better yet, they openly proclaimed themselves to be Christians. Not only did they keep aloof from all the indecencies and superstitions of their pagan kinsmen, but would not live in the same lodge with them, and on the warpath they bivouacked apart from the others. Buteux was with them at Montreal in some of these fights, and he tells us that usually on the journey, when he was reading his breviary, the Indians would stop paddling, if the wind was favorable, and keep him company by reciting their beads. They were very much admired by the pagans. On the other hand, they had a supreme contempt for the Christian Indians who did not live up to their professions.

Le Jeune, who was no longer Superior, had joined his friend Buteux at Three Rivers, and in the " Relations " of those years the familiar forms of de Nouë, de Brébeuf, Bressani and others cross the scene. Occasionally fugitives from the Iroquois country came with news about Jogues, and the report had got abroad that the enemy would gladly surrender him. In the vain hope that they might make some such proposition, the Governor kept boats going to the other side of the river to endeavor to meet some of the roving bands, but the approach of these scouts was only a signal for the Iroquois to disappear. They had no intention of relinquishing the prize.

CHAPTER II.

IN THE NORTH COUNTRY.

Up to the day of his death, Buteux lived in the midst of war's alarms. As a priest, he had the additional hardship of being compelled to battle against the corruption that usually reigns at a military post, a hardship which at Three Rivers was emphasized, because its geographical position made it a meeting place for the savage tribes from the east, west and north, with all their varied pagan superstitions and vices. It was also a resort for the wild *coureurs de bois*. As we have said, his Indians were remarkable for their fidelity to their obligations as Christians and their fearlessness in professing their faith. He never succeeded, however, in inducing his favorite White Fish to settle near the river; not that they were unwilling, but they were afraid. Nevertheless, with what instruction they received on their regular visits to Three Rivers, these timid and poverty stricken people became excellent Catholics. They were very devoted to him and resorted to all sorts of devices to have him visit their country.

At last, in 1651, he was told by his Superiors to make the attempt. It looked like trifling with life, for his seventeen years of the worst kind of hardship had been a dreadful strain on his physical strength, which from the very outset seemed on the verge of a collapse. Besides, a visit to the White Fish country meant a three months' journey, in the worst season of the year, through a region that was impassable except for a savage. Nevertheless, he made the attempt and succeeded. He has left us a journal of the expedition, which if not written by such a saint would be incredible. It is at the same time an astounding though unconscious revelation of his heroism.

56

JAMES BUTEUX

" I gladly accepted the work," he says, " and I informed the Chief, who was at Three Rivers, that I was at last able to go with him. He supplied me with a sled for my little baggage, and provided me with snow shoes and the like. On March 27th, M. de Normanville and myself started with two men and a band of forty Indians, big and little. A squad of soldiers went with us the first day as a protection against the Iroquois. The weather was fine, but it was bad under foot, for the warm sun had melted the snow and made our sleds difficult to drag and our snow-shoes were soaking wet. The ice was unsafe and in one place broke under my feet. The swift current would have carried me off if a soldier had not come to my assistance. The road that day ran along a succession of cataracts leaping from lofty precipices. There was false ice which was very dangerous and very annoying, for we had to walk with our feet and raquettes in the water. As a consequence the raquettes became very slippery and very dangerous when we had to crawl over the ice-covered rocks close to the rapids. We could only make six leagues that day, though we walked from morning till night. The end of the day was worst of all, for a cold wind sprung up and froze our shoes and stockings, which had been wet since morning. Our escort of soldiers, who were not accustomed to that sort of thing, were astounded, but still more so when, at night, we dug down into the snow and went to sleep. It was like entering a sepulchre.

" On our second day out we bade good-bye to the soldiers and continued up the river. About a league from our camp we came to a waterfall which blocked our way, and we had to climb over three mountains, the last of which was very high. It was then we felt the heaviness of our sleds and raquettes; to descend the opposite slope there was nothing else to do but to toboggan from the top to the bottom, and that brought us out into the middle of the river, which at one place was about 400 yards wide. At intervals of about a league we came to three other cataracts of a prodigious height and very terrible to look at, as they leaped down with a horrible roar and extraordinary impetuosity. We had to go through places which struck terror to every heart; we crawled over them on all fours. Finally, we halted on the top of a very steep mountain. In brief, it had been a hard day for all of us, and we were weary of trudging for eleven

57

hours through the snow, dragging our load as the horse does the plow, meantime taking no rest and no repast.

"The third day we started out very early and marched on the icy river which is there very wide. At two in the afternoon a mirage made some branches of trees which were buried in the water appear to be above the surface. They looked like men, and immediately everyone was sure it was a band of Iroquois awaiting us there. Scouts were sent out and they came back and reported that it was indeed the enemy. The Christians immediately prepared to go to confession and the catechumens to receive baptism. The chief exhorted them to fight like Christian soldiers, and to put their trust in God. His speech gave them courage and each man resolved to conquer or die. As we drew near, however, we found out our mistake and kept on our way very much relieved.

"On the fourth day I said Mass on a little island. It was the first time the Adorable Sacrifice was offered in these parts. There was a discharge of musketry at the elevation and after Mass a feast of Indian corn and eels. All our provisions for the forty people of our party consisted of about two bushels of corn meal, one of peas, and a little bag of sea biscuit. The difficulty of dragging our sleds had made us cut down our supplies. Besides, we had hoped to hunt a little on the way. But, as a matter of fact, we had scarcely enough to keep the life in our bodies. For myself, there was enough in the load, the road, and the fast which I was keeping, for it was Passion Week, to compel me to do without provisions. However, God gave me more courage than the young man I brought with me. He succumbed under the strain, and had to leave us and return with two Algonquin squaws. They went away two days later.

The fifth and sixth days were different; but yet alike in the difficulty of the roads. The first was rainy, the second fair, but the thaw which it brought clogged our sleds and raquettes, so that for the next ten days we had to start out very early in the morning before the ice and snow had begun to melt.

"On the seventh day we walked from three o'clock in the morning till one in the afternoon, in order to reach an island where I wanted to say Mass, for it was Palm Sunday. I succeeded, but I had a share in the suffering of the Passion of our good Master. My thirst made my tongue adhere to my palate. The extra burden which I had to shoulder, when my man left me, aggravated my pains. The Indians saw my weakness during Mass, and after it gave me some sagamité, which was made especially for me, and which consisted of some meal boiled in water. With it was half of a dried eel. After Mass we had public prayers, instead of Vespers. On the march each one said his rosary privately.

"On the eighth day, in order to avoid the rapids where the ice was beginning to break, and where we could not safely trust ourselves, we started through the woods in a valley between two mountains. It was encumbered at every step with trees which had been thrown down by the wind, so that the travelling was very difficult, as our raquettes were always getting entangled in the branches. Beyond this valley we reached a mountain which was so high that it took us three hours to reach the summit. Besides my sled, I had to carry in my arms a little boy, the son of the Indian who was taking care of me. I took that burden in order to help the mother, who had another child, and also had to drag all her traps on a sled. On the mountain we came to a lake which we had to cross. Every step made us think of death as we looked into its black depths. We were continually sinking up to our knees, and often deeper, through the soft mush, but were fortunately held up by stronger ice underneath. Often the surface was very slippery, and gave us many a hard fall, with the result sometimes of sending us head and heels into the water.

"The ninth day was notable for the length of the road. It ran between lakes and rapid rivers and down mountain sides. We walked from early morning till nightfall. Fear of the thaw made us hurry along till we were all exhausted. From time to time, so as to get courage, we sung hymns and kept our thoughts on God.

"The tenth day was spent in climbing and descending mountains, and at last we arrived at a lake whose banks were perpendicular rocks higher than any bluffs I have ever seen in France.

"On the eleventh day we left camp at three o'clock in the morning, so as to avail ourselves of the ice which the cold north wind had formed. The moon was shining brightly and when morning dawned we again struck for the woods and journeyed over hills and mountains and along lakes and rapid rivers.

"On the twelfth day, after the Office of Good Friday, and when I had heard the confessions of some Indians who were going to leave us, for they had to take another road, and first to make their canoes, we reached the top of the mountains and came to a little river where we found some beaver-dams. We killed six of the animals and continued our route over three great lakes, on the last of which is a small island where we slept on the snow with no shelter over us.

"The thirteenth day was the hardest of all. We started out at three in the morning by horrible roads through underbush so thick that it was almost impossible to find a place for our feet or raquettes. I was lost several times, because I could not find the trail of those who went ahead of me. Then we arrived at some lakes which were very slippery and yet dangerous to walk on without raquettes, which kept us from going through the ice. On the other hand it was hard to use them because of the melting ice and snow. At mid-day we stopped and I had the happiness of saying Mass, which was my only consolation. There I found strength in my weariness. To revive me, for I was very weak, they offered me a piece of beaver meat which had been left over from the day before. I did not eat it, but offered it to Our Lord, for I had not touched any meat from the beginning of Lent.

The fourteenth day of our journey was Easter Sunday, the 9th of April, and I was very much consoled at the piety displayed by the Indians. Our little chapel, built of cedar and pine branches, was extraordinarily decorated; that is to say, each one had brought whatever pictures and new stuffs he had and hung them here and there on the walls. After blessing them with holy water, and distributing the *pain bénit*, which was a piece of bread I had purposely kept, the chief made a speech to excite the devotion of his people. When Communion and thanksgiving were over, and the beads recited, they came to offer me a partridge and other food, which they deprived themselves of to give to me, in spite of the hunger that was gnawing their vitals as well as mine.

"On the 10th of April we started out early in the morning. The rain had fallen all night and had melted the surface ice of the lakes and the snow in the forests, so that we had to tramp in the water up to our knees, with our raquettes on our feet, so as not to go through the lower layer of ice. After crossing four lakes we arrived at the one where my guide usually lived. We built a shelter on a sand hill, under the pines, where the snow had melted. There we erected a chapel, where I said Holy Mass and planted a fine cross. Up to that we had merely cut crosses on the trees as we passed along, but now we lifted up our beautiful standard. We rested there all day, and should have had time to eat had there been the wherewithal. The snow was only half melted, and as the fish had not yet begun to run we were very straitened for food. My people set about making canoes, and they toiled at it from morning till night. I was astonished that they could work so hard, as they scarcely took six ounces of nourishment a day. What hurt them most was to see me in pain. Their own sufferings they offered light-heartedly to God.

" Seeing that everyone was occupied, I took up with an old man who was making snares for hares. One day I got lost in the forest and could not find the trail. I walked all day in places I did not know, across mountains and through lowlands full of water and melting snow without knowing where I was. Fatigue, the coldness of the water, and the approach of night, as well as the pangs of hunger—for I had eaten nothing all day—compelled me to throw myself at the foot of a tree to rest. I was soaking wet and my clothes began to freeze, for there was a frost every night. I gathered some pine branches to protect myself against the wet ground and then pulled some on top of me as a protection against the cold, but I had leisure enough to shiver all night. I was chiefly tormented by thirst and had to go down to the lake from time to time to drink. I finally fell asleep. On awakening and recommending myself to my Angel Guardian and to Father de Brébeuf, I heard the report of a musket. My people, who had been all night worrying about my absence, were out looking for me. I shouted a reply, and another shot was fired in response. I started to where the sound came from and arriving at the shore of the lake I saw M. de Normanville and my host coming toward me in a canoe. When I reached the cabin they looked at me as if I had risen from the dead. They gave me some fish which they had caught and I ate it without bread, or wine, or sauce other than what hunger gave, and that was enough.

" On St. Mark's day, after the procession and Mass, I

blessed the lake and called it after St. Thomas. I also blessed the canoes and dedicated each one to some saint. We painted the names on them in red letters. Before going to the tribe's meeting-place, everyone prepared himself for a general Communion which took place on May 1st. On the following day we got into our canoes, and until the 18th we were travelling over all sorts of rivers and lakes, which we had to reach by roads whose very names still make me shudder. Frequently it was only by climbing across portages of steep rocks with our canoes and baggage. We not only had nothing to eat, but had no hopes of getting any.

It was now Ascension Day, and after saying Mass on a beautiful flat rock in the middle of an island, and then travelling over passes which filled us with terror and dismay, we arrived at the general meeting-place where I was delighted to see towering above everything a great and well-made cross. We knelt and invoked the protection of our Angel Guardians and St. Peter, whom we made patron of the country. Then we discharged a volley of musketry, but were surprised to hear only the shouts of a few children in reply. A moment after the chief appeared and came down to the shore. 'Father,' he said, 'the reason we did not answer your salute was, not want of means to do so, or lack of esteem for you, but the people were at prayers in the chapel thanking God for your coming.' 'Splendid!' said I; 'but tell me who planted the cross?' 'It was put there long ago,' he answered, 'by the first Christians. And why should they not?' he continued; 'were not they as well as the French obliged to do so? But come, let us enter the chapel.'

"It was a small arbor-shaped structure made of bark. At one end was a sort of an altar, covered with blue stuff, on which were fastened paper pictures and little crucifixes. We all knelt down and said our beads together and then sung some pious canticles in thanksgiving.

"After that the chief men came to pay their respects, and to present their little children for baptism. We baptized about fifteen, but as it was already night, we put off the rest till the following day. The older people were so anxious to be instructed then and there that I had scarcely time to say my office. I began with the oldest and found some of them, eighty and a hundred years of age, who had never seen a white man, and who were so well disposed for the Faith that they seemed to me like St. Anne and Simeon waiting in the temple for the message of salvation.

"Although time was very precious and I was sorely in need of rest I had to let them have a dance in the cabin to show their gratitude and happiness after the fashion of the country; and next day, nothing would do but to take part in a banquet, where the viands were remarkable for their scarceness. It had not snowed much that winter and there was danger of a famine. Where we had expected to find abundance of food there was want. But the good will of the people was all the more acceptable on that account and their excellent dispositions served me instead of food.

"On the next day seven or eight families arrived with their babies to be baptized. I prepared the people for confession, and as there was a great crowd who had never been at confession before I thought I should have had a hard time of it, but they were so well instructed that it was like hearing so many French people. Every one had his beads and knew his prayers. They had instructed each other."

Father Buteux then tells us, at great length, how these good Indians kept the record of their sins; by notches on pieces of wood, or by painting them on pieces of bark or skin, or by beads and the like. He dilates with great enthusiasm on the solidity of their faith, which was evinced by their determination to expel any vicious person from their midst, their assiduity at prayer, their continual habit of preparing for death, and their love for the souls in Purgatory.

The cemeteries were kept with the greatest care. At the foot of the grave were two crosses. For men some warlike implement was laid upon the tomb, and for women an article of one kind or another from the household. At first they buried the rosaries with the body, but afterwards another custom was adopted. The dying person gave his beads to some friend with the agreement to pray for the soul of the giver. In one place the priest was startled by seeing some pots filled with meat hung in the graveyard. "It is not superstition," they hastened to tell him, "but an inducement to the poor who come there to pray for the dead in return for the public charity that is exercised in that way."

Resuming the journal, he says:

"After remaining some days in the place of the first meeting, I went with a convoy of thirty-five canoes to another place twenty-five leagues away. We had no other provisions than the fish we caught, and nine or ten ounces a day was all that any of us could get to eat. It was our bread, our meat, our entrées, our dessert. Our soup was the water in which we boiled our fish. At times, however, we had a little more abundant fare; but man can subsist on very little, and God sustains our bodies as well as our souls.

"The day after leaving we came to some frightful cataracts; one in particular, after roaring over a rocky bed, suddenly leaps down a precipice into a basin of stone a hundred feet long. There the river boils so furiously that if you throw a stick into it you see it sink out of sight and then rise high in the air forty or fifty feet away. To avoid these cataracts we had to carry our traps over lofty mountains; all the while skirting the edge of precipices on the narrowest kind of a trail. For a long time we were only one step away from death.

"On the third day we arrived at our destination and were received with a volley of musketry. When the chief had finished his short but affectionate harangue we were led straight to the chapel, which was made of the bark of odoriferous pine. No European had ever set foot in it."

The usual consolation awaited him there. Not only were the Christians faithful to their duties, but had been assiduous in instructing others in the Faith. Indeed, in his long account he chronicles many instances of remarkable piety. He regrets that he cannot recount them all.

"From the second assembly we went to a third, three days away," he says. "This time there were sixty canoes in the company. In this last place I experienced only sorrow, for the people came from a country where the Faith is regarded as the law of death, and where polygamy reigns. I did all I could to instruct them, and the Indians who had come with me gave me wonderful help. We got the people to erect a cross and build a chapel, and there I taught them from morning till night. They always came to listen, and put off the most urgent work to do so. They brought me all their drums and the other superstitious articles which they used in their conjuring. Even during the night they came to put questions to me. Several asked for baptism during the ten days I remained there, but I did not think it proper to grant their request, except for the very old people who I feared might soon die. I found one old blind man of eighty who was a marvel in the way he grasped the truths I taught him. He was never weary of teaching the others what he learned.

"Hunger broke up the meeting, but they begged me to return next year and asked so affectionately that I was very much consoled. Everyone wanted beads; some asked them for others whom they might meet in the woods. I sent some also to the various chiefs, and only regretted they were not of better material. It is wonderful what zeal these people have for conversions. If we could only go among the remote tribes we should have all we could do to take care of them.

"We returned by another road. It was over rapids and precipices and amid horrors of every sort. In less than five days we had to make thirty-five portages, some a league and a half in length. Our loads were heavy and our provisions light, but God gave us strength to reach home in safety. All the fatigues I had undergone did not affect my health. I arrived at Three Rivers on the 18th of June.

"In the spring time I hope to return and go as far as the North Sea, to find new people and bring them to the light of the Faith. However, since our return, the Iroquois have invaded the country. My poor people can embrace the cross only through persecution and death."

We are unable to say exactly how far Father Buteux went on this journey, but judging from what he tells us about his going from lake to lake to meet the different Indian assemblies, it would appear that he must have reached what are now put down on the maps as The Sources of the St. Maurice. This group of lakes is up at the Height of Land, or the crest of the watershed, one side of which slopes towards Hudson Bay.

In a letter which he wrote in the following November he

speaks of a massacre occurring at Lake Kisagami. That name does not appear on any of the ancient or modern charts, though there are some that resemble it, as, for instance, Lake Nattagame, which is very far to the north and at no great distance from Hudson Bay. Had he succeeded in reaching that place he would have anticipated Father Albanel by twenty years. There is another lake, however, called Kinougami, which is on the southern watershed and not far from the Aspamouachan River. It is impossible to determine, however, either the place to which he had first gone, or the other more important one where he was killed in the following year.

In the letter above referred to, he says that on leaving Sillery he was overwhelmed with spiritual desolation, but when he reached Three Rivers he understood the reason of it. It was to prepare him for future crosses. One reason of his distress was that some Indians had died without Baptism; another that the Iroquois were busy massacring his neophytes. That terrible foe had gone as far as Lake Kisagami, which was twenty days' journey in the snow, and some of the fugitives were already flocking into Three Rivers. Among them was an Indian saint. He had lost his wife, his father, three children, three brothers, and a sister; and yet not a murmur ever left his lips. The wife he was bereft of was a wonderfully holy person.

"She was the most beautiful woman," says Buteux, "that I have ever seen among these people, and also the most accomplished. She was a good housekeeper, extremely industrious, very liberal and courageous, and at the same time modest, charitable, wonderfully humble, and, above all, always on fire for the conversion of the Indians. Indeed, she lost her life on that account. She might have gone to Tadoussac, which was as yet unknown to the Iroquois, but the desire to help her people at Lake Kisagami prompted her to remain. She had already converted twenty-five families, and so wound herself around the heart of her husband that she changed him from a fierce savage into a holy man. For six years the happy pair never failed to make long and dangerous journeys together, to go to confession and Communion. They had intended to pass the winter at Three Rivers, to perfect their knowledge of the Faith, but death interfered with that." Whether the poor woman was killed or led into captivity we are not told.

The opening page of the " Relation " of 1652 is the concluding chapter of Father Buteux's life. He had passed the winter at Three Rivers, and in the springtime some poor people of the White Fish tribe who had come down to the settlement for instructions asked him to go with them to their country. He consented, and on April 4 started out towards the north. On the eve of his departure he wrote the following letter to Father Ragueneau:

" Dear Reverend Father:

" We are now planning our departure. God grant that they may not back out, at the last moment, and that we may leave for good and all. May Heaven be the term of this last journey! This is the hope laid up in my heart. Our party is a very weak one. The men are all ailing, and the rest are women and children, about 60 in all. The food and provisions of this little party must be furnished by him who feeds the birds. I am going accompanied by all my miseries, and I have great need of your prayers and those of the Fathers. I ask them in all humility. My heart tells me that the time of my happiness draws near. It is the Lord; let that be done which is good in his eyes."

Clearly Buteux knew of his approaching death, and this journey to the grave was a very painful one. They travelled about a month, suffering much from hunger and fatigue. Often not a morsel passed their lips for days. On Ascension Day they divided into two bands, for the purpose of finding food, but also to provide against total extermination by the Iroquois. If one division were massacred, the other might escape. It was a cheerless outlook. They made the best of it, however, and before bidding good-by to each other all went to confession and Communion.

With the missionary were a young Frenchman and a Huron. The snows had melted, and the rivers were free of ice. They were in a little canoe which they had made, and camped wherever the night found them.

On the 10th of May they had to leave their boat three different times, and as they were making their last portage, and bending under their heavy loads, they suddenly found themselves surrounded by Iroquois. The Huron, who was in the lead, was seized so unexpectedly that he had not time to make a single step backward. The priest and the Frenchman fell riddled with bullets. The savages then rushed upon them with their knives and tomahawks, stripped them naked and flung them into the river. The last word on the lips of both was " Jesus."

Two days afterwards, some other Christians, following the same trail, were also captured. One of them, an Algonquin, was burnt alive on the spot. The Huron who had been with Buteux was carried off to be tortured on the Mohawk, but after some days he succeeded in making his escape, and arrived at Three Rivers with the sad news. Some Christians went up the river, later on, to find the body of the priest, but they met with no success. However, they came upon the corpse of the young Frenchman half eaten by the crows and wild beasts.

" Father Buteaux," says Ragueneau, " had a wonderful power of instilling piety in the hearts of his neophytes. You could always recognize his Indians, by their tender devotion and their solid faith. He was a man of prayer, and of such constant mortification, that his life was a continual fast. He always slept on the ground, and gave himself only a few hours for that miserable rest. Though he was always weak, and never free from pain, he practised mortifications far beyond his strength. Hearing some one remark that it would be better to be put to death instantly, than to fall into the hands of the Iroquois, he said that although the tor-

68

tures would be terrible, he would prefer to die at a slow fire, no matter how cruel the savages might be; for grace prevails over everything, and an act of the love of God is purer in the midst of fire. Indeed he was a thousand times in places where the Iroquois might seize him, but he never quailed or even changed color; nor did any danger ever make him draw back a single step when there was hope of doing anything for the glory of God."

The whole life of this great missionary was so wonderful that the people of Three Rivers ought to petition for his canonization.

GABRIEL DRUILLETTES

CHAPTER I.

Down the Kennebec.

On the northern boundary of the State of Michigan, near where Lake Superior rushes over the rocks at Sault Ste. Marie and flows down to Lake Huron through the beautiful St. Mary's River, stands a monument which commemorates the official appropriation of the northwest territory by the delegate of Louis XIV in 1671. On the shaft, along with the names of the civic and military functionaries, we find those of Father Allouez, Louis André, and Gabriel Druillettes, all of the Society of Jesus.

If we are to accept the testimony of Rochemonteix and Gilmary Shea, Druillettes was at that time seventy-eight years old, having been born in 1593. But there is some doubt about the correctness of the date, just as there is about the place of his birth, some putting it at Gurat, or Garat, and others again at Beaulieu. In fact, we know little or nothing about the illustrious man's early life, except that he came to Canada, on August 15, 1643, on the same ship with Chabanel and Garreau, both of whom were subsequently slain by the Indians.

He was scarcely a year in the country, when he was sent out on the winter hunt with the Algonquins, many of whom were Christians. They had started ahead of him, and he got into his canoe with two young braves, and joined the party far down the river. As he was seen approaching, every one hastened to the shore to greet him. Negabamat, the great chief, made the customary speech of welcome, and a day or so after all rolled up their strips of bark, the ma-

70

terial, namely, for constructing a shelter at the encampments, and made for the woods in search of game.

At every stopping place, their first care was to build a chapel where Mass and morning prayers were said. Before starting out for the day's hunt, the Indians knelt for the priest's blessing, and at night prayers were recited. When shifting their quarters they always erected a great cross, around which they knelt to say their prayers and sing some simple hymn. At midday they halted for their meal, which was only dried meat, " as hard," says Druillettes, " as iron and as tasteless as hemp." Finally, at night they slept on the ground, with only the vault of heaven above their heads. " It was the sort of an inn," says the chronicle, " where you did not have to settle with the host."

During that journey Mass was said every day. Sundays and festivals were scrupulously kept, and many of the Indians went to confession and Communion. Christmas especially was observed with great solemnity, for the Algonquins had a great devotion to the Infant Jesus. They usually built a little side chapel of cedar and pine, where they went to pray, and to offer the acts of voluntary penance they had performed as a preparation for the feast. On St. Joseph's day they lighted a bonfire, " an easy thing to do," says Druillettes, " with the millions of tall trees around them," and on Good Friday they laid out on the snow a fine beaver skin, on which they placed a crucifix. Kneeling around it, they prayed most fervently.

Thus winter passed, and when the thaws set in the scattered bands all met on the banks of the St. Lawrence, and there erected a great cross as a memorial of their winter expedition.

Druillettes revelled in the spiriual joy which the piety of his Algonquins gave him, but he purchased his pleasures by a great deal of bodily suffering. He had nothing on which to rest his weary bones at night but a few pine branches laid on the snow, and nothing but a thin roll of bark to shelter him from the storms. He lived with dogs as well as human beings, for in those Indian camps every-thing is common for man and beast. He fasted more rigor-ously on Sunday in the woods than he would have done on Good Friday in Quebec. He had only enough to stave off death, but not enough to give him strength. As the "Relation" puts it, "filth was his cook and constant com-panion"; and in spite of his affection for these wretched creatures, and their love for him, he was their laughing-stock when he made a blunder of speech, or when he lacked skill in the craftsmanship of the savages. The strength of the ox and the fleetness of the deer were their ideals of worth, and they had only scorn for intellectual acquire-ments. There was no school of theology or philosophy in the forests.

In brief, the number and character of his sufferings con-vinced him he had not found the terrestrial paradise, and he thought once he was going off to the celestial one. The smoke of the wigwam had made him stone blind, his bones were racked with agonizing pain, and he was reduced to such a state of helplessness that it was determined to tie him on a toboggan and drag him along like luggage. But as he laughingly refused to be treated in that fashion, they gave him a boy to lead him on the trail. He grew worse, however, and then a solemn council was convoked to decide what to do with him. When the debate was over, the chief pompously approached the sufferer and said: "There is a woman here who can cure you, if you put yourself in her hands." It was a matter of blind obedience, so he assented. As an initial treatment, the squaw led him out of the wig-wam and said: "Now open your eyes wide and look at the sun." While he was staring in spite of the glare, the fair "oculist," as the "Relation" calls her, took a rusty iron and began to rasp at his eyelids. Her hand was not as light as a feather, and her skill was on the same level as her science; so she soon developed a running sore on the eye. In spite of the operation his sight was as dim as ever, and the lady admitted she had nothing else to suggest. She had exhausted her medical knowledge, so the victim turned elsewhere and determined to ask God to cure him. If his prayer was to be heard he wanted the savages to know it.

Blind as he was he determined to say Mass, for he knew the Mass of the Blessed Virgin by heart, and he summoned every one around and told them what he was going to do, bidding them to pray with him.

"Whether or not," says the "Relation" very cautiously, "God had chosen that time to be the term of the Father's sufferings, or whether it was a direct answer to prayer, it happened that, while he stood at the altar, a bright ray of light scattered the darkness that had settled on his eyes, and he not only saw perfectly, but all his bodily pains left him, and never after that did the smoke or snow cause him the slightest inconvenience." After some months he arrived at Quebec in perfect health.

He was in Montreal for a time after this expedition, and later was, as far as we can make out, laboring in Quebec about the time that Nicolet was drowned in the St. Lawrence. That disaster was the occasion though not the cause of a series of journeys which have given Druillettes considerable prominence in American history.

Nicolet had lost his life in an attempt to save some Abnakis from being burned at the stake in Three Rivers. He never reached the place, but when the Algonquin Chief Charles Meiaskwat arrived there with the news of the tragedy, Nicolet's wishes were respected and the captives were liberated and brought to Quebec. The Sisters in the hospital soon healed the wounds of the poor wretches, who had been horribly maltreated, and loaded them with presents when Meiaskwat went with them to the Abnakis country. The people heard with wonder what had happened, and an Abnaki sagamo immediately started off to see the wonderful White Virgins. Other Indians soon fol-

lowed, and in a few years there were Christians in every
village along the Kennebec.

Finally, on Assumption Day, 1646, two sagamos came to
Quebec for missionaries. Montmagny was only too anxious
to accede to their request, especially as peace had just been
concluded with the Iroquois; and hence, after much prayer
and deliberation, Father Jerome Lalemant wrote in his
"Journal," under date of August 21, 1646, as follows:
"To-day I held a consultation, at which Fathers de Quen,
Le Jeune, and Vimont were present. It was decided to
send Father Druillettes to winter among the Abnakis, and
Father Jogues among the Iroquois."

On the 29th there is another entry in the "Journal":
"Father Gabriel Druillettes set out for the mission of the
Assumption, with two canoes of savages, under the Chief
Claude, who is a good Christian. The name 'Assumption'
was given to the mission, because it was on that day the
Indians presented their petition." Father Jogues left for
his destination a month later, for we find the following entry
in September: "Father Jogues is to set out on the 24th to
winter among the Iroquois, along with Lalande, Outrihoure,
an Iroquoised Huron, and two or three other Hurons who
are going to visit some of their relatives held in captivity
there."

Druillettes was perfectly well aware of the danger, but
it mattered little to him, so with a light heart he stepped
into his canoe, and crossed to the other side of the St. Lawrence a short distance above Pointe Lévis, where the Chaudière empties into the great river.

The stream is tranquil enough when you enter it from
the St. Lawrence, but a little further up it runs furiously
down towards you through a deep gorge, for two miles or
more, at the end of which is a great cataract which leaps
over a precipice 130 feet above. The fall is split by an im-
pending rock just as the waters are about to plunge into the
fathomless gulf beneath, from which ascend clouds of vapor

74

THE LOWER CHAUDIÈRE.

that hover like the steam of a seething cauldron above the surrounding country. Hence, the name of Chaudière, or Boiling Cauldron.

Around this great waterfall the travelers carried their canoes, and embarked on the river which folds continually in on itself like a crimped ribbon on its way down from Lake Megantic. Whether the travelers followed it through all its course, or portaged over to Moose Head, out of which the Kennebec flows, we have no means of determining. At all events they reached the Abnaki region, " over roads," says the " Relation," " which seem to lead to hell, but in reality make for heaven." No white man had made that journey before Druillettes.

IIe passed the autumn and winter there, amid the usual horrors of savage life. Fortunately, we have a very detailed account of this first visit to the Kennebec. It is to be found in the " Relation " of 1647. A few extracts will suffice for our present purpose.

As soon as he arrived, all the savages from far and near came to visit him, " saluting him," he says, " with more heartiness and simplicity than politeness." The sick dragged themselves for miles to ask his prayers, and his amiability won the hearts of all. He was a man of very charming manners, and his interest in them was so sincere that they could not do too much to show their gratitude. His quickness in learning their language especially pleased them. It had very little affinity with the Algonquin, with which he was familiar, but he managed to master it so rapidly that every one was amazed.

Shortly after his arrival, he went down the Kennebec with an Indian to an English trading post, at Cousinoc, the present Augusta, where he was most cordially received by the Agent, Edward Winslow, who from that out became his affectionate and lifelong friend. He did not remain long, however, for his people needed him, and about the middle of October he bade good-by to Winslow and resumed his work among the redmen. He visited the sick, and even washed and cleaned and fed them, often going without food to give it to them. Old and young, men and women, continually thronged to his cabin to listen to him; and it is said that many miraculous cures were effected by his prayers. Indeed, he was more remarkable as a thaumaturge than any of the missionaries.

The Abnakis were very proud of him, and to please them he had to go a second time to Cousinoc, and then to the sea, where his Indians exhibited him all along the coast. He visited seven or eight English posts, and everywhere he was received with the greatest manifestation of respect. He journeyed as far as the Penobscot on this occasion, and he found there a small convent of Capuchin Friars. Charlevoix says that they had an establishment on the Kennebec, but there is no mention of such a post in the " Relations." The Superior at Penobscot, Father Ignatius of Paris, welcomed him cordially, as was to be expected from a man who was named Ignatius, and who was a Parisian and a Capuchin. Druillettes remained some time there, and then returned by way of Cousinoc, for he wanted to show Winslow the letters he had received from the Sieur de Chastes, whom he had met on the coast and who had supplied him with ample provisions for his journey home. Winslow was delighted with the laudatory tone of the letters, and had a copy made of them to show to the authorities of Plymouth and Boston. Meantime he gave the priest leave to go among the Indians at the fort, and even supplied him with timber to build a chapel.

Druillettes enjoined three things on these Indians. The first was to abstain from fire-water, which they all promised to do; and, what is better, they kept their word. The second was to put an end to the war with their neighbors, and in this he succeeded so well that a famous chief who had got into a quarrel in his own village scourged himself publicly, and begged the offended party to forgive him. The third was to throw away their manitous. Very many did so, and that put an end, for a time at least, to the nightly shouts and yells of the medicine men in their incantations over the sick. Some stubborn ones, however, still held out.

He remained there till the middle of January, and had the happiness of baptizing thirty dying persons, whom he had previously instructed; among them an old sorcerer, who got well as soon as he had discarded his conjuring-drum. Druillettes was a little uncomfortable when the old fellow recovered, for so far he had baptized only those who were at the point of death.

The impression he made on the Indians was so great that the squaws began to pray over their sick babies, and God often rewarded their simple faith. The medicine men were, of course, arrayed against him, and they were in great glee when the chief, at whose lodge Druillettes lived, fell sick. They were sure he would die, but to their intense regret he recovered. He had two or three relapses, but came out safely. After that Druillettes' reputation was secure.

But sorrow fell on the family of this much favored chief. His little boy, to whom he was very much attached, sickened and died; but instead of growing gloomy over it, the valiant man invited his friends to a banquet, where he made a great speech and expressed his delight that the child was safe in heaven.

Another case occurred of a poor fellow who relapsed into evil courses after his almost miraculous cure. He had gone down to Boston and indulged uproariously in fire-water, with the usual consequences. He fell sick again, but to vindicate the missionary, he summoned his friends to his cabin and declared that he richly deserved the punishment he was undergoing.

Druillettes was named "the Patriarch" by his Indians. They never tired of extolling his virtues, his fearlessness in facing contagion, his immunity from disease, his abstinence from food, for they saw him refraining from eating meat for months at a time, so as to give it to others, and, above all, his freedom from all suspicion that he was seeking personal gain quite captured their hearts. He was after souls, not furs. It was hard for them to understand how this scholarly man, who had always enjoyed the comforts of civilized life, could live in their hovels. They saw that he was venerated by the French, and, what was more surprising, respected by the English; yet he was always happy in an Indian wigwam, was intensely interested in Indian babies, was unwearied in nursing the sick, and was able to bear long journeys in the forests and over mountains as well as the most stalwart Abnaki.

In the winter they went up to Moose Head to hunt, and the medicine man predicted all sorts of misfortune for those who had accepted the prayer. They were sure to have a spell cast over them, or would be caught by the Iroquois, or would find no game. All these prophecies of evil failed. Druillettes accompanied them everywhere. He instructed his squad of hunters as they went along and made them pray, and so won their good will that everybody wanted to be near him. When the hunt was over the scattered groups met on the shores of the lake, and to their great delight not only was no one injured during all that time, but they had a plentiful supply of moose, elk, bear, etc., while the Indians who held off from the priest had no luck at all.

After remaining some time at the lake, they descended the Kennebec, and insisted again on showing their "Patriarch" to the English, "Houinslaud," as the "Relation" tentatively spells the name of the Agent. Winslow, who meantime had gone down to Boston and Plymouth, told Druillettes that he had presented Chastes' letters to the most important personages of New England, among others, to four ministers, and that all had not only expressed their delight at the arrival of the missionary, but had blessed God for inspiring him to devote himself to the work. They were most willing that he should build a house on the Kennebec, and promised not to molest him in the exercises of his ministry. "If you would remain here," he added, "some of the English would visit you," which would seem to imply, as the "Relation" suggests, that there were some Catholics in New England at that time. Could it be possible that Major Gibbons, who was so solicitous about Druillettes four years later, was of the Faith? At last, on the 20th of May, he bade good-by to "Houinslaud," and after going around to all the Indian villages, baptizing the dying and obtaining health for the sick by his prayers, he turned his face towards Canada. The Indians, old and young, reproached him bitterly. "You don't love us any more. You do not care if we die, for you are abandoning us." But he had to obey orders, and he departed for the north. Thirty braves accompanied him to Quebec, where he arrived on the 15th of June, in vigorous health, although his delay in coming made his friends fear that he had fallen sick on the way.

CHAPTER II.

IN NEW ENGLAND.

Druillettes expected to return to his Abnakis, but was told to dismiss all thoughts of it. The reason of this order is set down by Lalemant without note or comment in the "Journal" of 1647, and is as follows:

"On the 3d or 4th of August, the Abnakis asked to see me to thank me for Father Druillettes' visit, and to request his return. But as the last representatives of the Abnakis had brought letters from the Capuchin Fathers asking us not to return, I refused the Indians, and gave them the same answer that I had sent to the Capuchins."

What makes this opposition of the Friars particularly regrettable is that, according to Shea in his "Catholic Missions," they never attempted any work among the Indians. They were merely chaplains to the French. Nor did they remain long even in that capacity, for before 1650 they were carried off by de la Tour, who was fighting with Aulnay for the possession of Acadia. Indeed, their attitude was so unreasonable that, after some hesitation, it was decided to disregard it. Hence, we find another entry in the "Journal," that "in July, 1648, it was determined in the Consultation that if the Abnakis asked again for the Father he was to be sent."

Meantime, however, the upper Algonquins were again starting on their annual hunt, and wanted a priest. Druillettes was assigned to the work and passed another winter of terrible sufferings in the mountains of the St. Lawrence, down near the Gulf.

They first went as far as Tadoussac, and on the 8th of October crossed the great river to the south side. As the St. Lawrence is between twenty-four and thirty miles wide at that place, of course they had to wait for fine weather, but they finally reached the opposite shore in safety and then dispersed in the woods. Druillettes' squad consisted of about fifty people, not counting the very small children. They kept journeying in a northeasterly direction, till they arrived at the river Matanne, which flows into the St. Lawrence above the Restigouche, which the Inter-Colonial Railroad of to-day crosses at the head of the Baie des Chaleurs. At the mouth of the Matanne they left their two canoes and kept plodding onward, till they came to the mountains of Nôtre Dame, which are at the mouth of the St. Lawrence. The "Relations" furnish us with the interesting information, that when the ships from Europe sighted these mountains the passengers who had never seen them before had to go through the same unpleasant ceremonies that sailors subject people to when crossing the equator, dousing them with water, etc. These mountains were about four days' journey from the Matanne, "over roads," we are told, "more generously paved than the great highway from Paris to Orleans, but not so smooth or even. The stones were placed there by the hand of nature, and were of a most delightful variety; some as sharp as knives, others covered with moss; they were round, and square, and big, and little. In a word, it was a *chemin de fer*. "Over that road," continues the narrative, "we had to carry our houses and our provisions on our backs. We found our beds everywhere. He who made the earth and the woods and the rocks, had also made the mattresses and the sheets which the savages use when they set out on their journeys."

On the 7th of November, when they were eating the last handful of Indian corn that was left in their sacks, a chief addressed them. "Keep up your courage; now we shall have to starve. There are no porcupines here; the beavers are scarce; and the snow is not deep enough to hunt the elk." But the Indians did not seem to be distressed over the announcement, and the Christians among them offered their sufferings to God, and prayed that because of their hunger He would save them from the Iroquois.

When they reached the Mountains of Nôtre Dame their sufferings were terrible. Still they kept on, and one old woman surprised even the braves by climbing the highest of the peaks. "How did you do it?" they asked. "My Guardian Angel helped me," she said. "It was a great feat," they assured her. "And as you are about as old as this mountain, we are going to give you its name." From that out the venerable squaw was known as the Ouabask, a name that doesn't sound unlike one that was heard later, in the far West, the Wabash; but only the philologists can tell us if there is any linguistic kinship.

Food grew scarcer, but after a while the party that was in the section where there was supposed to be least game succeeded in killing many a wild beast, while the hide of an elk which old Noël had shot supplied material for snowshoes. That made hunting easier, for the snow was now very deep. Enough game was furnished by the hunters at least to support life.

During all this trip Druillettes continued his exhortations, and God seems to have given him almost miraculous powers in healing the sick. The Indians were enthusiastic, and one grateful savage planted a cross on the highest mountain in gratitude for what had been done to him in that respect. There was even a case of what seemed to be diabolical possession, and the victim was none other than the daughter of the chief. But she, too, recovered.

When the winter was over the tribes met again at the River Matanne, where they had left their canoes. It was the 3d of March, but they waited there till the 14th of April for the stragglers, and then made for Tadoussac, which was one hundred and twenty miles away. They were anxious to reach that place at the end of the month, to celebrate the feast of St. Michael, to whom the little chapel in the cove was dedicated, and though usually it would take a month to travel that distance, a favorable wind helped them to realize their hopes.

When they arrived at Quebec, Druillettes gathered them all around him, and with his crucifix held aloft gave thanks to God for the protection that had been vouchsafed during the winter. The white people looked on in silent wonder, some of them weeping at the sight of the poor emaciated and barefooted missionary, wrapped in his Indian blanket, exhorting his people who knelt before him as he gave them his parting benediction.

During his absence the Abnakis in Maine had sent delegation after delegation to have their beloved Patriarch return to them. They said they had secured the permission of the Patriarchs of Acadia (the Capuchins) for him to resume his apostolic work; and finally a letter came from the Superior on the Penobscot, Cosme de Mante, begging for the same favor. It was dated 1648, and ran as follows:

"We entreat your Reverence, through the holy love of Jesus and Mary, for the salvation of these poor souls towards the south who beg it of you, to give them every assistance that your courageous and indefatigable charity can bestow, and, even if crossing the Kennebec you should meet any of Ours, you will please us if you will make known your needs to them; and if you have none we ask you to continue your holy instructions to those poor abandoned barbarians as much as your charity will permit." It is curious that the Kennebec, which the English, later on, declared to be the dividing line between the French and English territory, was also proclaimed as an ecclesiastical demarcation.

In consequence of this return of good feeling, Father Druillettes, accompanied by a Frenchman, went with a party of Abnakis on his second trip to the Kennebec. It was September first. Unfortunately the old route was not followed, and they attempted one on which many Indians had previously lost their lives from fatigue or hunger. After fifteen days the provisions gave out and not a third of the journey had been accomplished. As usual, Druillettes brought the Lord to the aid of the famishing crew. He was just leaving the altar, when a young Christian Indian who had gone into the woods to find something to appease his hunger, came back with three elks and three moose. The savages devoured all they could, attacked the meat again and again, dried what was left, and then took up their paddles.

For some reason or another they had portaged into the River St. John, whose headwaters are not far from those of the Chaudière; and they had to return after finding their mistake. They were now working against the current, and there were so many rocks and shallows, besides portages of five or six leagues in length, that an Etchemin Indian who was in the party wanted to turn back and to follow the course of the river to where it empties into the Bay of Fundy. When he was remonstrated with, that such a course would be virtually abandoning the Abnakis, he relented, and for three days worked furiously in rounding and avoiding the cataracts that were met with continually. Then he lost heart again, and turned angrily on Druillettes, abusing him for having caused them to lose their way. The situation became so unpleasant that the priest had to get into another canoe. He even abandoned part of his baggage to lighten the burden. This concession mollified the savage. He took up his paddle again, and in the portages always trudged alongside of Druillettes and his companion. He was atoning for his bad temper. He never grew weary. Indeed, says the "Relation," "those Indians are like English horses: they will eat all night and travel all day. The priest had to imitate them, except for the eating. He would work all day long without a mouthful, and at night would take for his only meal a little bit of jerked meat, or perhaps a fish which he had managed to catch. The bare ground was his bed, and a log his pillow, but he slept more sweetly than if he were lying on feathers or down." After twenty-two or three days, he at last arrived at the village, as the " Relation " calls it, of " Naranchouak."

He was welcomed with a volley of musketry. The Chief Oumandarok embraced him, and after a long speech in which he thanked the Great Spirit for having sent him back, he inquired if he had been well treated on the way, and when some one told him of the bad behavior of the Etchemin, he grew very angry and, apostrophizing the culprit, said : " If you were of our tribe, I would make you feel the weight of the displeasure of every one here."

The poor Etchemin did not excuse himself, but acknowledged his fault.

" I had no sense " he said, " to have acted so; especially as his prayers saved my life. He watched all night at my side, and drove away the demon that was trying to kill me. He was not satisfied with carrying his own pack, but insisted on taking mine. He obtained from Him who made all things whatever he asked. When the water was low he prayed, and the rivers were immediately full, so that we could travel with ease. When we were hungry, he obtained from God more food than we could eat. He never ate meat when it was fresh, but used to go out to fish at night and he gave us the best of what he caught. When our canoes were in danger of striking the rocks in shallow water, he got out, and I have seen him walking for six days at a time in thick undergrowth, and over horrible rocks. He would eat nothing till nightfall and then he was fresher and livelier than any of us. He is not a man; he is a Niouskeou, an extraordinary spirit. When I cried out against him and blamed him for our sufferings, he never answered a word, or if he did, he was so sweet and kind that one would have believed he felt guilty. Yes, I had no sense, but I want to have, I want to love the prayer, and be instructed by the Patriarch."

No doubt after this discourse Druillettes affectionately embraced the penitent, and instructed him in the Faith.

The news of his arrival at Narantsouac brought all the savages who lived along the Kennebec and in the neighboring country to see him. They were all happy at his return, reproached him for having left them, and listened eagerly to all he had to say about "The Prayer."

But Druillettes had a very important political mission to fulfill just then, besides prosecuting his apostolic work among the Abnakis. He had been appointed by the Quebec Government to go down into New England and, if possible, make a treaty of mutual defense against the terrible Iroquois, and, as an inducement, he was to offer certain valuable trade privileges with Quebec in return for the alliance.

It is remarkable that this is not explicitly set down in the "Relation." He is represented as going merely as an envoy of the Abnakis to ask for English protection, but in a letter of Druillettes to Governor Winthrop, which Thwaites gives in full, surmising that it was probably written in 1651, the missionary appeals for aid against the Iroquois; but adds that "the Most Illustrious Governor of Quebec commanded me to offer you in his name the most ample commercial advantages and a considerable compensation for the expense of the war."

He also makes an admission which is notable, in connection with the claims made in Râle's time, seventy years later. Druillettes says that the Kennebec catechumens are inhabitants of New England, and the special clients of Plymouth Colony, which was an implicit abandonment of the claim which the French made later with regard to the Kennebec country, and it may explain why it is not stated in the "Relations" which were published in France. Perhaps it was expunged there. Whether this concession was made with the assent of the French Governor or not, is not explicitly stated, but it is not likely that Druillettes would have dared to make the statement without authorization. In all probability, the Governor of Quebec knew that if he insisted on French ownership of the territory he could have no hopes of making a treaty.

Garneau informs us that the proposition for a commercial treaty emanated from New England, and that a commissioner had appeared at Quebec with that end in view just prior to the second visit of Druillettes to Boston; and Hutchison, in his " History of Massachusetts Bay," says that " proposals had been made in the year 1648, to Monsieur d'Ailleboust, the Governor of Canada, for free trade between Massachusetts and that colony. The French professed to be greatly pleased, and a correspondence was kept up on the subject until the year 1650, when the French Governor sent an agent to Boston, not merely to settle the question of trade, but to form a league or alliance, defensive and offensive, between the Government of Canada and the colonies of Massachusetts and Plymouth." Hutchison does not tell us who the delegate was.

At that time the New England colonies were very far from enjoying a condition of internal peace and tranquillity. Cromwell had just beheaded Charles I, and while the other colonies were royalist in their sympathies, a letter from the General Court in Massachusetts Bay, dated 1650, reminds the honorable Parliament, that " as for our carriage and demeanor for these ten years, since the first beginning of your differences with the late King, and the war that thereafter ensued, we have constantly adhered to you, not withdrawing ourselves in your weakest condition, and doubtfullest time, but by our fasting and prayers, for your good success, and our thanksgiving, on days of solemnity set apart for that purpose after the same was attained, as also our sending over useful men (others also going voluntarily from us to help you), for which we have suffered the hatred and threats of other English colonies, now in rebellion against you."

Cromwell recognized this loyalty of the New Englanders to his cause, and thought he could not reward it better than by asking them to emigrate to Ireland, to take possession of the lands that he had devastated there. The offer was refused, whereupon the Protector, who evidently had a poor idea of New England's future, suggested to them to go to Jamaica. That invitation was also declined.

There were commercial troubles also with the adjoining colony of Connecticut, and in addition to all this the encroachments of the Dutch in that region caused considerable alarm. A certain number of Episcopalians were at the same time clamoring for their rights as English subjects; Roger Williams had left the colony in anger, and a little later the persecution of the Quakers was begun and two of them were executed. In 1656 the second execution for witchcraft took place. Ferdinando Gorges was also endeavoring to establish an independent colony in Maine, and an alarming growth of democratic spirit was revealing itself in the protests of the deputies against the autocratic power of the magistrates who constituted the Upper House.

As if all this were not enough of trouble, according to Hutchison, "the scrupulosity" of the good people of the colony was at its height. Soon after Mr. Winthrop's death, in 1649, Governor Endicott, the most rigid of any of the magistrates, joined with other zealots in an association against long hair, which was officially declared to be contrary to the rule of God's word, and it was enjoined that "the members of the Church should not be defiled therewith." Previous to that, namely, in 1646, the same "scrupulosity" had decreed that any Jesuits who persisted in remaining in the colony should be put to death. Hutchison does not mention this, as it is a little outside of his scope, but we find it in Gilmary Shea's collection (Vol. I, p. 269).

Such were the perturbed conditions of New England, social, political, and religious, when Druillettes went there. His "Narré du Voyage, 1650-1" is published entire in Thwaites, V, xxxvi, and is very interesting reading, especially for Americans. His shipwrecks in orthography are delightful, as there is no harm done except to some personal prejudices about how sounds should be written. Druillettes had his own ideas and carried them out. He was such an

amiable man that nobody cared. No doubt that amiability
stood him in good stead, for it is amazing that in those
troubled times a Catholic priest should have dared to show
himself in close-cropped Puritanical Boston. But it was
quite unlikely that he went there in his cassock.

On September 28 he was at Cousinoc with his friend
Winslow. The affection of that excellent man had not
waned. On the contrary, he assured Noël, after the chief
had made the usual speech, that " he would lodge Druillettes
at his own house and treat him as a brother." " This," says
the " Narré," " was because ' Houinslaud ' had a special zeal
for the conversion of the savages. Indeed, his brother
John was then appealing to the Parliament of England to
institute a brotherhood to train and instruct the savages."

Druillettes evidently did not seize exactly the precise
purport of John Winslow's scheme. He had not established a " confraierie," but he had organized a corporation
in England to supply funds to support the Indian missions
in the colony. This corporation was duly established, says
Hutchison, by an act of Parliament, which authorized collections to be made in England and Wales for that purpose.
Oxford and Cambridge took up the work, and called upon
the ministers to promote it. Even the army was enlisted
in the cause. Of course, as usually happens, great opposition was aroused, and the project was denounced as a
money-making scheme. Hugh Peters was accused of not
only refusing to give a penny himself, but also of discouraging others, because he had no hand in laying the plan.
In spite of all this, however, by the time Charles II came
to the throne, the corporation had a revenue of five or six
hundred pounds per annum, and because there were fears
of losing everything then, for the charter had been given
by the Parliament, and not by the King, a new concession
was obtained which assured the safety of the funds.

As Winslow had said that he would do everything for
" his brother " Druillettes, he was asked to accompany the

delegation to Boston. He agreed to do so, and started from Cousinoc by land to Merrymeeting, or "Marmiten," as Druillettes spells it, a distance of thirty miles. "That road," says the "Narré," "was very difficult, especially for the Agent who was already growing old, and he assured me he would not have undertaken it if he had not given his word to Noël.

On the 25th of November they set sail from Natsouac for Merrymeeting, and on the way met some English fishermen who complained that Winslow was conducting a French spy along the coast.

They were not able to reach "Kepane," or Cape Anne, until December 5th, and then had to go partly by land, partly by water in order to cross over the great bay to Charlestown. "We then went over the river, which separates it from Boston, where we arrived on the eighth." No doubt Druillettes mentally took note that he entered Boston on the feast of the Immaculate Conception. He puts down in his narrative that the principal men of Charlestown went ahead to announce his coming to Major-General "Gebin" or Gibbons.

Druillettes does not give us any information about the major, but we find in Hutchison, who quotes from Mather, that "in 1650 Edward Gibbons was made an Assistant or Member of the Upper House. He was one of Mr. Wollaston's plantation, and a very gay young gentleman, when the Massachusetts people first came to Salem, and happened to be there at Mr. Higginson's, at Mr. Shelton's ordination, and forming of the Church. He was so much affected by the solemnity of the proceeding that he desired to be received into the number. They had not sufficient knowledge of him, and encouraged him in his good intentions, and he afterwards joined into the Church in Boston."

The name of the "gay young gentleman" about whom the Puritans had "not sufficient knowledge" and who "joined into the Church" has a suspiciously Irish and Catholic ring to it. Perhaps the fact that he was friendly with Aulnay, a staunch Catholic, the opponent of de la Tour in the race for Governorship of Acadia, might indicate his spiritual attitude. De la Tour was the reverse of " staunch."

Gibbons received the missionary as a duly accredited ambassador of the Governor; " but," says the " Narré," " he gave me a key to an apartment in his house, where I could, in complete liberty, offer my prayers and perform my religious exercises. He begged me to take no other lodgings while I should sojourn in Boston."

We find in Charles Francis Adams' " Three Episodes of Massachusetts History," that the major was one of the fashionable set in Boston, and that his roystering habits often shocked the Puritans. He was once on the list of offenders in the matter of deep drinking and was heavily fined for it. At one time he disappears from Boston on one of his ships for a cruise, no one knew whither nor cared much. For those were the days when a gentleman pirate could go off as a privateer, and no one was very inquisitive about how the cargo on the return voyage was so valuable. Gibbons finally settled down and became one of the most prosperous and enterprising merchants of Boston. His house was in what is now Washington Street, opposite Cornhill. It was in that mansion that Druillettes was so hospitably received.

A little before that time we are told by Hutchison that " one Darbyfield, an Irishman, with some others, travelled this year, 1642, to the White Hills, which were supposed to be the highest in these parts of America. They reported that they had been on the top, where there is a plain sixty feet square; that on the west side is a very steep precipice, and all the country round appeared like a level very much beneath them. The glittering appearance of the rocks as they came near caused an expectation of something valuable, but they found nothing." We do not know if this acknowledged Irishman, Darbyfield, who was the first to reach the top of the White Mountains, and was looking at the glittering rocks, and found nothing, also happened to meet Druillettes in Boston. But he probably did.

The day after Druillettes' arrival, which, by an evident slip of the pen, is also put down as the eighth, the major conducted the priest to " Rogsbray," or Roxbury, to see Governor Dudley, who, after examining Druillettes' credentials, appointed the thirteenth for a general discussion of the matter by the magistrates. The thirteenth came and all the dignitaries, with one member of the Low House, met Druillettes at dinner, and when that was over devoted the whole afternoon to debate. They were in good humor when they sat down to supper, but the general verdict was that the clause about protecting the Abnakis would have to be referred to Plymouth, " as Boston had no interest in those Indians."

In consequence of this decision, Druillettes posted off to Plymouth, or " Pleimout," which he reached on December 22nd, Governor Bradford not only welcoming him, but, as it was Friday, inviting him to a fish dinner ; a very extraordinary act of courtesy on the part of the Puritan host, and the missionary was careful to make note of it. He was also well received by the principal merchants of the place. As their financial interests were involved in the Abnakis trade they strongly advocated the policy of uniting with the French for mutual help and protection.

Elated at his success, Druillettes returned to Boston. It was December 29th. The precise place in which he passed Christmas we do not know, for he left Plymouth on the twenty-fourth and did not reach Roxbury until the twenty-eighth. At Boston he lodged as usual at the house of Gibbons.

He made many friends there, one of whom he calls Ebens, whose identity has been somewhat of a puzzle to a few writers ; but as there was a distinguished man in the colony named Hibbins, there can be little doubt that he is the one indicated. He was a worthy man in many respects,

and a sad interest attaches to his name, because after his
death, and in spite of the esteem in which he had been held,
the Puritan superstition about witchcraft first vented its fury
on his wife. She had become moody and bad tempered in
her widowhood, and was soon regarded as a witch. In the
mind of her accusers there was little doubt about her com-
plicity with the Spirit of Darkness, because it was found
out that one day she passed two of the magistrates, who
were conversing in the street, and *guessed* that they were
talking about her. She was correct in her suspicion, and
was therefore arrested and condemned to death. A similar
test for witchcraft would convict nearly every Yankee since
that time. The unfortunate woman made her preparations
and calmly went to the scaffold. This was in 1656, *i. e.,*
only a few years after Druillettes bade good-bye to the
kindly "Sieur Ebens."

On the last day of the year he had a conference at Roxbury with Governor Dudley, who expressed his gratifica-
tion at Plymouth's resolution to subdue the Iroquois, and
promised to aid the movement with all his power. A few
days afterwards, Gibbons volunteered the assurance that,
although Boston would not participate in the war officially,
yet considerable private assistance might be relied on.

The indefatigable envoy posted off to "Marbletz," or
Marblehead, on January 9, and from there to Salem, where
he met Endicott. He found that grim old Puritan very
affable and spoke French with him, in which language he
tells us Endicott was very proficient. Very much to his
delight, he discovered a great deal of good feeling in that
important personage towards the French in general. "Seeing that I had no money," says Druillettes, "he paid my
expenses, and invited me to dine with the magistrates."
Indeed the Governor went further in his amiability. He
expressed his pleasure at the action of the Plymouth Government, and promised to send to Druillettes the report of
whatever conclusion he himself would arrive at. Quebec's

treatment of the envoy in sending him on an embassy without money was characteristic. Druillettes was at the mouth of the Piscataqua on January 24, and on February 7 he reached Temeriskau, where the fishermen who had taken him for a spy on his way to Boston now cordially welcomed him. As he went up the Kennebec the same friendly spirit was manifested by all the Englishmen he met. It was not until April 13 that his friend Winslow came back from his trip to Plymouth and Boston. He brought good news with him. He assured Druillettes (1) that all the Magistrates and the two Commissioners of Plymouth had resolved that the other colonies should be urged to enter into the league against the Iroquois; (2) that Governor Bradford had sent Captain Willet, who was greatly attached to the Abnakis, with letters to the Governors of Kenetigout [Connecticut] and of Nieufhaven [New Haven], and even to the Governor of Manate [Manhattan], to further the project; (3) that in ten days Endicott would be Governor of Boston, and that even if there were no official action, a great number of volunteers could be counted on for the expedition, and (4) that several Indian tribes, notably the Mohegans, would go out on the warpath. The Catholics of Maryland also were expected to at least favor the project. Such, in brief, were the results of Druillettes' embassy to the Puritans of New England.

It should not be forgotten that while he was there he met John Eliot, " the Apostle of the Indians," as American historians call him. " On the 28th of December I arrived at Rogsbray," he says, " where the minister Master Heliot, who was teaching some savages, received me at his house, because night was overtaking me. He treated me with great respect and kindness, and begged me to spend the winter with him."

As Druillettes was accustomed to spend the winter in quite another fashion, Eliot's kind invitation could not be accepted. He remained only that night, but the conversation of these two men, who were opposite types of mission-ary enterprise, must have been very interesting for both. Druillettes' method was to go out into the woods to hunt for the Indians; Eliot had them to come to him at "Rogs-bray." Protestant historians, while admitting the heroism of the outdoor kind, are fond of contrasting the results; always, of course, in favor of Eliot.

"If we compare the requisites," says Hutchison (I., p. 166), "to determine any one to be a convert, in Mr. Eliot's esteem, with those of the popish missionaries, it is not strange that their numbers exceeded his. Before the con-verts in New England were admitted to the ordinances, they were examined by some of the magistrates, as well as the ministers. The confessions of many of them, as taken from their own mouths, were sent to England, and printed, and there approved of; and, although the mission began in 1646, it was the year 1651 before the first church was gathered at Natick. Whereas with the Romish priests the repetition of a *Pater Noster,* or an *Ave Maria,* made them fit subjects of Baptism. The French *coureurs de bois* and others married among the Indians, and became savages them-selves, and the priests went into their country and dwelt among them, suffered them to retain their old customs and conformed to them themselves."

It would be interesting to know if Eliot thought that Druillettes, whom he entreated to stay with him all winter, had conformed to the savage customs of the Indians, or imagined for a moment that he would baptize any Indian who could do no more than recite a *Pater Noster* or an *Ave Maria.* As a matter of fact, the Catholic missionaries sinned in the contrary direction. They would keep Indians for years before baptizing them, and they are blamed, and per-haps rightly so, for undue rigorism in that respect.

How many Indians were converted in New England by Eliot's method we have no means of knowing, though we are told there were in 1660 ten towns of praying Indians.

In Martha's Vineyard there were ninety families on the list. At Natick, between forty and fifty communicants were counted. There were others at Stoughton, Marlborough, Nashope, Wamesut, Pautucket, etc. " The Massasoiets and the Naragansetts and the Wampanoags were averse to Christianity, but, they having been extirpated, we are told the rest lived in peace."

The large number of these Indian towns would make one fancy that in reality the number of Eliot's converts was greater than that of the " popish " missionaries, but we have no means of finding the number of individual conversions, nor do we know how severe was the test to which the Indians were subjected, prior to baptism, even if " the confessions of many of them, taken from their own mouths, were sent to England and printed." In our days " getting religion " is sufficient to admit almost anybody as a member of any sect, and probably such was the case then. Moreover, according to Converse Francis, even Eliot ascribed the knowledge of Christianity which his converted Indians possessed to some French priest who had been wrecked on the coast. As the savages were not clever in discerning doctrinal differences they probably considered Maitre " Heliot " as the lawful successor of the blackrobe.

In speaking of the Huron missions, Parkman inquires, somewhat scoffingly, of what use was such an expenditure of life that resulted in nothing but the few scattered Indian Christians which exist here and there? Hutchison's account of Eliot's labors might give the answer. He says: " It does not appear that the number of Christians have since decreased by the return of Indians to paganism. The Indians themselves are wasted, and their tribes or nations everywhere in Massachusetts and Plymouth extinct." He wrote this in 1770, and informs us that " at Nantucket, last year, there were ninety families, but now only fifteen." In neither case is the failure of the missions to be ascribed to the preachers.

GABRIEL DRUILLETTES

It may not be uninteresting to know that ten years after Eliot bade good-bye to Druillettes, the General Court of Massachusetts became a sort of Spanish Inquisition, and made an auto-da-fe of one of Eliot's contributions to literature. The good man had written a book and the Court found that " on perusal, though it was entitled ' The Christian Commonwealth,' it was full of seditious principles and notions, in relation to all established governments in the Christian world." Just like any benighted papist, " Eliot retracted and disowned his errors; the books were ordered to be called in and his acknowledgment was posted up in the principal towns of the colony."

As Druillettes was naturally and by training interested in educational projects, it is more than likely that while he was in Boston he took a glance at Harvard. Had he been present at one of the academic exhibitions he would have been surprised and delighted if he found that the collegiate exercises corresponded with the theses defended by the graduates of 1642. They are given by Hutchison (V. I., p. 510). They are in Latin, and the subjects discussed reveal the fact that the much derided scholasticism of the Middle Ages was in high honor in Harvard in its early days. Thus, among other pronouncements, we have: " Materia secunda non potest existere sine forma; Unius rei non est nisi unica forma constitutiva. Quidquid movetur, ab alio movetur," etc., etc.

In summing up the transactions of his diplomatic visit to New England Druillettes displays a joyous enthusiasm about the good results to be expected. He was sure he had succeeded, and when his friend Winslow returned from Boston to Cousinoc, with the intelligence that the colonists were quite ready to go out against the Iroquois, he hastened to Quebec with his report, and so impressed the authorities there that Godefroy and the old Indian Noël were dispatched with him on June 22, 1651, to make the final arrangements.

This Sieur Godefroy was an important man in the colony. He had come out to America at a very early date, and was employed as a clerk and interpreter of the trading company. He was present at the capitulation of Quebec, and had returned with Champlain to France in 1629. In 1636 he was again in his old occupation, not however at Quebec, but at Three Rivers. In 1644 he was a delegate of the Canadian colonists to France, along with the famous Pierre Le Gardeur, who was Nicolet's son-in-law. In the following year he was commander of a ship, and from 1648 to 1650 was Admiral of the fleet. He had just resigned that important office, and formed a trading company with several other conspicuous people in Quebec when he was deputed to go down to New England with Druillettes. Evidently the people on the St. Lawrence were deeply in earnest in furthering the alliance with the English.

Not much is said about this second embassy; possibly because of its failure, and we merely find in the " Journal des Jésuites " that Druillettes sent a letter back to Quebec, from Cousinoc, and also that Noël returned from Boston, before his associates. Godefroy finally appeared with his report on October 30. It turned out that the English were quite willing to make a commercial treaty with the French, but refused to engage in war against the Iroquois. Why should they? The Iroquois were not only destroying the other red men, but from all appearances would soon drive the French from Quebec. They were at that moment making raids around the very walls of the citadel.

In the " Relation " of 1650-1651 we have a letter of Noël to Father Le Jeune, who was then in France. The old Indian, very much impressed with his own importance, says: " I would like to go to France to see you, but I am prevented from doing so. I was sent to the countries of the Abnakis and of the English, who are their neighbors, to ask them for assistance against the Iroquois. I obeyed those who sent me, but my journey was in vain. The Englishman replied not; he has no good thoughts for us. This grieves me very much; we see ourselves dying and being exterminated every day."

This grief of Noël may explain the hatred which from that time characterized the conduct of the Kennebec Indians for the English. Up to that they seemed to have accepted the protectorate of Plymouth, which, according to Thwaites, came about in the following fashion: "The original grant of the territory was made to Bradford, Winslow and other Plymouth colonists, and was held by them until 1640, and then surrendered to the colony at large. The deed was known as 'The Kennebec Patent,' and is the original source of land-titles in that district. The patent was owned by the colony until October 27, 1661, when it was sold to John Winslow and others for 400 pounds sterling." Thus Druillettes' friends became the proprietors ten years after the delegation started from Quebec. But in Râle's time we find the Indians protesting that no one had a right to give away their lands, and they announced their determination to fight for them. Although the Jesuits were accused of urging them on in this contention, the contrary is true; for we find Druillettes' successors doing all in their power to induce the Abnakis to abandon the territory and establish themselves in the St. Lawrence. Even Râle, though commanded by the Governor and the King to support the Indians in their claim, thought he nevertheless had the right to urge his flock to withdraw.

CHAPTER III.

In the West.

Druillettes continued his labors along the Kennebec until March, 1652, when he ceased to work there, and a long gap intervenes until the coming of Father Bigot in 1685. But during all that period of non-residence, efforts were made to have the Abnakis come up to Sillery for instruction. In fact, the place had been already deserted by the Algonquins and was occupied exclusively by Indians from the Kennebec, and even a second mission called St. Francis of Sales had been established near the Chaudière. The small number of the priests and the constant fear of the Iroquois made missionary expeditions into Maine impossible at that time.

In 1656, a number of Ottawa Indians came down to Quebec, and professed to be eager not only to take the missionaries back with them to their country, but also to have the French establish a trading post or colony among them. As the Hurons had been completely exterminated, and fur-trading in that direction had ceased, the offer was gladly accepted by the authorities of Quebec, and fifty young Frenchmen volunteered to go as pioneers of the new enterprise. Father Druillettes and Garreau accompanied the party.

By the time they reached Three Rivers their enthusiasm had evaporated. The Iroquois were on the river and the general impression was that it would be wiser to return to Quebec. The Ottawas, of course, continued their journey homeward, and the two priests, a lay-brother and three of their domestics determined to keep them company.

Keeping up the St. Lawrence till they arrived at the Rivière des Prairies, they continued on their course until they fell into an ambuscade of the Iroquois. Garreau, who was in the forward canoe, was shot in the spine, and then dragged on the shore and left weltering in his blood inside of the stockade. The other canoes, in one of which was Druillettes, came up later, and a fight ensued. During the night, however, the Ottawas decamped, and, although Druillettes begged to be taken with them to the west, he was refused. What happened to him just then we do not know. He could not have been taken prisoner by the Iroquois, for they were then at peace with the French. Indeed, they carried the dying Father Garreau over to the settlement at Montreal, and protested that his death was the result of an accident. More than likely, after the Ottawas had refused Druillettes' offer to go with them, he and his companions made their way over to the settlement, which he knew very well, for he had labored there with Jogues twelve or thirteen years before, and he may have been present when the Iroquois came in with the bleeding body of Father Garreau. This, of course, is only conjecture, as there is no information at hand. The " Relation " is silent on this point. It gives a detailed account of the death of Father Garreau, but does not tell us who stood at his side when he breathed his last in the cabin at Montreal.

While Druillettes was endeavoring to reach the Ottawa country other Jesuits were laboring among the Onondagas, and had succeeded in establishing themselves at what is now Syracuse. They began their work in 1655, but in 1658, to avoid a general massacre, they abandoned the mission.

The most conspicuous man in that enterprise was Father Dablon, who on his return to Quebec settled down to ordinary parochial work in the city; but while there he met a Nippisirien chief who was continually talking to him about the region near Hudson Bay, especially about a great meeting of Indians, which was to be held in the summer of 1661. A large number of the Indians of Quebec and Tadoussac were going to take part in it.

Dablon was interested, for he considered it to be an excellent opportunity to obtain correct geographical notions about the place, and especially to find out if there was any truth in the report about a northwestern passage to the Sea of Japan; but most of all because it seemed to hold out some hope of establishing a mission there. The result was that he and Druillettes were assigned to go with the party, Druillettes being told to pass the winter with the savages, while Dablon was to report at Quebec.

They remained three weeks at Tadoussac, and on June 1, 1661, started up the Saguenay in forty canoes. We have already given an extract of Dablon's account of this interesting journey in Vol. I., but the entire story merits perusal as an extremely brilliant narrative of thrilling adventure far into the north in what was a totally un-explored country, where dangers on the rivers and lakes, as well as from starvation, stared them in the face at every moment, and where there was also the continual fear of the pursuing Iroquois. Dablon's letter is dated "Nekouba, a hundred leagues from Tadoussac, in the woods, on the road to the North Sea, July 2, 1661." It is in the "Relations."

When they reached Nekouba they found that the Iroquois had not only preceded them, but had completely exterminated the Squirrel tribe, which lived a few leagues further on. Reports of all this came in to the assembled Indians, and such consternation took possession of them that they flatly refused to go any further. The consequence was that the Fathers were compelled to turn back along with them, regretting indeed that they had not been able to explore the unknown regions of the North Sea, but above all that their apostolic purposes were again thwarted by the same terrible foe. Dablon, who had lived among the Iroquois in New York, calls them "the Turks of New France," and he was of the opinion that a holy war or crusade ought to be preached against them.

The failure of this expedition did not, however, dispel

the hopes of some day reaching the far away sea. Later on, Albanel was commissioned to make the attempt, and to guide him Druillettes sent to his Superiors a list of routes which might be followed. He had gathered the information from the Indians and also from his friends Radisson and de Groseilliers. The original was scrawled in lead pencil, and possibly Dablon, who transcribed it, did not keep the precious paper. What we have is his copy. We shall not trouble the reader with the list of places which could not possibly remain in the memory of any one not familiar with Indian languages, but we shall merely indicate the general directions which such expeditions should have to take.

The first was up the Saguenay to Lake Piouakouami, a distance of forty leagues, and then to another expanse of water with a name somewhat like the first, for a distance of sixty leagues, and from that another sixty leagues would be required to reach the sea.

The second would start from Three Rivers, and two hundred and fifty leagues would be the distance to the Bay of the Kilistinons. A traveler from that place told Druillettes that the sea was four days' journey further on.

The third might begin at Lake Nippising, and from there one hundred and fifty leagues further would be all that was required.

The fourth route would be from a river that empties into Lake Huron. It was reported that the Indians who lived there often went to trade with a tribe of the Kilistinons, whose country bordered on the sea. The journey was a matter of a few days.

The fifth was from the country of the upper Algonquins. Three days traveling would be enough to reach Lake Alimibeg and four others to arrive at the desired goal.

Finally there was a route from Lake Tempagami, between Lake Huron and the source of the St. Lawrence. After going some distance on the great river and traveling

fifteen leagues over small water courses you could reach
Lake Ouassisanik, from which the St. Maurice flows. That
was the route taken by the Nippisiriens on their journey
to Three Rivers two years previously.

It was not a geographical purpose that prompted Druillettes to make this study, for he hastens to tell his Superior
of the number of Indians to be found in those localities.
There were fourteen nations in all, some of them consisting
of only a few families, but others of them numbering twenty
and twenty-four thousand people. As the Huron Missions
were destroyed, and those among the Iroquois not yet
opened, he saw in these new regions to the north wide fields
for apostolic work.

When he returned from Nekouba he did not remain at
Quebec, but started off to evangelize the Montagnais.
There is no explicit announcement of it in the " Relations,"
but we discover his presence there in the account of Father
Nouvel, who was on his way to the Papinachois. " The
first of my flock to die," he said, " was a little girl baptized
by Father Gabriel." Later on the two missionaries met
unexpectedly in the wilderness among the savages. The
Indians had told Nouvel that there was a canoe a league up
the Esseigiou River, and in it were Father Druillettes and a
Frenchman. The joy of this meeting may be imagined.
But they did not remain long together. They discussed
their plans, and it was decided that Nouvel should keep on
towards the north, with his Papinachois, while Druillettes
would ascend the Saguenay to look after the Indians in
those regions. They then bade good-bye to each other, and
went on their separate ways.

Here we lose sight again of this wonderful man, but we
know that he was somewhere in those trackless woods until
1666. We find him afterwards at Three Rivers, and Marquette, who had just arrived from Europe, was put into his
hands to be inducted into the mysteries of Montagnais.
These two men, whose winning natures were so closely akin

to each other, and whose amiability exercised such a marvelous influence on the natives, must have been very congenial companions.

In 1668, Marquette, went to the west, and, in September, 1670, Druillettes followed him. He was thus again with the Ottawas, who had left him at night in the woods near Montreal sixteen years before. Father Allouez announces his arrival as follows: " To re-enforce the labors in this vast mission, Father Gabriel Druillettes, one of the oldest and most esteemed of our missionaries, was sent to us." He was assigned to Sault Ste. Marie, and there the man who had labored near the ocean and the North Sea was to spend what was left of his strength in the service of God. It is marvelous how much vigor he still retained. In all probability he was then nearly eighty years of age.

The abundance of fish in these waters attracted a great number of the neighboring tribes, and that was a strong reason for the missionaries to establish a post there. The natives of the place called themselves by the unpronounceable name of Pahouitingouach Irini. It was too much for the French, so the name *Saulteurs* was introduced. They were only one hundred and fifty souls in all, but they were related to three other nations who were allowed to live there, and who were about five hundred and fifty in number. In winter they roamed along both the north and south shores of Lake Superior. There were seven other nations besides who were dependent on this mission, but in spite of their name of " nations," they did not go beyond four hundred men, women and children all told. Finally there were wanderers from all directions who flocked to the Sault to fish. To this post Father Druillettes was assigned.

In order to induce the Indians to cultivate the soil, the Fathers laid out a farm, and built a little chapel, which they tell us was beautifully decorated for such a desolate place. It is a pity that we cannot find at the Sault to day the exact spot where that sanctuary stood. It would be far more precious assuredly than the foundries and factories and power-houses which now cluster around the rapids. However, there is a Jesuit church nearby, and one can find some little consolation in that, but only a few remnants of the aborigines are left. You meet them on the street, some of them gaudily tricked out in modern finery, but most of them slouching along in the cheap clothing of the working-man and engaged in the humblest employments. They keep by themselves and mingle very little with the whites.

The only difficulty in converting these Saulteurs in olden times was the Manitou. The old squaws were the worst victims of the superstition. But the power of Father Druillettes soon asserted itself, and his little church was filled morning and evening with people eager to hear him. As everywhere else, wonderful answers were given to his prayers, especially in healing the sick. The people were eager to live in the settlement, and built their huts as near as possible to the church.

Besides the Saulteurs, two or three distant tribes looked for spiritual help to St. Mary's. They were Chippewas, Kiskakons, and Missisagas. Old as he was, Druillettes did not shirk the work of looking after them. He passed the winter with each of them in turn, amid the privations and dangers of their hunting expeditions. It is marvelous how at his age he could have been equal to such a task.

A sad event cast a shadow over his last days. The fierce Dakotas had always been bitter enemies of the Indians of the Sault, but finally they sent an embassy for the purpose of making peace. They were received with every demonstration of joy, but while the council was in session, a Cree Indian slipped into the assembly and plunged his knife in the heart of a Dakota. Thinking themselves betrayed, the braves seized whatever weapons they could find, for they had entered the house unarmed, and made a desperate fight in self defense. They laid about them, slaughtering every one indiscriminately, and then barricaded themselves and began shooting at their enemies outside. The Chippewas, who had not been in the council, rushed to the fray. The battle became general, and raged furiously till every Dakota was killed. Meantime the buildings had taken fire, and soon the whole village was a heap of smoldering ashes. But that was not all. According to Indian ethics, the Chippewas, though not guilty of the murder of the deputy, were responsible for the crime, because it had been committed in their village. Hence, fearing a reprisal by the Dakotas, every Chippewa fled, and there was not a red man, woman or child left of all of Druillettes' once promising congregation. But little by little they drifted back; the chapel was rebuilt, cabins arose around it, and the old missionary resumed his accustomed labors, and under his kindly administration order reigned.

Before this tragic occurrence the Intendant Talon at Quebec had determined to fasten forever the claims of France on the western country and had ordered Saint-Lusson to take solemn possession of the territory in the name of the King.

Saint-Lusson arrived from the distant Kennebec, and Perrot, who knew the Indians well, was sent everywhere to summon the tribes to the meeting. He traveled along Lake Superior, into the remotest regions of Canada, and then down to Green Bay and succeeded in gathering a remarkable congress. In May, 1771, says Bancroft, " there were assembled the envoys of the wild republicans of the wilderness, side by side with brilliantly clad officers from the veteran armies of France. A cross of cedar was raised, and amidst the groves of maple and pine, of elm and hemlock, which are strangely intermingled on the beautiful banks of the St. Mary, where the bounding river lashes its waves into snowy whiteness, as they hurry past the dark evergreen of the tufted island in the channel, the throng of French, bowing before the emblems of man's redemption, chanted to its glory a hymn of the seventh century:

> " ' Vexilla Regis prodeunt,
>   Fulget crucis mysterium.' "

Bancroft does not mention the presence of the three illustrious priests whose tattered black gowns also mingled with " the brilliant uniforms of the officers " and the savage finery of the painted and feathered chiefs. The old white-haired Druillettes was there, and the splendid Allouez, and the young André, who had just begun his work among the Indians, nor does he speak of the glowing oratory of Allouez as he recounted the glories of the great chief Louis XIV., who wore scalps of numberless enemies at his belt, and made the oceans tremble with the thundering cannons of his great canoes. But Dablon in the account which he wrote in Quebec shortly afterwards tells us all about it.

Druillettes remained at the Sault until 1679. He had long before that passed the period of life when men need rest, and the time had come when even he could work no longer. So he stepped into his little canoe and journeyed over the thousand miles of river, and lake, and cataract, and tramped through the forests, which were still as full of perils as when he first started to the northwest. He finally reached Quebec, where, after two years, he went to heaven to claim the glorious crown that he had won.

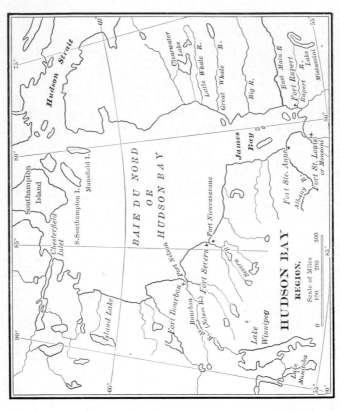

HUDSON BAY REGION.

CHARLES ALBANEL

CHAPTER I.

First Journey to Hudson Bay.

Father Charles Albanel was one of the very great missionaries among the aborigines. Although it was reported to the Superior of the Society that he was actuated more by a spirit of adventure than that of apostolic zeal, the charge is absolutely groundless. No one who reads the story of his life of hardships and privations can fail to see that at all times, and in all places, he was a man in search of souls. The accusation only afforded him one more opportunity to add new luster to his crown.

He was born in 1613, and belonged to the Province of Toulouse. Of his early life we have no details, but we know that he came to America on August 23, 1649, a few months after the martyrdom of Lalemant and de Brébeuf, and in the following year was at Montreal, which was then making its first fierce fight against the Iroquois. He remained there only a very short time, for we find him wintering that same year with the Montagnais. The awful sufferings which this kind of life entailed upon the young missionary just fresh from Europe is a sufficient evidence of Albanel's heroicity. When the spring came he went down to Tadoussac, where he took care of eight hundred Indians who were dying of a loathsome malignant fever.

He had a touch of the fever himself, but he forgot it in the enthusiasm he felt when he witnessed the wonderful piety of these dying red men. They were lying on their mats, in their wretched cabins, many of them clasping their beads and gazing constantly at the pious pictures or crucifixes which they had fixed on the bark walls of their miserable shelters. All of them accepted their sufferings with the most edifying resignation.

Just a chance notice in the "Relations" gives us the information that in 1659 Albanel was appointed to accompany Ménard on the fatal journey to the Far West, but he succeeded in getting no further than Montreal. His Indian companion was objected to by the Ottawas, and both he and Albanel found it impossible to join the party. Why the objection to the Indian should affect the priest is not stated. Ménard never came back.

For the next six years his labors were thus confined to the Indians of Tadoussac. As he had succeeded in raising a storm in Quebec, because he had married a Frenchman to an Indian woman without publishing the banns, it may be that to get him out of the way he was relegated to the Far West with Ménard, where banns might not be necessary. His inability to join the old missionary seemed to have compelled the Superiors to send him back to the Saguenay; for there he continued to labor for the following six years, when a change in the Government methods of dealing with Indians called for his zeal in another direction.

Wearied with the incursions of these relentless savages, the authorities at Quebec finally resolved to act aggressively, and in 1666 de Courcelles started out in midwinter for the Mohawk. His chaplain was the Jesuit Raffeix. He met no Iroquois, however, but, on the contrary, returned to Quebec, chagrined and disgraced, for he had left many of his own soldiers behind him dead in the snow. He attributed his failure to the unconcern or disloyalty of the Jesuits, who had not sent the Algonquin contingent to meet him, as had been agreed upon. The charge, of course, was prompted by the irritability of the old commander, and had no foundation, in fact. Indeed, the Jesuits were only too eager to get into the country, which Jogues had sanctified twenty years before; especially as

the destruction of the Huron missions had left them without
any field to work in. De Courcelles apologized for the
accusation later. He had spoken in his wrath.

In the following summer, de Tracy started out with
better arrangements for a successful raid, and also with a
greater number of soldiers. Albanel was on that expedition, with the former chaplain. They said Mass in one of
the villages of the Mohawk, and, of course, saw the place
where Jogues was slain. Very likely they brought back
some mementoes to Quebec of what, for them, was little
less than a sanctuary, but unfortunately the " Relations "
say nothing about it. Perhaps some future searcher in the
archives may discover a letter or a document of one kind
or another, which will give us the precious information.
Like de Courcelles, de Tracy saw no Iroquois. They had
all decamped, but the destruction of their villages had the
effect of inspiring them with such wholesome terror that
the French were left in peace for the ensuing fifteen years.

In 1668, Albanel was Superior at Sillery, but nothing
of importance is chronicled about that period, except that
he took part in the resuscitation of the pious old Chief Noël,
who had died some years before; not that the Indian was
called back to the flesh to walk the earth again, but his successor was appointed to the long vacant chieftainship, and
thus Noël was supposed to live again.

This poetic fiction was a very expensive piece of business for the new incumbent. All the tribes for miles around
assembled for the ceremony: Abnakis, Papinachois, Montagnais, Gaspesians, and the dispersed Hurons, all of whom
had to be placated by presents. His Royal Highness was
led into the great assembly, and, out of respect for the
French, he was appareled in civilized habiliments. Whether
they fitted him or not the simple son of the forest did not
care. He gave his first present to de Courcelles, the Governor, who was there however only by proxy. Father
Albanel was next honored, and made a great speech,

exhorting the new chief to reproduce in his life the virtues of the defunct. Then each tribe, in turn, received appropriate gifts, with the result that while the King won the hearts of his subjects, his exchequer at the end of the ceremony was empty. But his new honor consoled him for his want of provisions.

Albanel hurried down to Tadoussac, where a pestilence of smallpox was raging, on November 14, of the following year. The river must have been closed by that time, for it took him six days to reach the place. He arrived only to find that even the Indian with whom he was to lodge had a short time to live. It was a great loss for the missionaries, as well as for the tribe, for Theodore, as the chief was called, had distinguished himself by a life of holiness. Albanel prepared him for death, as he did the other sick people around, and then intimated that he was about to set out to visit the scattered huts of the Indians in the woods. "Not at all," said Theodore, "you will stay here till I breathe my last. I have served you for many years, and you shall not leave me, when I need you most." His only regret was that his condition prevented him from receiving Holy Communion, but he resigned himself to the privation. His last words were an act of love, and "he died," says Albanel, "with the marks of the predestined upon him."

His wife was as pious as himself. When death is of a particularly loathsome kind the squaw usually deserts her dying spouse; but not so Susanna. She never left his side, although the malady had already made him an object of horror to every one else. She not only cared for his bodily wants, but helped him to make his confession, and rehearsed all the things he had done, and the places he had been in. "Did you tell that and that?" she would ask, for the Indian man and wife keep no secrets from each other. The priest withdrew for a moment and Susanna continued to speak to him of God and hell and heaven. When he told her tenderly how sorry he was to leave her, she said: " Don't speak of that; I shall be with you soon," and so continued till the end, and afterwards. For when he was laid to rest the good old woman never let a day pass without going to pray at his tomb. She said her beads twice a day for him; and kept a rigorous Lent, and at other seasons fasted twice a week to hasten his release from Purgatory. " Many a French woman," says Albanel, " might learn a lesson of genuine conjugal affection from old Susanna, the squaw."

A French shallop arrived at Tadoussac with fifteen or twenty victims of the plague on November 28. They looked like monsters rather than men, so hideous were their disfigured and corrupting bodies. On December 4, four more canoes came, and increased the number of the sick. On the fifth a number of Frenchmen who had gone ashore at Green Isle, near Tadoussac, found a cabin full of stricken Indians, and sent a messenger in haste for the priest, but he could not leave Tadoussac until the tenth, and when he reached the place he found what he called " animated skeletons." They were not only ill, but starving to death. He helped them as well as he could with food, the French assisting him most heroically. He dosed them with " theriaque," which, he says, " was a sovereign remedy for that kind of ailment," and after giving them all the sacraments, he hurried back to Tadoussac.

Unfortunately on the twentieth some Indians from Gaspé, fourteen or fifteen leagues away, came to the infected village. They withdrew after they had all gone to confession and Communion, but they had scarcely reached home when nearly all of them fell sick and died. Albanel says: " It was a stroke of heaven, and a very particular grace "; not their death, but the reception of the sacraments.

It was now January, 1670, and all that month Albanel continued his work. " If I had only made use of my opportunities," he writes, " I could have practiced great acts of virtue, and especially of mortification, as I had to remain most of the time in a place where the stench was horrible." Most people will imagine that the occasion of mortification was not let slip by the holy missionary.

He started through the forests on February 3, to find some sick people who were far away from the river. The snow was light and the snowshoeing heavy, and it was only after a seven days' tramp that he reached the place. There he remained for two weeks, instructing the poor people and administering the sacraments. On the twenty-fifth he started off again for a village eighteen miles away, which some hunters had told him about, and it was not until the fifteenth of March that he came back to the Saguenay. It was then drawing towards Easter, and he prepared every one of his people for the sacraments, which, he says, "they all received with great piety." He speaks with enthusiasm of the devotion of the Frenchmen in helping the sick, and burying the dead. They even carried the disgusting carcasses on their backs; and he notes that by a singular protection of Providence not one of the white men caught the contagion.

"I was the last one who fell sick," he says. "My head was frightfully swollen, and my face was covered with pustules, like those of small-pox. I had a terrible pain in the ear, as well as a furious toothache. My lips were like those of a dead man, and there was a constant flux from my eyes. Added to it all, I had a great difficulty in drawing my breath. I promised to make a novena to St. Francis Xavier, and immediately I began to get better. Perhaps God had pity on the poor savages who needed my assistance. I end this letter," he says, "by recommending myself to your Holy Sacrifices and assuring you that I am your obedient servant in the Lord."

Another letter informs the Superior that in pursuance of orders he had set out for the northern missions, and had arrived there at the end of May. He cannot forbear casting a look back at Tadoussac, as he turns to the north, and expressing his grief that where he once saw ten or twelve hundred people scarcely a hundred were left.

On June third he met a party of one hundred and fifty savages from Hudson Bay, who told him that an English vessel had arrived there, and that the crew had maltreated and robbed the natives. The captain of the ship said he was coming back next year, and that he would have with him a number of Iroquois, who would murder the Algonquins if they were not on hand at his arrival, with plenty of furs.

Albanel reports that the Papinachois whom he saw on his journey were excellent Christians. He did not remain among them, however, but went further north to the Oumamiois. He reached the Black River on June 15. There the Indians had been expecting him for a month. After caring for them, he made for the River Godebout, where he met one hundred and thirty Indians, who had traveled six hundred miles to see him. He reports that they are a well built race, docile, peaceful, and clever, and that they led very decent lives. Polygamy they hold in abhorrence, and hate the sorcerers. They are wretchedly poor, however ; are clothed with caribou skins trimmed with porcupine quills, and also with feathers which are dyed in all sorts of colors. " But they are fast disappearing," he says, " on account of the continual famines. They have no firearms, and if they succeed in getting a net they consider themselves rich."

The morning after his arrival he built an altar and spread above it the sail of the boat. After Mass he began his work of instruction. On the twentieth of June he baptized twenty-one little children ; and some days later twenty-four adults. Night and day, these poor Indians clustered around him, listening to his instructions. One of them, an old man, gave him an almost unexpected and pleasant surprise. " Sixteen years ago, Father," he said, " you baptized me at

Tadoussac, and I have never failed to do what you told me." He had instructed his whole family in the Faith and had led a life of perfect innocence.

This is all we know of Father Albanel up to the time when the authorities at Quebec were looking for a priest to go to Hudson Bay. They thought of him, for his heroic life up to that had well fitted him for the work. It is at this point that he assumes a sort of international prominence.

Although it is very likely that some of the early navigators who were looking for the elusive northwest passage to China, by way of the Pole, were aware of the existence of Hudson Bay, nevertheless it is only from the great sailor who entered the Straits on June 24, 1610, and gave his name to the vast expanse beyond, that the world received any positive information about it. Thomas Button followed Hudson in 1612, and went as far as 65° north latitude. In 1631 Lucas Fox, whom Charlevoix calls "Lux" Fox, was so convinced that he was going to reach Japan by that route that he carried a letter from the King of England to the Mikado. He never delivered the missive, but he gained a few degrees of latitude on his predecessors. In the same year Captain James sailed south through the Bay and gave his name to the lower part of it. In 1646 the restless de la Tour, who for years had kept Acadia in a turmoil, visited those regions with some friends from New England, and ten years after that Jean Bourdon, the old companion of Father Jogues, an ambassador to the Mohawks, left Quebec and is said to have sailed into the Bay. Dionne, however, refuses to admit his claim.

Meantime efforts had been continually made by the French to reach Hudson Bay by a land route, but without success; Champlain had attempted it as early as 1615. In 1664, Fathers Dablon and Druillettes, with four Frenchmen, had ascended the Saguenay, crossed Lake St. John, and had gone as far as Nekouba on the Aspamouachan, but the

ASPAMOUACHAN FALLS.

Indians refused to go any farther. Couture, the Donné, who had been captured with Jogues, in 1643, claimed to have succeeded, but was not believed, and finally, in 1667, the famous Radisson and Chouart maintained that they had found the way. But they also were discredited. Finally, as the Intendant Talon was anxious to establish the feasibility of the route, he commissioned Father Albanel to make the attempt, and hence, on August 6, 1671, a year or so before Marquette sailed with Joliet down the Mississippi, Albanel left Quebec, and at Tadoussac met the two Frenchmen who were to go with him, Saint Simon and Couture. He kept a diary of the journey, which may be found in the "Relation" of 1672. We shall make a few extracts from it as we go along.

"I reached Tadoussac," he says, "on August 8th, and found no end of opposition to the enterprise. The chief had died a few days before, and hence I addressed myself to the uncle of the deceased, and by his help got the better of the ill-will of the braves. Indeed the chief came himself with us forty leagues up the river. We remained three days at Chicoutimi, the first two I heard confessions and gave Communion, and the third we packed up and portaged for over a league and a quarter. On the thirtieth, we reached Lake Kinougami, and on the first of September camped at a little lake called Kinougamichis, which was famous for its long-tailed and poisonous frogs; a curious thing, for in this country the toads, serpents and vipers are not harmful.

"On the second, we reached Lake St. John, or Pingagami. It is thirty leagues long, ten wide, and has twelve rivers flowing into it, and only one, the Saguenay, flowing out. The country around is fair to look upon, the country unbroken and the beautiful prairies are apparently fertile. Otters, elk, and beavers, and especially porcupines, abound. In fact, the Indians of that region are called Porcupines or Kakouchaes."

He tells us that in former times he had seen as many as twenty nations assembled there for trade, but war and pestilence had made sad havoc among them.

On the seventh he reached the end of the lake, and on

the seventeenth five canoes, filled with Whitefish Indians, were seen coming towards him. The savages reported that there were two English ships anchored in Hudson Bay; that there was a great deal of disorder in those parts; that one Indian had been killed, and that no one's life was safe.

This intelligence started a panic among Albanel's Indian guides, and they showed an unwillingness to go on. Indeed he himself seems to have suddenly discovered that it would be wiser not to proceed without passports from the Governor and letters from the Bishop of Quebec. Why, in view of a possible meeting of the English these two things were not thought of before the expedition started, is difficult to imagine. At all events, they had to be secured, and messengers were therefore sent back to Quebec for that purpose. The delay involved was, of course, considerable, and by the time the travelers had the documents in hand the bad season had set in, and the travelers settled down in winter quarters. "I have suffered many a hardship with Indians in their winter camps, but nothing like this one," writes Albanel. The misery, however, was not caused by lack of game, for there was abundance of it; but by the mean and discontented spirit of some Indians who were in the party, and chiefly the surly savage who had been selected as a guide. He and others did everything in their power to make the enterprise a failure, and to render further progress impossible. Finally Albanel discovered an old and needy Mistassirinin Indian, who for a consideration, chiefly of tobacco, undertook to lead the party to the Bay. It was already June, 1672, when the three Frenchmen and sixteen Indians got into their canoes to resume their journey.

"We had six days of rapids" says the chronicle, "and had to continually drag the boats against the current. We were compelled to go ashore frequently, to tramp through the woods, to crawl over rocks, to plunge into crevasses, to climb over precipices covered with stunted trees, tearing our clothes to shreds meanwhile and struggling painfully under our heavy burdens. Then rain came, and we had to make a two-days halt.

"The ninth was a trying day. We had to portage over a wide stretch of country intercepted with streams to reach Nekouba River. At times we were in water up to our waist.

"On the tenth we arrived early in the morning at Paslistaskaw, which is the dividing line between the north and the south. There we found two little lakes, from which two rivers flow, one emptying into the Saguenay, the other into Hudson Bay."

Here there was an attempt on the part of the Mistassirinins to stop him; but Albanel assumed a haughty tone and summoned the chief for a parley, and on the thirteenth of June eighteen canoes came to the place where the white men were waiting. The Indians were decked out in all their finery, and were grouped around the chief Sesibahoura, whom Albanel saluted with ten volleys of musketry as the dignitary stepped ashore from the canoe.

"Sesibahoura," said the priest, "you do wrong to prevent us from crossing your territory, after we Frenchmen have freed you from the Iroquois. Besides, God is sending me to preach the Gospel and He has rights which all other Indian nations recognize. Here is a present to lay on the graves of your braves whom the Iroquois have slain; and here is another to tell you that the Iroquois are now praying to God and to bid you do likewise. As I come to be your friend here and hereafter, I want you to stop trading with the Europeans who come to the Bay. Go down to Lake St. John, where you will always find a blackrobe to instruct you."

The chief collapsed. He gave a great banquet; made fine speeches in the usual Indian fashion, expressing his pleasure to be instructed in the truths of the Gospel. He wanted his training to begin immediately, but Albanel, while agreeing to baptize the babies, told the older people he would meet them at Lake St. John on his return.

"On the eighteenth, we entered the great lake of the Mistassirinins," he continues, "so extensive that it would

take twenty days of fine weather to go around it. It derives
its name from the prodigious rocks that everywhere crop
up, on its surface. Elk, bear, caribou, porcupines and
beavers are found in abundance on its beautiful islands. We
had travelled six leagues on the lake, when my eye caught
sight of a lofty peak, far away in the distance. 'Are we
going thither?' I asked. 'Silence,' whispered the guide,
'don't look at it, if you don't want to die. If you look at
it you will bring a fierce storm on the lake.'" It may be
noted here that this stretch of water is now called Lake
Albanel.

"On the nineteenth, we arrived at Makouamitikac, or
the place where the bears fish. It was great sport to see
bruin walking along the shore, scooping in a pickerel, a
whitefish or a little sturgeon. He was very skilful at it.
The twenty-second, twenty-third and twenty-fourth were
days of hardship, because of the innumerable portages, and
on the twenty-fifth of June at noon we arrived at Nemiskau,
a lake ten leagues in circumference, with a semi-circle of
lofty mountains from north to south. You see at the mouth
of the great river, which flows from east to north-east, vast
plains, which extend to the foot of the mountains, and are
so cut up by stretches of water, that they seem like lakes
dotted with islands. You find the track of beavers, deer and
porcupines everywhere. Five great rivers empty into the
lake, which is teeming with fish. On our way we came
across the gloomy vestiges of a raid of the Iroquois some
years before. On one of the islands they had built a fort
of great trees, and from there covered every approach. The
devastations they caused were so great, that the inhabitants
abandoned the locality altogether, though it was once a
great centre of traffic."

On the twenty-sixth the travelers were at Tehepimont;
a very mountainous country. On the twenty-seventh they
made many wearisome portages, and had to fight continually with swarms of mosquitoes, which left them no rest
night or day. "On the twenty-eighth," says the diary, "we
had scarcely gone a quarter of a league when we saw at our
left, in a little creek, a small coaster of ten or twelve tons
burden, floating the English flag, and carrying a lateen
sail." It was the first indication that they had reached the

great inland sea. He does not tell us if he went over to the little ship. Probably he did not. A quarrel might have ensued. But one would like to know who they were, and whence they came, and how they had dared to cross the wild ocean in a little coaster of ten or twelve tons with its lateen sail.

"About a gunshot away from it" continues Albanel, " we saw and entered two abandoned houses and there were signs that Indians had camped nearby.

"We kept on our way to a pond about six leagues from the English houses. There the tide was out, and the wind was against us; but we went ashore wading waist deep in the mud of a little creek to the right. Turning right and left, we at last came on two or three huts, but there was no living thing there, except an abandoned dog. From that clue however we gathered that the Indians were not far away, and had left only a day or so before. There we stopped, firing off our muskets over and over again to attract attention, and diverting ourselves by gazing out on the sea that we had suffered so much to reach, the famous Hudson Bay."

Albanel had accomplished his object and was a happy man.

But where were the Indians? Where could he look for them in those vast solitudes? On the twenty-ninth a canoe was sent out to hunt for them, at a place which he calls Meskoutenagachit. On the thirtieth the guide grew ill tempered, and insisted on returning home. It was now July. Albanel was in despair. To go back without seeing any of the people was to render useless all that had been done; it would make him and his party ridiculous on their return to Quebec, but especially for him as a priest the thought of turning his back on these people whom he had come to evangelize, and who might be within a few miles of him, was something that was intolerable. But he was at the mercy of this miserable Indian who would have left them there to perish in the wilderness. He controlled his feel-

ings, however, and early in the morning of July 1, 1671, he
called his Frenchmen and Indians around and began to prepare for the celebration of holy Mass; doubtless the first
time such an event had occurred in those frozen North
American regions. Some artist ought to make a picture of
it: the poor altar, with the weather-beaten and weary priest
in his sacerdotal robes, celebrating the solemn mysteries on
the shore of that wide sea; near him the battered wigwam
and the lonely dog; and kneeling around the altar the little
group of Frenchmen and the wondering Indians; the guide
perhaps standing aloof in anger.

After Mass, he took the reluctant savage in hand and
appealed to him. How would he dare think of returning
and run the risk of bringing on himself the curse of God,
for having deprived the poor people of those parts of the
message of salvation, which the priest had travelled so far
to bring them? He would certainly be punished in hell
for it.

" I have always noticed," writes Albanel, " that the fear
of hell exercises a great influence on the Indian." It was so
in this case. " Let us go," said the savage abruptly, and
immediately the party embarked in their canoes and paddled across the wide expanse, over which they had seen
the other boat disappear a day or so before. They had
hardly travelled six leagues when, lo! a canoe was seen
coming towards them. Was it their own? No, it was one
that belonged to the Indians who had been found by the
scout. They were only too eager to send one of their best
boats to bring the missionary to their settlement. No delay
was made in embarking. " From afar," he writes, " they
saw us approach, and ran out of their cabins to the shore,
crying with all their might: ' The black-robe! The black-
robe has come to visit us.' "

Banqueting and rejoicing followed, but in the midst
of it all Albanel detected a lurking suspicion among the
Indians that the Frenchmen with him were traders, and

just as at Lake Mistassirinin he had to disabuse them, by assurances that it was God who had sent him, reminding them also of how the French had delivered them from the Iroquois. He helped out his eloquence by means of presents, which was nearly always an overwhelming argument with the red men.

As in the former instance, there was a general request for baptism, the old chief, a remarkably intelligent man, being the most insistent upon it. Albanel forthwith began to teach them. The instructions were kept up night and day, and as the neophyte was not in danger of being spoiled by contact with the whites, he on July 14, 1672, poured the waters of baptism on the head of the great chief, giving him the name of Ignatius. He was the first native Christian in those parts of America.

Albanel gives us the outline of a wonderful speech made by the neophyte after the administration of the sacrament; in the course of which he showed how well he understood his obligations, and how determined he was to fulfill them. He was anxious that all the tribe should follow his example. Indeed every one was eager to do so, and though Albanel was not able to remain long with them, he baptized sixty-two persons, children and adults, before he turned his face homeward.

Apologizing for the incompleteness of his information, because of the briefness of his stay and his absorption in ministerial duties, he gives, nevertheless, some idea of the country which he had succeeded in reaching.

" The river by which we entered Hudson Bay " he says, " flows out of Lake Nemiskau, whose name it keeps. It is very beautiful. It is a league or more in width, in certain parts, and is about eighty leagues in length, flowing from southeast and northwest. It is very swift and its course is broken by eighteen cataracts. Its tides are very regular, but the distance which the sea recedes from the shore at low tide is amazing. The Indians put it at twenty leagues. At all events the water of the river is lost to sight. As far as the eye can see there is nothing but mud and rocks. The river that flows into it disappears in the mud, and there is not water enough a little way from the shore to float a canoe. The mouth of the river is at 50° latitude."

Then follows a list of the tribes, in the adjoining regions; but as they are unpronounceable and unrememberable, they may be omitted here. There was any amount of game, and the savages told him, though he doubts the story, that in some places the birds shed such abundance of plumage when they moult, that other birds and sometimes men, are smothered in the heap. The only fruits he found were blueberries, small red apples, diminutive black pears, and any quantity of gooseberries. There was plenty of game, but on the other hand he saw many trees stripped of their bark. The Indians had gnawed it off when they were in want of other food.

"It is a mistake," he says, "to fancy that the climate makes the place uninhabitable, either because of the ice and snow, or the lack of wood to build or to burn. Those who think so have not seen these vast and dense forests, the beautiful plains, these wide prairies, along the borders of rivers, and covered with herbage which is most suitable for live stock. I can assure you that, on the 15th of June, I have seen wild roses as fragrant as those at Quebec. Indeed, the season seemed more advanced, and the temperature mild and pleasant. While we were in those parts, there was no night; dawn succeeded twilight immediately."

A recent visitor there assures us that the same conditions still prevail at the foot of Hudson Bay, and he urges his countrymen of Canada to emigrate thither and take possession of the land. We do not know if the copper-plate on which Albanel cut the arms of France, and which he planted at the foot of a great tree to proclaim that Hudson Bay belonged to Louis XIV., has ever been dug up.

On the sixth of July the travellers started homeward; the journey up the river being of course harder than going down; but in four days he reached Nemiskau, where he erected the arms of the King on the point of an island in the lake. He met two canoes on the fourteenth and the Indians told him that one hundred and fifty Mistassirinins were near by waiting to be instructed. "I was on fire with eagerness to go to them," he writes; "but my ill-tempered guide, who pretended to be asleep, while the Indians were talking, started up as he saw me departing and cried out: 'Where are you going, Black-Robe? We cannot wait; let us go on.' It is a wretched thing to be dependent on the humor of a savage, but there was no help for it; I had to submit."

Later on he met another party of two hundred Indians who wanted to be Christians, and all he could do was to tell them to meet him at Lake St. John, the following spring. However he baptized thirty-three of the little papooses.

"On the nineteenth, at 2 o'clock in the afternoon," he tells us, "I planted the arms of our puissant and invincible monarch, on the banks of the River Minahigouskat, as a protection for these people against the inroads of the Iroquois. On the twenty-third we reached Lake St. John, where I found a number of Mistassirinins who had been waiting for me a whole month. They were the party we had first met on our way up, and whom I had requested to meet me there."

He was thus back again within reach of civilization, and it is worth noting that it took him only seventeen days to cover the distance from Hudson Bay to that point. He had established the practicability of the route. Saint-Denys, the Commandant of Tadoussac, met him at Chicoutimi on the twenty-ninth, took him aboard a vessel and started for Quebec, which he reached on August first, and gave an account of the expedition to the authorities.

Albanel was very much elated over his success; almost too much so in fact for such a holy man. He was convinced that God had set him apart for the task; because, when, at the solicitation of his Superior, he had devoted himself to the northern missions he was miraculously cured of a serious illness. Whether God had especially appointed him or not, matters little. He deserved to succeed, for he had been endeavoring for eighteen years to find the road that led to Hudson Bay. Before him, three expeditions had made the attempt and failed. He had reached the goal. He had travelled eight hundred leagues, passed two hundred cataracts, and had crossed mountains and morasses, where his life was in his hand at every moment. He was virtually alone, for the authorities at Quebec did not think it worth while to give him a single soldier to protect him from the red men on the way, or from the Englishmen, at the end of the route. History is silent as to the temporal recognition by the Colonial authorities of the information given by the explorer, which was very valuable for commercial purposes, but in all likelihood the silence is due to the fact that the Government did nothing at all to acknowledge the service.

CHAPTER II.

FINDING RADISSON.

Albanel made a second journey to Hudson Bay in 1674. As the "Relations" had suspended publication two years previously, it is of course impossible to obtain any official account, not only of the details but even of the main facts of this expedition or indeed of the twenty-four subsequent years of Albanel's adventurous career. Fortunately, a recent work on "The Conquest of the Great Northwest" furnishes us with some valuable information about what happened in 1674.

On this second trip to the Bay he met with a serious accident. Some unpublished documents of the Society inform us that Father de Crespieul, who was laboring among the savages in those parts, heard of the mishap, and he, of course, immediately left his own post and hurried over mountains and lakes and rivers to bring help to his companion-in arms. A heavy load had fallen on him and had nearly broken his back. In the story of Crespieul we have given a detailed account of this romantic meeting in the woods. They were together off and on, for about three weeks, and then Albanel resumed his journey to the north. In spite of many hardships, which in his battered condition of health must have required heroic patience and courage to overcome, he at last arrived at Hudson Bay.

There he met the Frenchman, Pierre Esprit Radisson, who was acting as the chief agent of the English Hudson Bay Company. Indeed, the main object of this second expedition was to effect that meeting, for, though no one knew it then, nor till very recently, Albanel was acting as the secret agent of Frontenac, the Governor of Quebec, and if he succeeded in inducing Radisson to abandon the service

127

of the Hudson Bay Company the consequences would be momentous both for England and France.

To understand this situation, it will be necessary for us to interrupt the story of Albanel's life at this point, and to give somewhat at length an account of Radisson's career, although we have already said something of this remarkable man in the other volumes. This historic personage first appears in the territory which is now the state of New York.

In September, 1653, the Jesuit missionary, Father Joseph Antoine Poncet de la Rivière, was carried down in a mangled condition to Albany, or Fort Orange, from the same Mohawk village where Father Jogues had been put to death seven years before. While he was waiting for his wounds to heal, a party of Indian braves arrived at the Fort. Among them was a young French lad painted and plumed like the rest. Poncet speaks of him as being very serviceable as an interpreter, but forgets to give his name. We find, however, in an account written later on by this white savage himself, that he was no other than Pierre Esprit Radisson, who was destined, in the course of his life, to embroil England and France in a bloody and protracted struggle for what is now known as the Hudson Bay Territory. He acquired the additional distinction of being the most detested and perhaps the most maligned man in Canadian history.

He had come to America in 1651 and in the following year, on account of his reckless disregard of danger, which was his characteristic through life, he was captured by the Mohawks. Instead of being scalped he was adopted by an old chief, whose wife was a Huron, and consequently well acquainted with the French, possibly even knowing something about Christianity. She loved him as a mother and called him " Orimah " after a son whom she had lost. The name fitted him; for curiously enough " Orimah " means Pierre. Later on, the Algonquins called him " Porcupine

Head." After a while he was initiated as a member of the Mohawk tribe and thus became a full-fledged Iroquois. He had two Indian sisters.

He seemed to be about as savage as his red brethren; for he, himself, informs us that soon after his capture, when out hunting with three of the braves, an unknown Algonquin came upon them in the woods and was hospitably admitted to their temporary shelter. He took Radisson aside and said: "Do you love the French?" to which Radisson replied: "Do you love the Algonquins?" which probably meant, "Of course I do." "Why don't you escape then?" inquired the Indian. "Impossible," was the answer. "I am a captive." "Very easy," rejoined the Algonquin; "we can murder these three Mohawks while they are asleep and get away to the St. Lawrence together."

The ghastly proposal was accepted; and three Mohawks lay dead in their cabin that night. The assassins reached the great river, and even succeeded in crossing Lake St. Peter, but just as they landed, a band of Iroquois, who were on the war path, started out of the bushes. They were not aware of the crime that had been perpetrated, but they shot the Algonquin on general principles and led Radisson back to the Mohawk, along with three other white prisoners, one of them a woman, and a dozen or so of Hurons.

Radisson's Indian father and mother were in consternation, for, like the other captives, he was to die by torture. The first day the executioners tore off four of his finger nails; on the second a brutal savage made him put his thumb into a calumet on top of burning tobacco, and then proceeded to smoke the horrid mixture until the end of the thumb was reduced to a cinder; through his feet also was thrust a skiver of hot iron. While this was going on, a four-year-old child was doing his best to chew off one of Radisson's fingers, but without success. Finally he was tied to the stake, but as the flames ate into the thongs he was free for the moment, and then the old chief interfered

9

and saved him from death. He was thus taught how unwise it was to try to escape from his Indian relatives.

The precise age of this singular lad at that time we have no means of determining. Some one has given 1620 as the date of his birth, but that would have made him over thirty when he arrived at Fort Orange, which is contrary to the general belief. There is a conflict of opinion also about where he was born. Mr. Scull, who wrote the preface to the Prince Society publication which printed Radisson's diary, pronounces for St. Malo. Dionne admits that, at least, his family lived there: while Judge Prud'homme of Winnipeg favors Paris.

When the Dutch Commandant urged this boy-savage to take off his paint and feathers he was met with a positive refusal. An offer of a ransom was also rejected. Radisson said he was very much attached to the Mohawks, and besides he wanted the opportunity to travel, and so he went off with the Indians. Possibly he remembered his former effort to desert. But about three weeks later he changed his mind and stole back to the fort, where he was received with open arms. The Governor dressed him up as a white man and then led him away, for the Indians were on his trail. They arrived very soon after him, but were not admitted to the fort. His two Indian sisters also came to plead with him to return. He did not see them but could hear them outside crying piteously: "Orihma! Orihma!" He grew a little sentimental at the sound of their lamentations but braced himself up and persisted in his resolution.

He tells us that while there he went to confession to Father Poncet, or Father "Noncet," as the printer's copy of his MS. puts it. The poor fellow was in sad need of being shriven, as well as of getting instructions in fundamental ethics. It is curious to note how Dionne, with so many other proofs at hand, eagerly seizes on the incident of confession to prove that Radisson was a Catholic. No doubt he performed other pious acts besides going to confession, and of course his penance was a heavy one. When Poncet started for Montreal by way of what is now Herkimer and Ogdensburg, Radisson sailed down the Hudson to Manhattan, where he remained three weeks, and then took ship for Amsterdam, reaching that port on January fourth, 1654. He was back in Three Rivers the next year. Whether he married or not at that time historians are not agreed, but in any case he certainly did not establish a home in the colony, for he was one of the most persistent rovers that Canada ever produced.

He appears, in the " Relations " of 1655, where we read that: "on August 6th, 1654, two young Frenchmen, full of courage, having received permission from Monsieur le Gouverneur to embark with some of the Indians who had come down to the French settlements, began a journey of more than five hundred leagues under the guidance of these Argonauts, not in great galleons, or long-oared barges, but in little gondolas of bark. They fully expected to return in the Spring, but the Indians did not conduct them home until towards the end of August, 1656. Their arrival gave a great deal of joy to the whole country, for they brought with them five hundred canoes laden with goods which the French come to this end of the world to procure."

The two young men who made this wonderful journey were Radisson and his friend Chouart. The enormous amount of furs which they brought back to the colony meant a great deal for them financially, and that was their object of their expedition, but it is very much to their credit that while they were among the Indians they talked constantly to them about the missionaries, and whenever they found a dying papoose they made haste to baptize it.

Before they went west, Father Le Moyne, at the peril of his life, had visited the Onondagas to make sure that they were sincere in their request for a missionary. As Le Moyne's report was favorable, Fathers Chaumonot and Dablon undertook the work of evangelizing the Indians of that part of New York, but they soon found that it was not a craving for religious instruction that agitated the hearts of these savages. The red man wanted a trading post, and hence in the spring of 1656 Father Dablon made his memorable journey, on foot, from Onondaga to Quebec to obtain volunteers for this commercial enterprise. As we have said elsewhere, permission was given by the authorities, and on July eleventh a flotilla of canoes, carrying fifty white men and a motley crowd of Onondagas, Senecas, and Hurons, sailed over Lake Ganentaa. Cannons and musketry roared their salute as the barks approached the shore, banners fluttered on the breeze and songs and cheers awoke the echoes of the forest as the fifty Frenchmen beached their boats at a place now known as Liverpool, and began the first permanent establishment in Iroquois territory.

Radisson had not yet returned from the West, or he would certainly have thrown in his fortune with these adventurers. He reached the St. Lawrence only after their departure, but later on we find him going up the St. Lawrence to Onondaga with Father Ragueneau in August, 1657, and witnessing somewhere on the river a horrible butchery by the Iroquois of the unfortunate Hurons, who had been invited to the new settlement. Ragueneau saw on reaching the place that the same treatment was to be meted out to the whites; not indeed by the Onondagas, who were well disposed, but by the Mohawks and Oneidas. After considering the situation it was decided that the only course to adopt was flight. How to do so was a problem. "A young Frenchman," as the "Relations" described him, came to the rescue. Very likely this "Frenchman" was Radisson. He had a dream, or said he had, in which he was commanded to spread a great banquet, at which everything was to be eaten, otherwise the ghost would kill him. It was good news for the hungry redmen, and they agreed to keep the contract.

Enormous quantities of food were laid before them,

and they gorged themselves heriocally, but never reached the bottom of the pot. The supplies were inexhaustible. They pleaded for pity, but the dreamer asked: " Do you want me to be killed? " They assured him that they did not, and they went to work again until they were almost filled to the lips, dancing and singing and screaming meantime, until at last, to the sound of French fiddles and fifes and cornets, they all fell off in a stupor. With their enemies thus reduced to helplessness, the Frenchmen slipped out on the lake and paddled down the Oswego River, cutting their way through ice, portaging around cataracts, and through woods and swamps, until they reached Lake Ontario. They left Onondaga on March twentieth and arrived at Montreal on the evening of April third, 1658.

Ragueneau has left us a very graphic description of his adventure and Radisson also gives us his story. He informs us that the fugitives were anxious to murder the sleeping Indians, as the only way to prevent pursuit, but that the priest forbade them to carry out the ghastly proposal. Quite possibly the suggestion came from Radisson himself. He had disposed of his enemies in that fashion before.

He was hardly in Three Rivers, when he began to pine, as he says himself, for "life in the bottom of a canoe." He did not pine long, for he and Chouart started about the middle of June for the great lakes. There were sixty Frenchmen in the party, and some western Indians who were going home. At Montreal eight Ottawas and two Frenchmen joined them. As they were paddling up the St. Lawrence an Indian suddenly appeared on the shore and warned them to be cautious about discharging their firearms. They paid no attention to him, and on the following day a handful of Iroquois attacked them, killed thirteen men and scattered the rest in all directions. All the white men returned to Montreal except Radisson and Chouart, and they, with a few Indians, continued on their journey to the west. They went to the end of Lake Ontario and then entered Lake Huron. Arriving at Sault Ste. Marie, they wintered there, but traveled a great deal meantime among the tribes, going as far as Green Bay, and carrying on a brisk trade. At the Sault they met the Crees, who told them about Hudson Bay.

The next winter they were again at Green Bay, and then reached the end of Lake Superior. The Canadian Government map marks the place as near the present Duluth and puts the date as 1659. From the "Minnesota Historical Collections" (Vol. I, p. 38), we find that they were invited by the Indians of Mille Lac and the headwaters of the Ste. Croix River. They proceeded westward along the Knife Sioux Trail, and were at what is now known as Pine County in January, 1660, "securing from the Indians a description of the Forked River, which is very reasonably understood to be the junction of the Mississippi and Missouri." They then returned and reached Three Rivers in the spring of 1660, after a journey of twenty-five days, which was a remarkably speedy trip from Lake Superior. They had three hundred Indians with them, and two hundred thousand francs' worth of furs.

It is sometimes alleged that the travelers had on this occasion discovered the Mississippi, and had, therefore, anticipated Marquette and Joliet. Indeed, Perrot (p. 28) declares that "they saw it, but did not recognize it under its Sioux name." Dionne merely says they learned of its existence, and in the "Relations" of 1660, Dablon, who talked with the travelers after they returned, writes that they told him they had met a band of dispersed Hurons, and that these Hurons spoke of their having seen a river as "wide, as deep and as beautiful as the St. Lawrence." Chouart and Radisson did not assert that they themselves had seen it. In his own narrative Radisson does indeed say that "by the persuasion of some of the Indians we went into ye great river that divides itself into two parts, where the

Hurons, with some Ottanake, and the wild men that had wars with them, had retired. *This nation have wars against those of the forked river.* It is so called, because it has two branches; the one towards the west, the other towards the south, which we believe runs towards Mexico, by the tokens they give us."

The " forked river " is evidently the junction of the Mississippi and the Missouri; but, far from saying that he went that far, Radisson implies the contrary. He speaks of it as being far removed from the place where he actually was with his Indian friends.

The account in the " Relation " is certainly more reliable in any case than the one written for King Charles II, which was never intended to be published, and in which Radisson would be prone to make much of his own exploits. With Perrot we may say that he saw the headwaters of the river, but did not know it. He would be more likely not to exaggerate when speaking to Dablon and Perrot, who were his friends. It is gratifying to hear that on this journey they baptized two hundred Algonquin babies; " forty of whom went straight to heaven." Evidently these Frenchmen were not Huguenots.

So far they had only heard about Hudson Bay. They were burning with a desire to visit it in person, and asked Avaugour for the requisite permission. The Jesuits interceded for them, but the Governor could not be budged. Whereupon they took French leave, traveled over Lake Ontario and Lake Erie, and made their way to Mackinac. They saw Keweenaw Bay, and in the winter of 1661-2 they camped on the shores of Lake Superior at Chagouamigan Bay. They stayed there, however, only twelve days, and started out again. Possibly they visited the Lake of the Woods. They inform us that they also went with some Crees to the shore of the sea, where they found the battered ruins of an old shed, and learned from the Indians that the whites used to visit the place. From there they reached the

Aspamouachan, which is the prolongation of the Saguenay. Dionne credits them with having reached the shore of James Bay, spending the spring of 1663 in piling up stores of furs. They finally arrived in Quebec in the summer, after an absence of two years.

Unfortunately the intractable Avaugour was still at Quebec, though on the point of being recalled. He arrested Chouart, who had been commandant at Three Rivers, and had absented himself without leave. A fine of 4,000 livres was imposed on the pair for the purpose of building a fort at Three Rivers. "He told us for our consolation," says Radisson, "that we could put our coat-of-arms on the fort. He laid on us another fine of 6,000 for the public treasury, but the bugger (sic) wanted to fatten his own ribs with our money. He then exacted a fourth part of the pelts, which was the usual tariff; so that we had to give up 46,000 livres, and were allowed to keep only 24,000. Isn't he a tyrant to treat us in that fashion after we had within two years brought 40,000 to 50,000 pistoles into the country."

What about Radisson's claim to have been the first to reach Hudson Bay by the land route? There is little doubt of its being unfounded, for we read in the "Relation" of 1672 that "the sea which is north of us, to which Hudson gave his name, has since then always prodded the curiosity of the French to discover a land route to it in order to ascertain its relative situation, and to become acquainted with the people who live there. Anxiety to know these things has increased since we heard from the Indians that certain ships were there engaged in fur trading. On that account M. Talon, the Intendant, decided that we should do our best to make the discovery, and for that purpose Father Charles Albanel, an old and tried missionary, was chosen for the work. He left Quebec on August 6, 1671."

Then follows the diary of Albanel, which enables us to follow him step by step, until he reaches Hudson Bay in the summer of the following year. At the end of his narrative he informs us that three attempts had been made, and that he and his companions, two Frenchmen and six Indians were the first to open the way. The very detailed account, in which every portion of the march is noted, would seem to intimate that the authorities at Quebec did not believe that Bourdon or Couture had gone as far as Hudson Bay, and attached much less credence to the story of Radisson and Chouart.

Whatever views may be taken of the claims of Radisson and Chouart as discoverers of Hudson Bay, there is no doubt that they were unjustly and cruelly treated, not by their fellow Canadians, but by the mulish and wrong-headed Avaugour. In hope of better things they went to France, but all that could be obtained there was the promise of a vessel to continue their explorations. It was not full reparation, but at least it would enable them to retrieve their fortunes.

Believing what they were told, they returned to America and waited for the vessel at Isle Percé, in the Gulf of St. Lawrence. But a Jesuit missionary was sent to inform them that the Government had changed its mind. Of course, there was no use going to Quebec, so they made their way to Cape Breton, where they were mobbed. They then fled to Port Royal, in Nova Scotia, which was at that time under English rule.

Now begin the accusations of treachery and apostacy. Charlevoix calls them *des transfuges,* but if they were, every unfortunate emigrant who leaves his country to improve his fortunes is likewise a deserter. It is a perversion of truth to describe them at this stage of their career as " Huguenot adventurers," as Douglas calls them in his " Old France in the New World " (p. 516). Up to that time both had been conspicuous as missionary helpers; the Jesuits had been interceding for them at Quebec, and Chouart, who had accompanied Father Ménard to the Far West, is described by Dionne as a Jesuit *donné,* or oblate. Whatever may be the truth about Radisson, this is the only instance which we know of in which Chouart is accused of leaving the Faith.

At Port Royal they succeeded in inducing Captain Zachary Gillam to attempt the journey to Hudson Bay, but Gillam lost courage when he found himself in the ice of the Straits and turned back. The Frenchmen, however, did not give up. They had some little money left, and with that they chartered two vessels, but one of them went to pieces off Sable Island, and that disaster landed the unfortunate navigators in a lawsuit in Boston. Though they won the case, they were left absolutely penniless. Finally good luck or ill luck brought them to the notice of Sir George Carteret, the Royal Commissioner, who persuaded them to go to England with him.

They left America on August 1, 1665, but when off Spain they were captured by a Dutch privateer, The Caper, after a desperate two hours' fight. Carteret had just time to fling his private dispatches overboard when a bayonet was pointed at his breast and he gave up his sword. Every effort was made to induce the two Frenchmen to go over to Holland to tell their wonderful story, but they refused to leave Carteret, and all three were put ashore somewhere on the coast of Spain, and from there made their way to England.

They were presented to the King, who was then at Oxford. The good-natured monarch listened with delight to the account of their travels, and a little later, when he went to Windsor, he had them accompany him, and saw that they took chambers somewhere in the neighborhood. Like a true Stuart, Charles had no superfluous money, and all he could do for these two great men was to give them £2 a week for their maintenance. It was the time of the great plague, the London fire, and the Dutch war, and thus something besides the King's own extravagances had drained the country's exchequer.

CHARLES ALBANEL

It was then that Radisson wrote from his memoranda the story of his travels. It is a great book. As he had but a scraping acquaintance with English, he plunges through its spelling and grammar with as much glee as if he were careering down the cataracts of the Ottawa, hitting the rocks at times, and swirling in the eddies, but swimming out unconcernedly, and then starting in again for another race down the stream. The manuscript was found with the Pepys papers, part of it in the Bodleian, and part in the British Museum, and published with all its horrors of syntax and orthography by the Prince Society of London. It is one of the curiosities of literature, but, as he was writing to amuse a pleasure-loving King, and to exalt his own importance, absolute confidence cannot be placed in his assertions.

Prince Rupert had already come upon the scene at Oxford and developed a lively interest in the rovers. But it was the King himself who issued a letter of instruction to his brother, the Duke of York, afterwards James II, to detach a vessel from the fleet for the enterprise. This information, which is given to us by Laut, is of great value, for hitherto all the credit of sustaining Radisson's scheme, was attributed to Rupert, whereas all that he did was to co-operate with a half dozen friends in victualling the ship and paying the wages of the sailors. Radisson's old friend, Gillam, of the Nonsuch, was to join the Eaglet, which the Government supplied. The Royal munificence again poured itself out lavishly by bestowing a gold medal on Radisson, and a small title of nobility on Chouart. The nobility in question was that of the Garter. Marie de l'Incarnation gives us this information, and she adds that besides knighthood, Chouart received a gift of 20,000 crowns. Why this discrimination was made in favor of Chouart, she does not state, nor why he assumed the name of de Groseilliers.

While these preparations were being made, a spy came from Holland and tried to bribe the Frenchmen to join the

Dutch service. When he failed to win them over he accused them of counterfeiting money, but, as he could not prove his charge, he was incontinently thrown into prison.

It was now five years since Radisson and his friend had discovered the North Sea, or had said they did, and at last, at June 3, 1668, they sailed out from Gravesend, Radisson on the big ship Eaglet, and de Groseilliers on Gillam's smaller craft, the Nonsuch, but before they were out very far the Eaglet was dismasted and limped back to port, while the Nonsuch kept on its way and reached the Great Bay.

It remained there all winter, and, as no news came to Radisson about its successful passage across, he secured another vessel, the Wavero, and started out to search for the missing ship. Unfortunately the Wavero in turn was disabled, but when Radisson, now in the very depths of gloom, entered the Channel on his return to England, he had the unexpected pleasure of seeing the Nonsuch before him. The little vessel had crossed and recrossed the ocean.

She must have brought back a rich cargo, for a trading company was immediately organized, and with the greatest secrecy application was made for a royal charter, giving to " The Gentlemen Adventurers Trading to Hudson Bay " a monopoly of trade in America for all time to come.

The request was granted, and it would be hard to find in the documents of any government a more splendid generosity in disposing of the earth than the deed of gift made by Charles II to his friends and cronies, who made up the original Hudson Bay Company. Laut says " it was practically deeding away half America, namely, all modern Canada except New France," which they were ultimately to take, and most of the Western states beyond the Mississippi.. The grantees were to have " all the trade and commerce of all those seas, bays, rivers, creeks and sounds in whatever latitude that lie within the entrance of the straits called Hudson's Straits, together with all the lands, countries, and territories upon the coasts and confines of said straits, bays, rivers, lakes, creeks, and sounds not now actually possessed by any other Christian states." They were even given power " to make war against other princes or peoples that were not Christian, and to expel any other Englishman who should intrude on their territory, and to impose such punishment as the offense might warrant. Admirals, judges, sheriffs, and all officers of the law in England are charged by the charter to aid, favor, help, and assist the Company by land and sea." Signed at Westminster, May 2, 1670.

The applicants for the charter were Prince Rupert, the Duke of Albemarle, the Earl of Craven, and others less conspicuous. They were in great part also the stockholders. The capital did not exceed £10,500, and most of the shares were not subscribed in cash. But neither in the list of incorporators nor shareholders do we find the name of Radisson, who really had created the company. Later on his name appears with £200 to his credit.

The first vessels sent out were the Wavero, the Shaftesbury, and the Prince Rupert. On reaching the bay, Radisson took the Wavero, which was the smallest craft, and sailed along the south shore, and afterwards north to Nelson, where he erected the arms of the English King. He then continued on to Moose and Cape Henrietta Maria, and when he had accomplished that much he left Groseilliers in America and returned to London as advisor of the company. In the summers of 1671 and 1672 he was again in the bay, and when he returned to London in the fall of the latter year he committed the offense of marrying the Protestant, Mary Kirke, the daughter of Sir John Kirke, who was the representative of the Huguenot family which had driven Champlain from Quebec in 1629. This alliance is considered proof enough for some of Radisson's critics, but not for others, that while taking a wife he accepted her religion.

The year 1674 was the beginning of the disillusionment

of Radisson. He was again in the bay, and, although he saw vast fortunes accumulated around him, he found himself regarded merely as an employee. He had taken the oath of fidelity to the company, but that was not enough for his English friends; nor did his marriage with Mary Kirke avail to convince them of his trustworthiness. He was still considered to be a Catholic, and, indeed, Laut always describes him as such throughout the narration. There can be very little doubt that had he been an out-and-out Protestant and Englishman, he would have been the recipient of more worldly favors, and not looked down upon as a hireling.

Just then something occurred. It was in the fall of 1674. He was at his work, when suddenly a Jesuit missionary, Father Albanel, appeared and handed him a letter. It was from no less a personage than Colbert, the Prime Minister of Louis XIV, offering him a position in the French navy, the payment of all his debts, and a gratuity of £400, if he would return to his allegiance.

There is a scene for a novelist: a traitor and an outlaw in the icy desolation of the North, thousands of miles from civilization; a dark-robed Jesuit mysteriously appearing, secretly slipping a letter in the fugitive's hand, making offers of wealth and advances from the Grand Monarque, etc., etc., etc.

The weavers of romance have not lost sight of this opportunity, and they have spun fine yarns of how the absent Governor unexpectedly appears and sees the two Frenchmen hobnobbing with the Jesuit; dark suspicions arise; he demands the Jesuit's passport; finds it is from Frontenac, and is compelled to extend official courtesy to him; but in a rage he knocks down both Frenchmen; they reply in kind; and then flee to the woods, and after a thousand dangers arrive palpitating with excitement at Quebec.

The real story is more romantic. Radisson had pocketed the letter before the Governor arrived, and he was too sleek an individual to betray himself subsequently. As soon as he got the chance he slipped back to England, and from there crossed over to France. He accepted the offer of a place in the navy; went with d'Estrées on an expedition to the West Indies; was in the squadron that ran on the rocks at Curaçoa, when three out of the six ships were lost. Returning to France, he was recommended by d'Estrées for a gratuity of one hundred louis d'or.

He then tried to get his wife to join him in France, but she refused. By a curious process of logic, Colbert and his son, Seignelay, interpreted this unwillingness of the lady as meaning that Radisson was too much attached to England, and they forthwith began to frown on him. The poor fellow probably convinced them of his loyalty later on by sending to the Government a *supplique* signed by the Marquis de Belleroche, declaring that his wife had adjured Protestantism. This important paper is quoted by Dionne, who refers us to the "Collection of Documents," pp. 314, 315, 316, in the "New York Colonial MSS.," Vol. IX. It shows conclusively that Radisson was not a Huguenot.

What became of Father Albanel? There is no information forthcoming from any of the published "Relations" of the Society; but fortunately the author of "The Conquest of the Great Northwest" fills up the gap with two very valuable letters, dug up from the Hudson Bay archives. One is dated "London, September 25th, 1674," though the writer's name is not given; but it is addressed to the Secretary of State. It runs as follows: "This day came The Shaftesbury Pink from Hudson Bay, Capt. Shopard. Ye Capt. tiles me he found a ffranch Jesuit that did endeavor to convert ye Indians and persuade them not to trade with ye English, for which reason they brought him away with them. Capt. Gillam we expect to-morrow."

Later: "This day arrived Capt. Gillam. I was on board of him; they were forced to winter there and spend all their provisions. They have left only four to keep possession of the place. I see the French Jesuit is a little, ould man."

There is no mention whatever of Albanel's tampering with Radisson, nor was it necessary to communicate that information to Captain Shopard. There was reason enough in that he was "converting ye Indians." It may be noted that, besides giving us the knowledge of these very important facts, the letters also furnish us with a pen picture of the famous missionary's personal appearance. We are told: "He was a little, ould man." As a matter of fact, he was only sixty-two, but the hardship of his missionary career had, no doubt, left its scars on him. In addition to this, Dionne, in a paper read before the Royal Society of Canada, tells us something else about the "little, ould man." He notes that in the journal of Thomas Gorst, the secretary of Charles Bradley, Governor of Port Nelson, it is stated that on April 3, 1674, "there arrived at Fort Charles a Jesuit missionary, *born of English parents.* He brought a letter from Frontenac to Charles Bradley, in which the wish was expressed to have the Jesuit treated with all respect due to his position. The missionary also gave a letter to Chouart from his family at Three Rivers." Probably because Albanel was of English parentage and spoke English he was chosen for the mission to Hudson Bay.

These two letters fill up a gap in the story of the great missionary's life. It is said that for two years his Superiors knew nothing of his whereabouts. How could they? He was a prisoner at Hudson Bay and in England, and his disappearance from view may also explain the harsh judgment about Albanel's propensity for travel, rather than for apostolic work in converting the Indians. He appears to have been a much wronged man, even among his own.

We have no details about his prison life in England, nor is there any explanation at hand of how he was set free. We know only that he was in France in 1675, and on July 22 set sail for America. He was on the ship with

CHARLES ALBANEL

Father Enjalran, and, although the voyage was very tempestuous, he was quite immune from the distress of seasickness, which nearly killed his companion, though, on the other hand, had it not been for Enjalran, Albanel might have been brained by a stack of guns which had been detached from its place by the battering of the waves against the side of the vessel, and which came near falling on the missionaries.

Enjalran, in his long letter, narrates an incident which occurred at their departure from Gaspé, which at first sight reflects somewhat unfavorably on Albanel's courage. As they were leaving the shore to go up to Quebec a Christian Indian girl implored them to take her with them, as she feared for her virtue from the Frenchmen at Gaspé. She even leaped into the shallop and took her place at the side of the priests. The most prominent individual of the post pursued her, and dragged her out of the boat, in spite of her protests. Enjalran wanted to interfere, but Albanel, who is called by his companion " our dear and gracious leader," bade him to say nothing, and the unfortunate girl was hustled ashore. It was very distressing for the priests, but, on the other hand, they understood her very imperfectly. She may have been deceiving them, and merely wanted to go to Quebec. Besides, it might have compromised the reputation of both the missionaries if they had carried off a lone Indian girl from one of the French settlements. At this distance of time any judgment in the matter would be temerarious.

Albanel had scarcely arrived when he was sent to the Far West to replace a Father who was leaving for the Illinois. Probably he was given that destination to remove him as far as possible from the danger of meeting the English. He was likely to be seized again, for in the Public Record Office of London there is recorded in the " Colonial Entry Book," Vol. 96, p. 42, a protest of the Hudson Bay Company in the proceedings of the Royal Council, against

" some ill practices of Charles Albanel, a Jesuit; de Grose-
liers, a Frenchman, and Radisson, an Italian. The Council
resolved to request the French Government to hinder the
Jesuit, and the two persons aforesaid, undertaking anything
that may be prejudicial to the trade or interest of the aforesaid Company."

Whether or not the knowledge of this complaint of the
company had reached Quebec we do not know, but on
general principles it was prudent to have him out of the
way. It is curious to hear Radisson described as an Italian
by his old English associates. Of Albanel's work among
the Ottawas we find nothing but a casual reference. While
he was laboring there, the fight of the English and French
for the territory around the bay was in progress; Radisson
had a second time abandoned the French allegiance, and
gone over to the enemy. The romantic expeditions of Iberville to recover the trading posts, were filling the Canadians with alternate enthusiasm and despair, for the multi-
plied conquests of that remarkable man between the years
1687 and 1697, splendid as they were, only ended in the
loss of the entire country. No doubt Albanel heard of it
all, in his far away seclusion of the west, for the news of
such events travelled fast among the aborigines. The end
came at last, and the heroic missionary, who was described
as " a little, ould man " in 1674, went to heaven from Sault
Ste. Marie as late as twenty-two years afterwards, on January 11, 1696.

CLAUDE ALLOUEZ

CHAPTER I.

THE UNWELCOME PASSENGER.

Claude Allouez is often spoken of as the Francis Xavier of the American missions. No distance was too great, no danger too threatening, to make him desist from his pursuit of the souls of the red men. He was the first to follow Ménard to what was then the farthest west. "Do you notice the shape of Lake Superior or Lake de Tracy?" asks Dablon in his "Relation" of those apostolic enterprises. "Its northern shore is bent like a bow, the southern side may do for the string, while midway in the three hundred and sixty miles of water a great peninsula juts out, which, with a little effort of the imagination, will seem to you like the arrow, even if it does not go all the way across the one hundred and forty miles, which is the width of the lake at that place. At the extreme western end of that inland sea Father Claude Jean Allouez established his mission of La Pointe du St. Esprit." The place is now simply La Pointe. Indeed, it was sometimes so designated in missionary times.

Allouez was born at St. Didier, in France, June 6, 1622, and was only a lad of seventeen when he entered the noviciate at Toulouse. He made his studies in the same city, and subsequently at Billom and Rodez, and we find him in the last named place engaged chiefly in preaching. When he was thirty-six years of age he set out for Canada, on the same ship with d'Argenson, who had been made Governor of New France. Like all the other missionaries, he was first engaged at different posts along the St. Lawrence; in 1660 he was Superior at Three Rivers, and while at that

147

post was named vicar general of the Northwest, an appointment which was perhaps the first act of the ecclesiastical organization of the western country.

He started from Three Rivers for Lake Superior in 1664, but on reaching Montreal he found that the flotilla of canoes had already gone up the river, and he was compelled to retrace his steps and wait for the next expedition, which left in the following year, on August 8, 1665. It consisted of a party of more than four hundred savages. They were of no particular tribe, but were an aggregation of the various nations who had fled westward from the pursuing Iroquois. Besides Allouez there were six other Frenchmen; they in quest of furs, he of souls.

It was a hard journey that he had set for himself, and he naturally blamed the devil for all the troubles he had to wrestle with. Even at the start the haughty savages gave him the uncomfortable assurance that he would never reach his destination, but would be abandoned in some lonely place on the way up if he persisted in going. However, he was not to be balked. He and the Frenchmen had a canoe of their own, but by the time they reached the Rivière des Prairies, which flows behind Montreal Island, they unfortunately smashed it, and the crowd of Indians went on without them, being only too glad to be rid of any white companions. The boat, however, was repaired, and they paddled fiercely after the retreating savages, and succeeded in joining them two or three days later at the Long Sault on the Ottawa.

The effort, however, was too much for them, especially as the canoe was in a deplorable condition. That night Allouez made a speech to the Indians, entreating them to take the white men in their canoes. He won his case for his friends, but he himself was not wanted, and the next morning when he attempted to embark, the occupants of the canoe drove him off, and left him standing on the shore, while they paddled rapidly away. He was heart-broken, but knelt down and prayed for the brutal men who had left him to starve to death in the wilderness. His repulse, however, was providential, for the canoe from which he had been expelled went to pieces later on in the rapids. Had he been in it the dark waters of the Ottawa would have closed over him forever.

While he was resigning himself to God's will he saw three of his French friends coming up the river. He hailed them, and, of course, they came ashore to rescue him from his plight. Together they repaired the old canoe, and started after the party, which had long since vanished from sight. It was a dangerous thing to do, for they were traveling up an unknown river, where ignorance of the currents meant at times almost certain death. The passage at the Chat Rapids was particularly perilous, but doubtless they were helped by the prayers of the missionary, and they not only made it safely, but succeeded in catching up with a party of six of the Indian canoes.

Allouez thought it was high time to lay aside his meek and humble demeanor, and he began to berate the Indians soundly. "Do you know that I represent Onontio?" he asked; "that I hold his voice in my hands and that I am going as his ambassador to speak to all the nations of the West?" They looked at him in amazement. He had succeeded in frightening them so much that they let him journey along with them, and at noon that day they caught up with the rest of the flotilla.

Encouraged by his maneuver in terrorizing the first detachment, he tried the same tactics on the whole assembly that afternoon. But he failed; for one of the chiefs rose up to reply, and succeeded so well in allaying the fears of the others that, although the laymen were taken aboard the canoes, the priest was again repelled, the reason alleged being that he did not know how to paddle and could not carry a load at the portages.

Utterly discouraged this time, the abandoned man withdrew to the woods to pray, and perhaps to die, but after a little while he returned to the shore, he scarcely knew why, and there to his amazement he saw out on the stream the very Indian who had treated him with such contempt coming back to ask him to get into the canoe. "I did so immediately," says Allouez, "before he could have time to change his mind."

Seated in the canoe, a paddle was thrust in his hand, and he was bidden to get to work. "I felt like a malefactor condemned to the galleys," he tells us, "and had to work all day long, but, though thoroughly exhausted, God gave me strength to keep at my task far into the night." But he was treated with undisguised contempt; he was the butt of the whole party, and they stole everything they could from him. Hunger added its pangs, and the putrid meat and bitter roots which he occasionally received left their taste in his mouth for days. But, he wrote, "it is a pleasant thing to be hungry on Fridays."

The portages were especially difficult for him, on account of the heavy packs that were put on his shoulders. When he stumbled and fell he was abused for his lack of strength; nor were the two or three hours' stretch which he allowed himself on the rocks calculated to rest his tired frame, especially as he went to sleep supperless.

When the party had passed Lake Nipissirinien and were descending a little river they were startled by mournful wailings and death songs in the distant woods. They approached and to their horror found eight young Ottawa braves lying on the ground mangled and dying. A powder keg, ignited by a spark, had exploded. As far as we are aware, this is the only accident of the kind recorded in the "Relations." Four of the poor wretches were at the point of death, and Allouez endeavored to prepare them for baptism, but he had no time, for the Indians would not wait; they took up the wounded men and made all haste to reach the entrance of Lake Huron.

ALLOUEZ'S OSTENSORIUM.

CLAUDE ALLOUEZ

On the twenty-fourth of the month a hundred canoes met at the rendezvous and the jugglers forthwith began their incantations to heal the wounded men. Others who were not jugglers offered what the missionary thought to be a sacrifice to the sun. They lighted a fire out on the point of a rocky islet, where ten or twelve of them solemnly sat around in a circle, and, while the smoke of the fire ascended to the sky, they made the air hideous with their cries, finally bringing the ceremony to a close by a pompous speech which the most influential and oldest chief addressed to the sun.

Allouez hesitated a long time as to what he should do to combat their superstition. If he angered the savages he and his French companions would very likely be killed or abandoned, but, plucking up courage, he went up to the jugglers. An animated debate followed, ending with the change of heart of one of the victims of the accident. He promised to have nothing more to do with such superstitious practices. It was a triumph and a comfort for Allouez, but the defeated medicine man howled all night around the missionary's hut, and then vented his rage on him by smashing to pieces the poor old canoe that had given such trouble all the way up the river.

It was not till the second of September that they reached Sault Ste. Marie. He tells us that the journey up what is now St. Mary's River had been comparatively pleasant as far as the scenery could make it, but that the savages were surly, because the fish they expected to catch in abundance refused to enter their nets. At last they launched out upon Lake Superior, to which Allouez then gave the name of the Governor, de Tracy, a designation which may still be seen on some of the old maps.

"The savages," he writes, "regard this lake as a divinity and offer it sacrifices, but whether it is on account of its size, or because of its goodness in furnishing a supply of fish to make up for the lack of game in those parts, I do not know. As you sail along over its clear waters you can see far down at the bottom of the lake pieces of copper, some of them as much as ten and twenty livres in weight. The Indians keep bits of the metal about them as manitous, and hand them down as precious heirlooms to their children."

He was anxious to find the great rock of pure copper' which he had been told projected far out of the water; but as he saw nothing he surmised that the frequent storms on the lake had covered it with sand. It may be of interest to the reader to know that this same copper rock is now in the Smithsonian Institution, in Washington, D. C.

Allouez met on the lake representatives of twelve or fifteen nations. They had come from north, south, east and west, chiefly for fishing. For him it was a dispensation of Divine Providence, as it enabled him to do some fishing of another sort. During all the journey, of course, he had been unable to say Mass, and he informs us that it was only in the month of September, when he was alone with the Frenchmen, that the desired opportunity presented itself.

After Mass he crossed the bay to which Father Ménard, who had preceded him in that far away wilderness, some years before, had given the name of St. Theresa, and on the first of October he arrived at beautiful Chequamegon Bay, or Chagoumigong, as he calls it, where he found a great village, which could send out on the warpath no less than eight hundred warriors. They were a sedentary people, however, and cultivated the land, and, strange to say, though composed of seven different tribes, they lived in peace with each other.

The exact spot of this mission is still a matter of dispute. It may have been at the mouth of what is now Vanderventer's Creek, and not far from where the famous trapper Radisson camped four years before. Verwyst, however, locates it near Whittlesey's Creek, on Shore Landing.

The only trouble in the place was the dread of the Nadouessi, a warlike tribe, their next neighbors, who were threatening to go to war with them. Allouez was invited to the council that was called to discuss the situation, and he willingly accepted, but, while assuring them of the protection of Onontio, who, he told them, was just then setting out for the Mohawk to crush the Iroquois, he contrived to insert in his discourse a great deal of information about the Christian faith. What was the result of the council he does not tell us, and we do not know if hostilities began at that time. We learn, however, that later on the Nadouessi triumphed and the mission of La Pointe was temporarily abandoned. But that was after Allouez left it, and when Marquette was in charge.

Like the rest of the savages, these Indians were a bad set; they were polytheists, with a particular devotion to the sun, the delusion varying in its manifestations from what it was further east. He tells us that he saw in one village an idol to which a dozen dogs were sacrificed for the purpose of putting an end to a pestilence. Tobacco also was a common oblation. It was offered by throwing it at the object venerated. They believed also in a certain kind of metempsychosis, and were particularly devout to a wonderful beast which they called Missibizi; a creature, however, which no one had ever seen except in a dream. The usual savage debauchery was associated with these religious rites. Polygamy reigned, and men, women, and girls were all wildly profligate. Of medicine they had no idea and usually submitted to the absurdities of the juggler, though a feast in honor of the sun was considered the most sovereign remedy for all the ills that flesh is heir to. Whatever the fate of the patient, it was sure to be profitable for the medical practitioners.

After some time he thought he discerned some decrease in the debauchery of the people, and was so delighted that he plucked up courage and planted his little chapel in the very center of the village. But he made a mistake, for it brought him face to face with the worst of their disorders, and inaugurated a bitter struggle with the chief of the jugglers, who treated him with the utmost scorn and contempt. That, of course, was to be expected, but unfortunately the people imitated their medicine man, and soon made a wreck of the little chapel, so that the weary man had to withdraw to his former secluded abode.

He set out, on May 6, 1667, for far away Lake Nipigon, or Alimibegong, which was fifty or sixty leagues from the North Sea. The purpose in view was to visit the Nipissiriniens, many of whom were Christians. They had fled northwards to get out of reach of the terrible Iroquois, and for twenty years had never seen a priest. The route was across the western end of Lake Superior, which was the most dangerous part of the journey, for he and his men had to paddle incessantly for twelve hours a day in order to make the most of the fair weather. If they had been caught in a storm on that great inland water they would never have returned to La Pointe, for when Lake Superior is in its fury it is like the ocean. Indeed, so rapidly did they travel that in a single day they made a run of eighteen leagues. The amazing part of it is that, though all the time they had very little to eat, their strength did not give out. They fished when they could, but it was only on the twenty-third that they succeeded in getting anything. But on that day there was such a plentiful haul of sturgeon that they had to leave much of it behind.

They were now on the north shore, and after winding through the beautiful islands, one of which was twenty leagues long, they left the lake and attempted the ascent of a river, but there were so many difficult rapids to pass that the Indians gave it up in despair. Moreover, they heard that Lake Alimibegong was still frozen over, and they, therefore, resolved to rest where they were for the next two days.

When they resumed their journey they met some Nipissiriniens in the woods. It was then Whitsuntide, and the missionary gathered his Christian Indians together and, erecting a bower in which he built an altar, he celebrated Holy Mass, and gave his little congregation an instruction. "They listened," he wrote, "with as much piety and decorum as our Indians at Sillery." It was on this occasion that he met two women, a mother and daughter, whose previous adventures would furnish a blood curdling theme for an Indian romance. They had been captured by the Iroquois, and once had succeeded in making their escape, but, having been recaptured, a close watch was kept on them. One day, however, it happened that they found themselves in a cabin with a single Iroquois. The others had gone out to hunt. It was their only chance, and they put their heads together for a plot, and when everything was arranged the girl asked the unsuspecting brave for a knife to help her to dress a beaver skin which had been given her to prepare. Unsuspectingly, he handed her the knife, but in an instant it flashed before his eyes only to be buried in his heart. He sunk at her feet and the mother finished the work by beating out his brains with a block of wood. They then fled to the forest and made for their country, which they succeeded in reaching after incredible suffering. It was not thought much of, however, for it was a common occurrence among these wild people.

Leaving these wanderers in the woods, Allouez paddled around the lake for six days, seeking some way of going farther north. He found an outlet at last, and on June 30 came upon the village of the Nipissiriniens. Most of them were idolaters, but there were twenty Christians among them, and with both classes he had his hands full for the two weeks he was able to remain with them. He then started for home, which he reached in safety, having made a journey which, including the detours, was a mere trifle of about fifteen hundred miles.

Meantime his people at La Pointe were not responding

to his efforts for their improvement, and he determined to try what effect a little fear might have on them. He summoned a general council and gave vent to his feelings. "You are an ungrateful people," he said; "I have been two years laboring among you, and you have treated me with no consideration whatever. I am going to leave you; I will shake the dust from my shoes," and, suiting the action to the word, he took off his shoes and shook them violently.

The Indians were alarmed. It was not, however, entirely regret for the loss of his ministrations that worried them, but fear that the French would leave them to the mercy of the Iroquois if the missionary went away. The temporal and the spiritual seemed to have an equal share in determining them. At all events, an entire tribe, the Queues Coupés, promised to embrace the faith. As a matter of fact they abandoned their superstitious practices and renounced polygamy, but their conversion, however, was not as abrupt as it might at first appear. Years before Allouez appeared among them, de Brébeuf and his companions had dealings with the tribe down at Lake Huron, and Ménard had met them in his lonely wanderings in the west.

Seeing such rich harvests before him, as he thought, he started for Quebec to ask for help. It was fortunate that he did so, for as no news had come of him since the day he left Three Rivers with the four hundred Indians, two years before, his Superiors thought he was dead. He was welcomed, of course, and succeeded in getting Father Nicholas as an assistant, but he remained only two days with his brethren and then set his face again for Lake Superior. Five Frenchmen volunteered to go with him, but the Indians would take only three, and insisted on such a small amount of luggage that the white men stepped into the canoes with the greatest misgivings. It looked as if they should never reach the western country. However, no misfortune befell them.

156

CHAPTER II.

Green Bay.

In 1669 Allouez again went down to Quebec; this time with a number of Iroquois, whom he had ransomed. His stay in the colony was as brief as on the former occasion. Apparently, however, he did not return to La Pointe, but, after reaching Sault Ste. Marie, set out on another journey, this time to the south, to discover new fields for apostolic endeavor. Evidently war was raging at La Pointe.

The opportunity came to him in a complaint lodged by some Pottowotamies against five or six traders, who had established themselves in the vicinity of the Baie des Puants, or Green Bay. Where there was trading, argued Allouez, of course there were people, and with the double purpose of making the traders behave themselves and establishing a mission, he, with two white men, pushed their canoe off the shore of the Sault on the third of November, 1669, and paddled down the St. Mary's River towards the Straits of Mackinac.

It was already late in the season, and the ice was forming, but these hardy men made light of the fact that, although the cold was intense, they could have no other place to sleep than the bare rocks on the shore.. Allouez notes incidentally that they were a little uncomfortable one morning when they woke up and found themselves covered with snow. Their boat was coated with ice, and they had to walk in the freezing water in their bare feet, dragging their canoe after them, so as to prevent it from being crushed by the cakes of ice. About the fourth day out they reached the bend in the river, where it turns towards Lake Michigan. Allouez called it the *Detour*, and such is its name to-day.

Not in that fashion is the journey made at the present time. In the course of an afternoon you are carried in a fine steamer down the beautiful St. Mary's and over the wide stretches of Hay and Mud Lakes, on neither of which beautiful expanses of water do you see either mud or hay. On the contrary, the eye rests with delight upon islands dotting the surface, while the far away shores sometimes almost fade from view in the distance. Again and again great steamers, seven and eight hundred feet long, are seen speeding along with their precious freight towards the gigantic locks at the Sault, to be lifted like toys into the western sea of Lake Superior. You hurry along through a panorama of forests, and mountains, and islands, and towards evening you land at Detour, not to pass the night on the rocks, but in one of the big hotels which look out on the Straits towards the Island of Mackinac.

The old travelers whose itinerary we are now following were detained for some days on one of the little islands off Detour, and only on the eleventh of the month were they able to resume their journey. They were warned by some Indians and Frenchmen whom they met not to make the attempt, but they kept straight on, and after bravely undergoing a great deal of hardship and danger the huge bulk of Mackinac loomed up in the sky behind them. His sufferings, however, did not prevent the light hearted missionary from being amused by the stories his Indians told him about Michilimackinac.

The god of the place is Ouisaketchak, or the Great Hare. He created the earth, the natives say, and then, very inconsequently, they add, he also invented fishing nets, the idea being suggested to him by watching a spider spinning its web. As the god was a mighty hunter, it suited his fancy once upon a time to go out after beavers. He started up the St. Mary's River, traveling eight leagues at every step. There used to be a dam midway in the river, but he stepped on it and crushed it. That's the reason why there are no rapids there. He was in a hurry when he reached the Sault, and hence trod very lightly on the obstruction at that place, which explains how you do not find it a cataract, but merely rapids. When he entered Lake Superior the beavers saw him and scurried away to the North Sea, intending to swim to Europe, but when they tasted the salt water they were disgusted and turned back, and that is the reason why there are no beavers in France.

On the twenty-fifth and twenty-seventh they met some Pottawotamies, but were unable to accept their invitation to eat with them, for there were not provisions enough to go round. On the twenty-ninth they reached the mouth of a river, up which they intended to go, but it was frozen. They waited till the wind broke up the ice, and on the second of December, the eve of St. Francis Xavier's feast, they found the post of the French traders. The day, of course, suggested the name, and the place was thereafter known as St. Francis Xavier's. Until recently this place was believed to be the site of the present city of Green Bay, but that is a mistake, for Allouez says distinctly that he reached the mouth of the Menominee River only in the spring time. That mission post was eight leagues away from St. Francis Xavier's, which was probably at the entrance to the Oconto River.

He passed the winter among the Pottowatomies, whom he found wretchedly poor and deplorably stupid. They had not wit enough, he said, to make a dish or to scoop out a ladle. He started for the Menominees on April sixteenth, and consequently was on his way to Lake Winnebago. There were plenty of rapids to pass, and, among other things he makes note of the weir which the Sacs, who were about four leagues up the river, had constructed for catching fish, a device which, with very little modification, is used by the whites of to-day. The apple trees and vine stocks which he saw as he passed along are noted down in his diary, and he describes the eclipse of the sun which occurred on the nineteenth. Finally, on the evening of that day, he launched his canoe on the waters of the lake, which he also called St. Francis. The first Mass in that territory was said on the following day, which was Sunday. This was at the confluence of the Upper Fox and Wolf Rivers.

It is very delightful to note with what minuteness Thwaites describes the various obstacles which Allouez had to face on his way up the river, now known as the Fox. They were the Rapides des Pères; Little Kakalin, now known as Little Rapids; the Croche, above Wrightstown; Grand Kakalin, at Kankauna; Little Chute, which still preserves its old name; the Cedars at Kimberly; Grand Chute at Appleton, and Winnebago Rapids, at Neenah. Allouez would be astounded if he visited those scenes to-day to see the thriving manufacturing towns and villages all along the river, which he toiled up so laboriously two hundred and thirty years ago.

He had but a limited time to work in those regions, for he had to report back at the Sault, but he has left us some precious information about the fertility of the soil, the abundance of game, and the character of the various tribes. He was regarded by the Indians as a manitou. They often entreated him to save them from their enemies, and he had great difficulty in preventing them from offering sacrifices to him. Their favorite oblation was tobacco. It was then he was told that the river of the Oumanis would lead him in six days to the Mississippi. He would gladly have gone to explore it, but was under orders, and could not yield to his own inclinations. We should not forget, however, that it was he who marked out the route which his great successor, Marquette, was so soon to follow. Finally, on the twentieth of the month, he embarked with an Indian and a Frenchman, and made his way back to Sault Ste. Marie.

Father Dablon, who had just been named Superior of the missions, arrived at the Sault on September 6, 1670, and went with Allouez to the Green Bay country. The journey has been already described in the sketch of Dablon, in Volume I, and there is no need of repeating it here. On June fourth of the following year there took place at the Sault the solemn official act by which the northwest territory was declared to be subject to the King of France. M. de Lusson, who had been delegated by the Government at Quebec to preside at the ceremonies, had arrived at the mission post the month before, and summoned the tribes for a hundred leagues around to signify their approval of the act of possession by taking part in the proceedings. As has been related elsewhere, the occasion was invested with all the pomp and solemnity possible. It is only necessary to recall that the orator of the occasion was Father Allouez, who, evidently elated by the importance of the occasion, pronounced a perfervid and picturesque discourse, dilating chiefly upon the glories of the Grand Monarque beyond the seas, Louis XIV. The choice of Allouez indicated the esteem in which the great missionary was held both by the Indians and whites, and the brief résumé of the topics he dwelt upon, as well as the local color with which he invested his thoughts, showed that the holy man was a master of barbaric imagery, which counted for much in an Indian council.

An event now occurred which is somewhat puzzling when looked at from a merely human point of view. Both the Home and the Colonial Government had determined that the Great River must be found at any cost. Joliet had been chosen for the expedition, and a priest was to go with him, but the one selected was not the tried veteran Allouez, who had already been so near the Mississippi, and who not only knew every step of the intervening country, but was inured to every hardship by long years of missionary toil. It was the young and comparatively inexperienced Marquette, who had been only a few years in the west. Was it some mysterious dispensation of Divine Providence that set aside the older soldier and chose the young recruit? Who can tell? At all events, in the year 1671, Marquette and Joliet started out to find the Mississippi, and Allouez went back to Green Bay, and up the Fox River, to establish the missionary post of Des Pères. Father André, a recent arrival, was named as his companion. The name of Allouez is still in benediction at De Pere, as it is now called. The full name used to be Rapides des Pères, or Rapids of the Fathers, but it has now assumed its present abbreviated and singular form.

The remembrance of the great missionary is not likely to fade from men's minds in that part of the world. For the State Historical Society of Wisconsin has built a monument to him on the sloping river bank, quite close to the site of the old house and chapel which he occupied. It is a huge granite boulder, resting firmly on a pedestal of native limestone, and a bronze tablet records the fact that " Near this spot stood the chapel of St. Francis Xavier, built in the winter of 1671-72 by Father Claude Allouez, S. J., as the centre of his work in Christianizing the Indians of Wisconsin. This Memorial Tablet was erected by the citizens of De Pere, and unveiled by the State Historical Society of Wisconsin, September 6th, 1899."

Bishop Messmer of Green Bay, now Archbishop of Milwaukee, who read a paper on this occasion on the " Early Jesuit Missions in the Fox River Valley," must have felt his heart thrill with delight when he held in his hand the old mission ostensorium which was given to the Fathers in 1686, by Nicholas Perrot, who was then Commandant for the French in the west.

De Pere was the center of Father Allouez's work until the news came that Marquette had succumbed to the labor entailed by his journey down the Mississippi, and had died after attempting to inaugurate a mission among the Illinois. " A successor was needed," says the " Relation," " no less zealous than Marquette," and Allouez was ordered to the front. It was at the close of October, 1676, that he set out

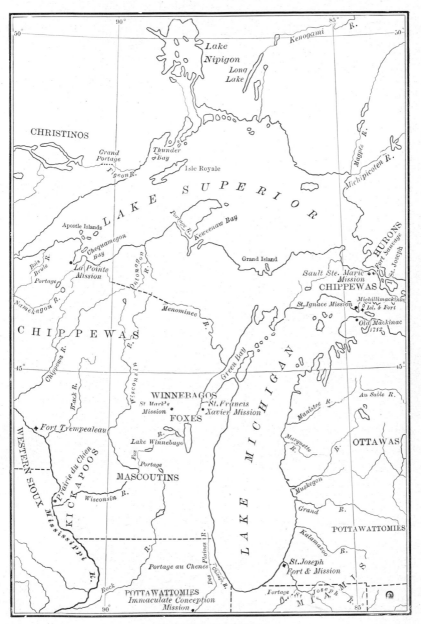

OTTAWA COUNTRY.

with two men to go to the country assigned to him, and which he already knew, but the winter was early that year, and they were compelled to go into a camp until the ice was strong enough to bear them. It was not until the month of February that he was able to resume his journey, and then, says he, "the mode of navigation was very unusual. Instead of putting the canoe in the water, we placed it on the ice, over which the wind, which was in our favor, and a sail, made it go as on water"—the first example of "ice-boating" that, as far as we know, appears in American history. On the eighteenth of March, the eve of St. Joseph's day, he found himself on the shores of Lake Michigan, and, of course, he gave it the name of the saint. He notes that it was a bitter cold day, the wind was high, the ice formed on the paddles, and the canoe was nearly crushed between the shore ice and the cakes that were driven in by the gale.

On the next day he found the famous "pitch rock," which he said gave them material for caulking the canoe and sealing his letters. The exact locality of this rock has been identified by Dr. Hobbs of the University of Wisconsin, as being in Whitefish Bay, a few miles north of Milwaukee. It rises slightly above the water, and in it there are many cavities filled with a semi-fluid, tar-like bitumen.

He journeyed seventy-six leagues over the lake before he reached the Illinois country, where he was received most hospitably. Eighty Indians came out to meet him. At their head was the chief, holding a firebrand in one hand, and in the other a calumet, tricked out with feathers. Advancing about thirty steps in front of his braves, he made one of the characteristic Indian speeches and conducted the missionary to the wigwam that had been made ready for him.

He arrived at Kaskaskia on the twenty-seventh, where he had been the year before. It was the largest of the

Illinois villages, and consisted of three hundred and fifty one cabins, all ranged along the river bank. It was an unhealthy spot, but was well adapted to give the people a chance to see an approaching enemy. He did not stay with them long, however, for this expedition was only to prospect in order to determine the most advantageous place for the central mission. He returned again in 1678, and during his absence the Iroquois had made their appearance, but had been put to flight by the watchful Illinois. There Allouez passed the remaining years of his life. He wrote much about his mission; always graphically and interestingly, and one reads with the greatest delight the account of the events that occurred there, his description of the country, the habits of the people. He remained eleven years in this apostolic field, and on the night of August 27-28, 1689, near what is now Niles, Michigan, on St. Joseph's River, among the Miamies, he died. He was sixty-seven years old, and he is credited with having instructed during his apostolic career 100,000 natives, 10,000 of whom he baptized. He had earned his name as the second Xavier.

JAMES MARQUETTE

It was a gloomy and depressing day when we set out on the journey from Detroit, up through the Michigan peninsula. The country was flat, desolate, and sparsely settled, with only an occasional town to break the dead monotony. To the right and left were never-ending swamps and lakes and bays, and beyond them forests, over which fierce fires had passed. The sky was like lead, and mists were hanging over the low meadows and marshes. For a long time we were skirting the shore of Mullet's Lake until we reached Cheyboygan, and then, veering to the northwest, were hurried along the South Channel of Lake Huron, where you could see Bois Blanc Island beyond. At Mackinaw City the train rumbled in on the deck of a huge steamer, and we were soon ploughing across the Straits of Mackinac, whose waters are sometimes as tumultuous as the sea, for there Lake Huron and Lake Michigan rush together. You feel the battering of the waves against the hull, but you see nothing, for the walls of the steamer shut you in as in a tunnel. At last the boat grinds against the groaning wharf, and we land at Pointe St. Ignace, or " St. Igniss," as they call it in those parts. You are free to make your choice of pronunciations, just as you can say Mackinac or Mackinaw, as it suits your fancy. St. Ignace is not wonderful architectually, commercially or socially, but for the historian and the Catholic it is a sacred place, for it guards the precious remains of Father Marquette.

At the eastern end of the village or town or city of St. Ignace, you will find a little enclosure, somewhat triangular in shape, near the base of which stands a modest stone shaft, which tells you that you are standing above the grave of the great discoverer. It is all so humble and unpretentious that you look into the eyes of your guide, and are tempted to be skeptical about the truth of the story. Is not the place rather on beautiful Mackinac Island, where the rich people of these parts who resort thither in the summer have erected a great statue of Marquette—a copy of the one that stands in the Capitol at Washington? No; this little out of the way village possesses the treasure, and there can be no serious doubt about it whatever.

In the year 1877 an excellent Catholic Irishman, named Patrick Murray, concluded after a great deal of deliberation that it would be a proper thing for him to clear up a patch of ground adjacent to his house and convert it into a garden. It was covered with a tangle of undergrowth, with an odd cedar tree here and there, but, although bordering on the public road, no one ever crossed it, for there was a tradition among the Indians, which the whites seemed to share, that a great bishop had once been buried there. Perhaps the story about the bishop gave new energy to the loyal son of the Church who had undertaken the work. At all events, in the course of his digging, he came upon the foundation of a house, and midway in what must have been the lower room his spade struck the decaying remnants of a birch-bark coffin.

Had he found the body of Father Marquette? It was just possible, he thought, and he hurried off to the parish priest, Father Edward Jacker, who was an admitted authority on all that related to the old Indian missions. Careful investigations were made; studies of the Jesuit "Relations" were resumed, measurements were taken, historians were consulted, with the result that the grave was admitted to have been really found. Pointe St. Ignace was no longer a place which the traveler might pass with unconcern.

Strangely enough, pieces of the coffin had been scorched by fire. How was that to be accounted for? Had the Indians burned down the chapel? No; it was the Jesuits

MARQUETTE'S GRAVE.

themselves who had applied the torch. Those who are familiar with the "Relations" will remember that when St. Ignace was deserted in consequence of the action of Cadillac in withdrawing the Indians to Detroit, Father de Carheil set fire to the whole establishment, so as to preclude the possibility of its ever being desecrated by the roving bands of Indians. He could not, of course, have removed the body of Marquette, which in any case he thought was safe from the flames. He was mistaken, indeed, for the humble casket was disintegrated, and the bones were all scattered in the clay. Perhaps God wished to put His stamp on the treasure, so as to be the means of its identification later on by leaving this reminder of the conflagration.

It is worth noting that this discovery was made in 1877, just two hundred years after Marquette was buried there; for it was in 1677 that the Indians came in their canoes to the shores of St. Ignace with the hallowed remains, which' they had taken from the hill on the Marquette River, near where it empties into Lake Michigan. They delivered their precious burden to Fathers Pierson and Nouvel, who placed it reverently beneath the earthen floor of the little chapel—a fitting resting-place for such an apostle.

The uncertainty which always confronts a man not in quest of human glory is very strikingly illustrated in the life of Father Marquette. He had been only a very few years on the missions, and yet on none of the priestly pioneers of Christianity in America has the world lavished more honor. There were others among his associates who were apparently better qualified to accompany Joliet in discovering the Great River, yet in the Providence of God they were set aside and the youngest and most inexperienced of all was chosen for the work. But neither he nor they were looking for the world's esteem. It was another who was disappointed—Joliet.

James Marquette was born at Laon, in France, a fortified city about seventy-four miles N. E. of Paris. It was an ancient place, and even Cæsar makes mention of the isolated hill called Mt. Bibrax, on whose steep slope it stood. Queen Brunehaut had made it her residence in 575, and the French kings often went there to live, previous to the rise of the House of Capet in 987. In the Middle Ages, Anslem and Abelard taught and studied at Laon, and later on it made vigorous resistance against the white-plumed King of Navarre. Napoleon, too, is associated with Laon, and in 1870 the Germans occupied it in the great war which so deeply humiliated France.

The Marquette family was among the most distinguished of the city, but its glory culminated in the son who saw the light there on January 10, 1637. When he was a boy of seventeen he left home and entered the Jesuit Novitiate at Nancy. That was on October 8, 1654. In 1666, after his term of studies and teaching at Pont à Mousson, Rheims, Charleville, and Langres, he came to America,. just when de Tracy and de Courcelles were marching down with the Carignan regiment to subdue the Mohawks. The usual time for studying Algonquin at Quebec and elsewhere along the St. Lawrence was accorded him, and then he set out for the far away west. He was assigned to the post which had been established a few years before by the old and tried missionary, Claude Allouez, at the furthest extremity of Lake Superior. He was then only thirty-two years old. About one hundred and ten years after that time four of the Marquette family fought for American independence, three dying in battle for the cause. It is also worth recording that by his mother Marquette was a relative of the saintly founder of the Christian Brothers, John Baptiste de la Salle.

The conditions at La Pointe to which he was first sent were not as bright as Allouez had painted them. His knowledge of the language was as yet necessarily imperfect, and perhaps he did harm to his prestige by apologizing to the Indians for his deficiency in that respect. The red man had never much respect for the virtue of humility, and the young missionary was treated rather contemptuously by many of the degraded wretches whom he was trying to regenerate. Still he toiled on manfully in his lonely and isolated mission.

There for the first time he saw the Illinois. They came from their own country to visit the place and told him wonderful stories about the great river which he and all the other missionaries had been longing for years to explore. He made up in his mind from what they said that it did not empty its waters into the Atlantic, which was one of the theories then current about it, but he was still wondering if it would not, if he ever embarked on it, lead him through California to the Pacific. "We shall go there next year," he wrote to his Superior, "in order to open the passage to those of our Fathers who have been awaiting this good fortune for so long a time. This discovery will give us a full knowledge of the South Sea or the Western Sea." He did not go next year, as he thought he would. On the contrary, after remaining for two years at La Pointe, he got into his canoe and paddled back to Sault Ste. Marie, for the Nadouessi had dug up the hatchet, and the war made it impossible for him to remain at his post.

In 1671 he went to the Straits of Mackinac. He called the new place St. Ignace, and began to labor with greater success than had attended his efforts at La Pointe, for the Indians at St. Ignace were chiefly Hurons, who had fled from Georgian Bay after the death of de Brébeuf and his companions. At first they had settled, some on Mackinac Island, and some on the mainland, but later on went off from both places to the Noquet Islands. In 1671, however, they returned to Mackinac and established themselves on the mainland at the place where Marquette found them. There he remained for the two following years. The vision of the Mississippi seemed to have been dispelled forever.

There is nothing special to chronicle about his work at the Straits, except that it was the usual round of hardships, dangers, and disappointments, though doubtless there was more spiritual consolation than elsewhere, for the Hurons were mostly Christians. But just as he was beginning to think that his dream about the great discovery could never be realized, there came to St. Ignace—Marquette is careful to note that it was on the eighth of December, the feast of the Immaculate Conception—his friend Joliet, who had just been commissioned by the Colonial Government to find the Mississippi, and he brought with him the delightful intelligence that Marquette was to be his companion. It was like an order to conquer an empire.

Dablon in his account tells us that Joliet was particularly well adapted for the work. He was a man of education; he had followed the course of studies at the Jesuit College of Quebec, and had even entered the theological seminary with the idea of becoming a priest, but, changing his purpose, he set sail for France, where he prepared himself for his future career as an explorer by a course of engineering, hydrography, and whatever else was available in those days. Previous to that he had lived among the Ottawas, and was conversant with many of their languages. As winter had already set in, it was out of the question to think of starting till the ice had broken up, and hence it was not until May 17, 1673, that he and Father Marquette, with five Frenchmen, pushed off their two little canoes from Pointe St. Ignace, "fully resolved," writes Marquette, "to do and suffer everything for so glorious an undertaking." A little smoked meat and some Indian corn constituted their whole stock of provisions.

Their route lay through the Straits of Machinac, across the headwaters of Lake Michigan, and up to Green Bay, just as Allouez had gone before them. "I placed our voyage," writes Marquette, "under the protection of the Blessed Virgin Immaculate, promising her that if she granted us the favor of discovering the Great River that I would give it the name of the Conception."

The Wild Oats Indians were the first to be met with. They were startled at the audacity of the white men, and drew dreadful pictures of the dangers that would have to be encountered. They had weird stories about the savage men, the monsters on the rivers, and the huge demon who was waiting on the river to swallow up every one who came near him. Marquette must have smiled at most of these fancies when he thanked them for their good advice, and, bidding them good-bye, paddled up the Baie des Puants.

Ascending the Fox River, the travellers arrived at the villages of the Maskoutens, Miamis, and Kickapoos. "The Miamis," says Marquette, whose diary we shall quote frequently, "are gentlemen; the Kickapoos and Maskoutens, boors." He tells us that he found a plant in the neighborhood which was a specific for snake bites, but modern botanists have been unable to trace it. It had several stalks, long leaves, and a white flower, something like the wall flower. Among the Maskoutens he saw, to his delight, "in the middle of the village, a handsome cross, adorned with bows and arrows and peltries, which these good people had offered to the Great Spirit to thank Him for having had pity on them during the winter by giving them plenty of game when they were very much in fear of starvation."

But "that was not a Christian cross at all," says W. J. Hoffman, in the "Bureau of American Ethnology Reports" (1885-6; p. 155), "and Marquette was *without doubt* ignorant of the fact that the cross is the sacred post, and the symbol of the fourth degree of the Midewiwin, a Society of Midé, or Shamans, designated as the Grand Medicine Society, which is found among many Algonquin tribes. Its ritual and the traditions of Indian genesis and cosmogony constitute what to them is a religion even more powerful and impressive than the Christian religion is to the average man. This symbol of the cross had *probably* been erected and bedecked with barbaric emblems and weapons months before anything was known of Marquette."

Perhaps it may not be out of place to interrupt the course of this narrative for a moment to animadvert upon these amazing utterances of the " Bureau of American Ethnology Reports."

In the first place, no where in the " Relations " is there any mention of this General Medicine Society, and had there been any such association the old missionaries would certainly have made note of it. Secondly, instead of the cross being a sacred thing for the Indians, it was a constant source of dread and suspicion. Thirdly, it is astonishing to be told that " the cross had *probably* been there for months before Marquette was heard of." As Marquette had been living at St. Ignace for two years, it is more than probable, or rather it is very certain, that not only had the Indians heard of him, but knew him. Finally, it is going far afield to conjure up the cross as a sacred emblem of a secret society of medicine men when Marquette's predecessor, Allouez, had been for two years before that going through the country erecting crosses in every Indian village. We say nothing of the extraordinary sentiment expressed by the writer, viz., that the indecent and degrading ritual of Indian incantations " was a more powerful and impressive religion than Christianity is to the average man."

These Indians on the Fox, like the others below, were horrified when they understood the nature of the expedition. But, though warning the wayfarers of the dangers to be met with, they gave them two guides to conduct them to a river nine miles away, which emptied into the Mississippi. The distance was not great, but the country was so broken up by swamps and small streams, whose channels were hard to find, that guides were indispensable; and so, on June tenth, Marquette and his companions bade good-bye to the great crowd that gathered on the bank to see them off. They reached the Fox-Wisconsin Portage in safety, and then launched out upon the Wisconsin River. "We left the waters flowing towards Quebec," writes Marquette, "to float on those that would take us to strange lands, but before embarking we began a new devotion to the Blessed Virgin, and after mutually encouraging each other we entered our canoes." The Miami guides left them at that point and returned home.

In the diary there is an accurate description of the Wisconsin, with its islands and sand banks, the woods and hills and prairies on either side, with their oak and walnut and basswood trees, and "others whose branches are armed with long thorns." But the travellers saw no game or fish, though there were plenty of deer and cattle. They noted an iron mine as they passed along, and, at last, "after proceeding forty leagues by this route, we arrived at the mouth of our river, and at $42\frac{1}{2}°$ latitude we safely entered the Mississippi, on the seventeenth of June, with a joy that I cannot express."

Marquette did not see the league-wide river which the Indians had told him about, for it is narrow where the Wisconsin empties into it. Further down, he says, "it is at times about three-quarters of a league across." He saw herds of buffalo as he went along and also wingless swans; a tiger cat made its appearance at one time and startled the travelers, and again, when a huge catfish dashed against the canoe, they thought that they had struck the submerged trunk of a tree; but no where did they see any trace of human habitation, though they had already journeyed three hundred miles, counting the distance on both rivers. At night when they landed to cook their meals they made only a small fire, so as not to attract attention, and then withdrew to their boats, always, however, leaving a sentinel on guard. Finally, on the twenty-fifth of June, they perceived the tracks of men, on a narrow and somewhat beaten path, leading to a fine prairie.

"We stopped to examine it," he says, "and thinking it

was a road leading to a village, we resolved to reconnoitre. Leaving the two canoes in charge of our people, M. Joliet and I undertook the investigation, a rather hazardous one for two men who exposed themselves alone to the mercy of a barbarous and unknown people. We silently followed the narrow path, and after walking about two leagues we discovered a village on the bank of a river and two others about half a league from the first. Then we heartily recommended ourselves to God, and, imploring His aid, we went farther without being perceived, and approached so near that we could even hear the savages talking. We therefore decided that it was time to reveal ourselves. This we did by shouting with all our might, and then stopped without advancing further. On hearing the shout the savages quickly issued from their cabins and, having probably recognized us as Frenchmen, especially when they saw the black gown, or, at least, having no cause of distrust, for we were only two men, and had given them notice of our arrival, they deputed four old men to come and speak to us. Two of these bore tobacco pipes, handsomely ornamented and adorned with various feathers. They walked slowly and raised their pipes to the sun, but without saying a word. They spent a long time in covering the distance between the village and us. Finally, when they had drawn near they stopped to consider us attentively. I was reassured when I observed their ceremonies, which with them are performed only among friends, and much more so when I observed that they were clad in cloth, for I judged thereby that they were our allies. I asked them who they were. They replied that they were Illinois, and as a token of peace they offered us the calumets to smoke, and then invited us to enter their village.

"At the door of the cabin in which we were to be received was an old man who awaited us in a rather surprising attitude. He stood erect and stark naked; his hands were lifted toward the sun, as if he wished to protect himself from its rays, which nevertheless shone upon his face through his fingers. When we came near him he paid us this compliment: 'How beautiful is the sun, O Frenchman, when thou comest to visit us. All our village awaits thee and thou shalt enter all our cabins in peace.'

"The people crowded around us, devouring us with their eyes, but all in profound silence. We could hear, however, these words, which were addressed to us from time to time in a low voice: 'How good it is, my brothers, that you should visit us.'"

Then followed the smoking of the calumet, at which at least a pretense of smoking had to be made. A visit to a grand council in the next village followed, and as the Frenchmen passed along, the people ran ahead and then lay in the grass to contemplate the wonderful strangers, repeating the act again and again. At the entrance to the village the great chief, with an old man on either side, stood at the entrance of the cabin, all three in the garb that nature gave them, and holding their calumets up to the sun. The same ceremonies were performed as before, and when Marquette had spoken to them about the truths of Christianity the chief arose, and, having thanked the Frenchmen for having come to see them, said: "Never has the earth been so beautiful or the sun so bright as to-day; never has our river been so calm, or so clear of rocks, which your canoes have removed in passing; never has our tobacco tasted so good or our corn appeared so fine." He then gave them a little slave to sit near them, and begged them not to proceed on their journey.

Attention has been frequently called to the fact that Longfellow, in his Hiawatha, has taken this scene from Marquette's diary almost word for word. It may be useful to quote it here:

From the distant land of Wabun,
From the farthest realms of morning,
Came the Black-Robe chief, the Prophet,
He the Priest of Prayer, the Pale-face,
With his guides and his companions.
    And the noble Hiawatha,
With his hands aloft extended,
Held aloft in sign of welcome,
Waited, full of exultation,
Till the birch-canoe with paddles
Grated on the shining pebbles,
Stranded on the sandy margin,

Till the Black-Robe chief, the Pale-face,
With the cross upon his bosom,
Landed on the sandy margin.
    Then the joyous Hiawatha
Cried aloud and spake in this wise:
" Beautiful is the sun, O strangers,
When you come so far to see us!
All our town in peace awaits you,
All our doors stand open for you;
You shall enter all our wigwams,
For the heart's right hand we give you.
    " Never bloomed the earth so gayly,
Never shone the sun so brightly,
As to-day they shine and blossom,
When you come so far to see us!
Never was our lake so tranquil,
Nor so free from rocks and sand-bars;
For your birch-canoe in passing
Has removed both rock and sand-bar.
    " Never before had our tobacco
Such a sweet and pleasant flavor,
Never the broad leaves of our corn-fields
Were so beautiful to look on,
As they seem to us this morning,
When you come so far to see us! "

The council was followed by a feast, of which Marquette writes: " The master of ceremonies filled a spoon three or four times with sagamité, and put it in my mouth, as if I were a baby. He did the same to M. Joliet. The second course was fish, and the same dignitary took a few pieces, removed the bones, and then, blowing on the fish to cool it, put it in our mouths, as if he were feeding a bird." The third course was a dog, but, as the pale-faces gagged at that, it was removed. The last was wild ox, the fattest morsels being placed in the mouths of the honored guests. On the following day six hundred people gathered to bid farewell to the travellers, and loaded them with presents; the chief distinction being accorded to Marquette, who received a sacred calumet. It was to be of great use further down the river.

JAMES MARQUETTE

Near where Alton now stands they saw painted on the rocks two hideous figures, on which no Indian would dare to fix his gaze. They were as large as calves, and had horns as big as those of a deer. Their eyes were blood red, like a tiger's; they had human faces; bodies covered with scales, and their tails wound around their bodies, then over the head, and finally curled backward between the legs. The end of the tail was like that of a fish. Marquette made a copy of this work of art and sent it to France.

The inrush of the Missouri, or the Pekitanoui, an Indian name for Muddy River, was a dreadful menace to their frail canoes, as it swept down huge trees and masses of earth. Nevertheless, Marquette wrote: "I hope to ascend it some day, and perhaps we may discover the Vermillion Sea." He never realized that hope, but he was sure when he saw the Pekitanoui's course that the Mississippi, whose current it swelled and defiled, did not empty into the Pacific. The Ohio also, or the Ouaboukigou, as he calls it, which he met twenty leagues further down, and coming from the east, cleared up the doubt about the possible eastern mouth of the Great River, which he was now tolerably certain poured its waters into the Gulf of Mexico.

Meantime the tall reeds on the banks began to show themselves; swarms of mosquitoes pursued them night and day; but the first feeling of terror came over them when they saw, on the bank before them, a crowd of Indians, armed with guns, and awaiting their approach. But Marquette held up the calumet, and after a parley they all went ashore and found that the savages had been as terrified as themselves. Being reassured, the Indians laid aside their fears and spread a feast for the wonderful newcomers, who learned, to their delight, that the sea was only ten days away. Leaving this kindly tribe, they kept on down the river. Cottonwood and elm and basswood lined the shore, and the bellowing of great herds of buffaloes could be heard in the distance.

When the canoes were nearing the mouth of the St. Francis River in Arkansas, a village on the water's edge was perceived, and crowds of savages, armed with bows and arrows, hatchets and clubs, were seen hurrying to their boats. Some were already in the water, swimming out to intercept their progress. Every one was uttering frantic yells, inciting each other to battle. Indeed, it seemed already begun when a huge club flung from the shore passed over the Frenchmen's heads. Marquette held up the calumet to plead for peace, but it was of no use, and the braves stood with their arrows drawn to the head, when suddenly some old men standing near the river bank made out the sacred pipe, and, keeping back the warriors, came to cast their weapons at the feet of the white men. " We landed," says Marquette, " not without fear, but unfortunately none of the Indians could understand any of the six languages which I spoke. At last we found an old man who could say some words in Illinois, and with his help we made the rest understand the purpose of our journey. They could give us no information about the river, but told us we could find out all we wanted to know at a village called Akansea, which was eight or ten leagues further down. We passed the night among them, with some anxiety."

On the following morning, preceded by a canoe containing ten savages, they proceeded on their way. Arriving within half a league of Akansea, they saw two canoes coming to meet them. Standing in one of the boats was a chief, holding aloft a calumet. He joined the Frenchmen, singing as he came, and gave them tobacco to smoke and bread to eat. He preceded them to the village, and led them to a platform, which was very clean and well covered with fresh mats. The council assembled and Marquette spoke them on religious matters, with such good results that a general desire was manifested to have him remain with them altogether.

Inquiries were, of course, made about the sea, and the

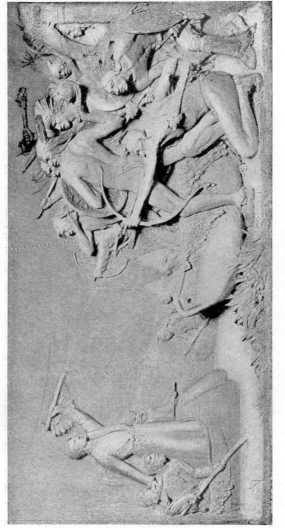

THE CALUMET.

travellers discovered that they could reach it in five days, but, learning that the Indians in the lower country were evidently in contact with Europeans, it was decided that it would be unsafe to proceed further down, as it was likely the explorers would be killed by the hostile Indians, or kept as prisoners by the Spaniards, who were on the Gulf, and thus all the fruit of their expedition would be lost. Hence it was decided to return to the north, as the course of the river had been satisfactorily determined.

They had assured themselves that it emptied neither into the Atlantic nor the Pacific Ocean, but into the Gulf of Mexico. Their return was prudent also for another reason. The very night they arrived at the last village some of the young men had determined to kill and rob them. But an old chief discovered the plot and forbade it, and then came to dance the calumet before the visitors to assure them of complete protection. In spite of that, however, Joliet and Marquette, after a day's rest, turned their canoes up the stream and began their journey homeward. It was then the seventeenth of July. They had spent one month in descending the river.

Naturally, fighting the current on their way back involved considerable labor, but Marquette gives us no account of this part of his travels, except to say that they did not continue on as far as the Wisconsin, but took the Illinois River, which he merely calls "another river," and by that route reached Lake Michigan, thus passing over the site of the present Chicago. At the end of September they reached the mission of St. Francis Xavier at Green Bay, and there, when the ice broke up, Joliet left them and started for Montreal, but unfortunately was wrecked in the Lachine Rapids, and lost all his maps and papers, barely escaping with his life, for he was four hours in the water clinging to his canoe. Of course, his unsupported declaration that he had reached the Mississippi was valueless without documentary proofs, and only a year later, when

Marquette's charts and narration reached Quebec, did the public believe that the great exploration of the river had been made. It was, after all, the papers of Marquette which dispelled the doubts about the success of the expedition, and thus his name, and not Joliet's, is most frequently mentioned in connection with the great discovery, though in reality Joliet was chief of the enterprise.

That summer Marquette was down with dysentery, the result of his hardships and sufferings on the Mississippi. But by September he considered himself cured, and on October 25, 1674, about noon, he started for the Illinois country with two Frenchmen, Pierre and Jacques, their ultimate destination being the village of Kaskaskia. He did not go further than the mouth of the Illinois River that winter, and passed all those terrible months suffering untold hardships from cold and exposure. Meantime the recurrence of his ailment was rapidly exhausting his strength.

He foresaw his approaching death, and in the miserable cabin, which his two faithful companions had constructed for him, he made his annual retreat. In spite of the danger of perishing on the way he started in the spring up the river. It was then March twenty-ninth, and after eleven days he reached the great village. It was composed of five or six hundred fires. A vast assembly was convened to meet him, and his first instruction was delivered on Holy Thursday. He then said Mass. He celebrated again on Easter Sunday, but, as his strength was rapidly failing, he deemed it wise to set out for home. With profound regret they saw him go, and a great many Indians went with him a distance of thirty leagues down the river. A journey of one hundred leagues lay before him, and he was already so feeble that he had to be lifted like a child.

All the time, however, his sweetness and gentleness never deserted him. He was continually communing with God or instructing his companions. Every evening a meditation on death was read to him, and, though his sight was fast failing, he contrived to recite his breviary till the day of his death. He prepared the holy water for his burial, and the night before he died told his friends that he would leave them on the morrow. He instructed them as to the way to conduct the burial services, and selected the spot for his interment.

They were proceeding up the lake when he saw a hill rising close to the river bank. "There," he said, "you must lay me in the grave, and be sure to put a cross above me." As the day was fair they thought they might go a little further on their way, but the wind drove them back to the place he had indicated. So they carried him ashore, built a little shed above him, and laid him down on the ground, making him as comfortable as they could; they were so heartbroken that they scarcely knew what they were doing. He gave them his last instruction, bade them ask pardon for him from all the Fathers, and entrusted to them a slip of paper, on which he had written all the faults he had committed since his last confession, enjoining upon them to hand it to the Superior of the mission. He heard their confessions, promised not to forget them in paradise, and then sent them off to rest, assuring them he would awaken them when he was about to die.

Two or three hours passed, and he entered into his agony. His companions drew near him and he embraced them, their tears pouring down their cheeks as they knelt to kiss his feet. He asked for holy water and his reliquary, took off his cross and told them to hold it before him. He made aloud his profession of faith, thanked God for all His favors, and then, repeating the sacred names several times, he riveted his eyes on the Christ and breathed his last, his countenance all aglow with happiness and peace. They buried him on the summit of the hill, planted a cross to mark the spot, and sadly turned their canoe to the north. The river on whose banks he was buried was named after him, but his blessed remains were not left there. By a peculiar coincidence a party of Kiskakous whom he had instructed some years before in the far away mission of La Pointe, on Lake Superior, were hunting on Lake Michigan. As they were returning in the spring they passed by his grave, and determined to bring back the body to St. Ignace. They disinterred it, and, according to the Indian custom, removed the flesh and exposed the bones to dry in the sun. Then, placing them in a birch bark coffin, they set out for St. Ignace.

Thirty canoes in regular order formed that funeral procession over the great lake. A goodly number of Iroquois had meantime joined them, and with great solemnity they approached the strand on which stood the mission which Father Marquette had founded. Fathers Nouvel and Pierson saw them as they slowly approached, and put the usual questions to make sure that it was really the body of the venerated missionary. There could be no doubt about it, and before it was brought to the shore, and while thirty canoes were still out on the water, the priests entoned the *De Profundis,* and then carried the blessed remains to the little church. It was Whit-Monday, the eighth of June, and all day long the body lay covered by the funeral pall, and on the following day it was lowered into the small vault in the middle of the little church. There, two hundred years later, it was found, and there it rests to-day.

The name of Marquette will ever be venerated in America. You meet it everywhere. There is a city named after him and a county, and a township, and a river and several villages in Michigan, Wisconsin, Kansas, and Nebraska. His Jesuit brethren of the twentieth century have built a Marquette University in Milwaukee, which rejoices in the possession of some of the relics that were given to it when the grave was opened at Pointe St. Ignace. Again, though Marquette never descended the Mississippi as far as New Orleans, the Jesuits of that city thought they could do no better than imitate their brethren of Milwaukee, in giving

DEATH OF MARQUETTE.

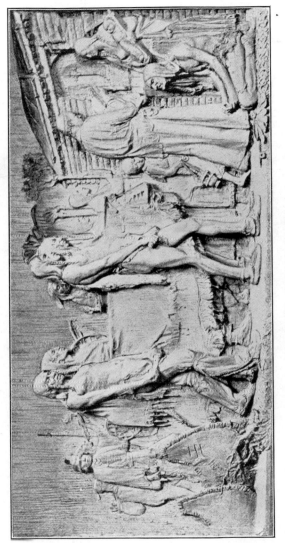

BURIAL OF MARQUETTE.

the same name to their own great educational establishment. But perhaps the most curious illustration of this popular desire to commemorate the glory of the illustrious discoverer is given by one of the great railroads of the country. You are almost startled as you see speeding over the vast prairies of the Far West long trains of cars belonging to the great railway system which proclaims itself, not in English, but French: "Père Marquette." One cannot help thinking how times have changed since Marquette himself trudged across those same prairies with his pack on his back, or launched his bark canoe on the lakes and rivers on whose shores the wolf and the wild cat skulked, or the wandering Indian erected his wretched tepee. In every city of the country, from New York to San Francisco, these engines and cars, with their picturesque and historical name, recall the story of his achievement.

His portrait is in all the school books. It is conventional, of course, for there is no duly authenticated likeness of him extant. The sturdy and somewhat bulky man whose picture Thwaites suggests as a possible portrait cannot be Marquette, for he left his home when a mere boy, and ended his life when he was a little beyond thirty. The anxiety to secure a genuine portrait of him is an indication of the world's anxiety to know him better.

A statue has been erected in his honor on Mackinac Island, though as far as we know he never pitched his tent there. Still it is very likely that he often visited the Indians of that place, for it was very near to St. Ignace. Finally, when the State of Wisconsin wanted to exercise its privilege of erecting in the Capitol at Washington a memorial of one of its illustrious sons, it chose Marquette. There was some delay in the acceptance of the statue, but to-day the marble figure of Father Marquette, in his cassock and cloak, with his beads and his crucifix in his belt, stands beneath the great dome, by far the most artistic in its conception and execution of all the group of the notables of the nation.

FRANCIS DE CRESPIEUL

In 1658 a brilliant young man of twenty entered the Society of Jesus at Tournay. His name was Francis de Crespieul. He was born at Arras, on March sixteen or seventeen, in the year 1638. During his studies, he attracted unusual attention by the brilliancy of his intellectual endowments, and the strength and energy of his character. He had much to expect in Europe, but he was on fire with enthusiasm for the Canadian missions. He came to Quebec in 1670, before finishing his theological course, and when he had passed his final examination was assigned to the Tadoussac mission, arriving there on October 28, 1671.

The Indians received him with unusual manifestations of friendship, and that feeling in his regard never waned. Doubtless, he communicated some of his own effusiveness to them, for he was characteristically optimistic. Thus he tells us, with some commendable exaggeration, that "the feast of All Saints, which occurred a few days after my arrival, was celebrated by the savages with all the practices of devotion that are observed in the holiest Christian communities."

He started up the Saguenay on November sixth, but after a day's journey was stopped on his way by bad weather, and compelled to seek shelter in a bay of considerable size, while the storm raged with unabated fury for four days on the river beyond. It was his first chance of becoming acquainted with the hardships of Indian life. He was in the woods in mid-winter. The cold, the blinding smoke from the half decayed wood which made his eyes run water all day long, the damp air, the biting wind, and the want of food, all this de Crespieul describes as "his little martyrdom, his happiness and bliss."

FRANCIS DE CRESPIEUL

His enjoyment of it was helped by the fact that these trifles failed to extinguish the devotion of the savages. They insisted on hearing Mass, every one of those four terrible days, although the fire had to be put out meantime, for the smoke would have stifled the priest, who had, of course, to stand erect in the midst of it. Indeed, when there was a fire in the hut, the only way to breathe at all was to crouch as near as possible to the ground. One old missionary used to say that the only way to avoid drinking smoke, was to eat dirt.

After saying Mass on the eleventh of November, and planting a cross to commemorate their sojourn there, they sailed north with a favorable wind, though the pelting rain was drenching them, and the piercing wind was penetrating the very marrow of their bones. Towards evening they reached another bay, which was shut in by thirty high mountains. At the foot of the tallest peak the travelers built their bark hut, and remained there through another five days of cold, "calculated," he says, "to put one's patience to the test." It was not only a "test of patience," one might fancy, but of endurance. However, "a picture of my beloved St. Francis Xavier," says de Crespieul, "and a reliquary, in which there was a piece of the true cross, greatly ameliorated my little sufferings." In the hut he offered the tears which the smoke wrung from his eyes, "to extinguish the flames of some souls in Purgatory."

On the twenty-first he was tramping through the forests, for the ice had formed on the river. While climbing the icy mountains, the Indians killed a moose. "They showed me her fawn," he says, "which was no bigger than my thumb"—evidently the embryo. "After studying carefully the entire anatomy of this little animal, I was struck with admiration at the wisdom of the Creator who can enclose in so small a compass so many different parts, all so well adapted to their functions. Had the creature been larger, it would have relieved the hunger that beset us, and

185

which until the first day of December caused us no less
suffering than the cold and smoke." But the extreme fondness displayed by his Indians for religious exercises and
instructions made him forget his pains. As soon as they
were up in the morning, every one, even the little children,
flocked around him for the lessons which lasted all day long.
"It was only during the silence of the night, when our savages cease their singing and talking, that I had leisure to
commune with Our Lord in those solitudes."

The hermits of Thebais had a comfortable time of it
when compared with this nocturnal solitary in the Saguenay woods. Incidently, one is tempted to ask how the
Indians could contrive to sing in such surroundings. Like
de Crespieul, they, too, must have been optimists.

Here a Christian family of Esquimaux appears on the
scene. They were fugitives for the Faith, for their amiable
compatriots used to strangle any one who accepted baptism.
One would like to know how many martyrs of that kind
there were in Labrador in those days, and who had baptised
these refugees, but no record is to be found. Onward they
tramped, the Esquimaux with them, over the ice and snow.
At this stage of the journey, de Crespieul thanked God
that, besides his own pack, he had to shoulder the burden
which a poor sick girl had been trying to carry. However,
the additional load was a help, he said, for it prevented him
from plunging into a crevasse where he might have lost his
life, or at least fractured his limbs. He notes also how they
celebrated the feast of the Immaculate Conception with confessions, Communions, and spiritual songs, and, of course,
with the celebration of holy Mass.

They kept on till Christmas Eve, following the moose
tracks in the snow, and hoping to bring down some game;
but they found no moose, and were all spent with hunger.
"At length, however," he says, "the good God, who takes
pity on His servants in their necessities, helped us, after
many a day of bitter suffering, to shoot two elks and four

beavers. It happened seasonably, for the Indians would not have hunted on Christmas Day, out of reverence for the festival "—a bit of strictness which ought to make even a Sabbatarian wonder. But what is more incomprehensible, is that although they were starving, they would not touch the meat on the eve because it was a fast day. Evidently the Indians were exceedingly pious, or de Crespieul was a rigidist. Nor were their devotions confined to the festival itself. They sat up all night, and had midnight Mass, at which a young man and woman made their First Communion.

There was gloom in the hut, however, when a little boy, who on account of his fondness for catechetical instruction was a special pet of the priest, died in spite of all the care they lavished on him in his sudden illness. But "the little angel's death fell in the week of the Holy Innocents, so that he might go," says the priest, "and swell their numbers in Heaven." Indeed, firmly believing the child was in Paradise, the Indians invoked him without ceasing. He was buried with all the ceremonies of the Church, "to the great consolation of the savages, and before leaving the place the child's father went and knelt on the grave, commending himself to his boy, and entreating him thenceforth to exchange with him the place of a parent."

Hunger drove them onward over the mountains, which were piled high with snow drifts, and over lakes, where they were sometimes up to their waists in icy waters. A cold wind beat against their faces, and they were in constant danger of having cheeks and feet and hands frozen. "It was hard," he said, "to set out on such a tramp without a morsel of food for breakfast, and to have nothing during the day, and then to wait at night for three or four hours, while the cabins were being built, before a fire could be lighted." In this fashion they passed the whole month of January, on one Friday of which they were particularly pressed with hunger. "We besought Our Lord by His sacred wounds to have pity on us. Our prayers were not displeasing to Him, for on that day He gave us five beavers in a very short time after our asking the favor. They restored our strength, and prepared us for greater hardships. So we continued our journey. As it was Friday, one is prompted to inquire if this stern spiritual Father permitted his neophytes to eat these quasi-amphibians on that day.

January came to a close, and then the weary days of February began, when the cold was greatest. March was well on its way, but they had not yet reached their destination; and though the weather was milder, the smoke in the huts was more pungent. But the moose were now plentiful, and the holy man says " God seemed to lead them with His own hand to our cabin, to reward our savages for their fidelity in daily attending the Holy Sacrifice of the Mass which I offered there."

Seismologists will be interested to learn that during the last two months of this dreary tramp two moderate earthquake shocks were felt. They were thought to be a continuation of the great earthquake which had occurred throughout Canada in 1662, which the missionary assures us took place at intervals up to the time he was writing about them. That was 1672, so that they had a ten years' succession of quakes. The journey came to an end at Lake of the Cross, so called from its shape; but to proclaim its name to the Indians who might pass that way, Father de Crespieul and his people planted a great many crosses along the shore. It was Holy Week, and the locality suggested that more than usual devotion should be displayed in the ceremony of the adoration of the Cross.

" It will, perhaps, excite astonishment," he says, " that for the proper celebration of the most august mysteries of our religion, we were able to find room in our poor cabin for everything that conformity to the Church during Holy Week requires. We accomplished it, however, so as to bring our winter to a happy end and to consecrate those

. rocks and mountains by all that we possess that is holy
and venerable. Thursday, Friday and Saturday of Holy
Week, converted our forests into a church, and our cabin
into a repository, where very few of the ceremonies observed by Christians all over the world were omitted by
our savages. Above all, they showed profound respect for
and maintained a religious silence in the cabin where the
Blessed Sacrament was placed during the night of Thursday and Friday, so that in the depths of that desert this
august mystery was honored without ceasing, by continual
prayers that suffered no interruption in the darkness of the
night."

Easter Sunday crowned it all by a general Communion
and more than usual devotion. " The Indians," he said,
" wanted to make me forget all the hardship I had suffered
with them during the winter."

They finally reached the Saguenay, and on May 17,
1672, arrived at Tadoussac, which they had left six months
before. But it was not to give rest to the weary bones of
the apostolic man. " It was the season," he writes, " for
the mission to the Papinachois, for which Our Lord had
left me sufficient strength. Its situation is thirty leagues
below Tadoussac, and I reached it safely just when the
savages were returning from their winter hunts."

There he baptized thirteen children, and administered
whatever sacraments the adults were prepared for. Among
them were two old squaws, who had been baptized by
Father Le Jeune many years before and had led a life of
perfect innocence during all the intervening time. De
Crespieul ends his letter to his Superior by asking for what
he calls " the same happiness next winter, when I hope that
God will give me courage to make amends, by fresh sufferings, for the errors I may have committed this season."

He went to Quebec for his final vows, on Assumption
Day, 1673, for, says Dablon, " he preferred to postpone it
until then, rather than lose the opportunity of wintering
among his beloved savages. He invariably falls ill when I

recall him for a little rest, and no sooner has he returned
to the labors of his mission than he is restored to health."
His Superiors afforded him the opportunity he asked for,
and at the end of September, 1673, he set out again for the
Papinachois country, intending to go from there to Chicoutimi, and afterwards to Lake St. John, where he was to
pass the winter.

In October he was down at the Jeremie Islands, two
hundred miles below Quebec, a little west of the mouth of
the Betsamites River. He remained there for six or seven
days, instructing and baptizing, and on the twenty-first
made for the Saguenay. The journey was a rapid one, for a
storm which lasted for ten hours, and threatened every min-
ute to send them to the bottom, swept them like the wind
along the coast. Calm weather came again, and they traveled up the river to Chicoutimi, where there was a gathering
of Indians waiting for the priest. On All Saints Day,
nearly all the savages and Frenchmen confessed and went
to Communion, and on November twentieth, after performing their duties to the souls in Purgatory, the French got
into their bark and set sail for Quebec. That evening de
Crespieul started off with six canoes of savages, and spent
the night " near the rapid of the large river that flows from
the Lake St. John into the Saguenay."

The experiences of the preceding year were repeated,
and it is therefore unnecessary to rehearse them here. They
are all set down in the diary sent to his Superiors. It will
be sufficient to say that he found in this region also, more
vestiges of the great earthquake of 1663. Forest fires had
likewise devastated the country, in some places to the extent
of two hundred leagues. Intelligence was brought to him
on January fourteenth that Father Albanel, who was making for the North Sea, had met with a serious accident and
was not far away.

" I set out, therefore, on January sixteenth, after Mass,"
he says, " along with two Frenchmen and an Algonquin

chief. We made five leagues on snow shoes, but the snow was soft and clogged our feet. At the end of the five leagues we were on a frozen lake, four or five leagues long, over which a blinding snow was driving, so that we could scarcely see each other or make out their bearings. After a league and a half our strength began to give out, and we went back to get some fir branches to build a shelter. We tried to light a fire but failed. The cold penetrated to our bones, the darkness was intense and the wind howled fearfully. To keep ourselves from dying of cold we resumed our march on the lake, not knowing whither we were going. After a league and a half we had to stop. I thought of Father de Noüe, who, in similar surroundings, was found dead in the snow, kneeling, and with his hands clasped in prayer. This thought aroused me. I made the sacrifice of my life to God and united my death, which I thought to be near, to that of the pious missionary. The Frenchmen cut some fir branches, which they laid on the snow, and we threw ourselves down on them, after saying our prayers, and taking for our supper a little theriac and seven or eight raisins which we happened to have with us. Fatigue caused us to fall into a slumber, but the wind and snow and cold did not allow us to enjoy it very long. We remained awake during the rest of the night. Fortunately, on the following morning two Frenchmen, from Father Albanel's cabin, arrived very opportunely, and kindled a good fire on the snow. One of them went for some water to quench our burning thirst. Then we resumed our journey, and in spite of the wind and snow, which drove into our faces, we reached the place where the Father was. A serious injury of the loins, caused by a heavy load falling on him, prevented him from moving, and, of course, from performing any of his missionary duties."

De Crespieul remained with his suffering friend for two days, meantime instructing the people he found there; and then tramped back to his own place, a distance of ten leagues over the snow, to administer the sacraments to a dying squaw. He was back again with Albanel on February second, and remained till the sixth. A report came just then that the Iroquois were in the neighborhood. The result was that the whole party started off to a place twenty leagues away, where they found that the people had thrown up defenses in view of a fight. Soon, however, the scouts came in, and reported that it was a false alarm. The enemy were far away at Lake Piecouagami.

Off went the indefatigable man, with his party, to the Mistassinis; and having toiled and suffered there for a considerable time, he joined a delegation of Indians who were going to pay their respects to Frontenac at Quebec. This journey, however, was not a matter merely of courtesy. The region in which he was laboring had been appropriated by the Government and was called the King's Domain. No white man could enter it without a passport, and the punctilious Governor was in a high dudgeon because de Crespieul had presumed to go into that wilderness without permission. It was an absurd assertion of authority, of course, and Frontenac might have been better occupied. But de Crespieul went down to mollify the great man, and humbly petition to go back to his martyrdom.

In 1686 he writes from the cabin of Louis Kistabistichit, at Pastagoutchichwusipiou, and gives some valuable information about the character of the people in those parts, and he also imparts useful advice for future missionaries. He begins by citing several examples of God's judgments on the Indians who were unfaithful to their marriage relations, or who took to drink. The wife of Tall Charles, for instance, was guilty of the latter offense, and ended her career by hanging herself; but, on the other hand, he is glad to note how completely some of his Indians have changed their ways.

He tells us that there is generally a great deal of kindness and consideration shown in the wigwams, although several families may be huddled together in their narrow limits. On the trail they do not lose their temper or swear, like the French, if an accident happens. They merely laugh. They have a horror of theft, but are very jealous, and easily calumniate each other. They are modest in their dress, and

FRONTENAC.

even when sleeping are decently covered. They are not only safe in the presence of fire-water, but often give proof that they can be trusted even with kegs and flasks, more so than many a Frenchman. He is indignant with some people in Quebec who fancy it is useless to attempt to convert these Indians; but, however, he warns all the missionaries never to grow angry with an Indian, and not to be discouraged by failures at the outset. Visits to the cabins are always acceptable, but it would be very unwise for the priest, except for a grave reason, to enter a wigwam at night where there are women. The danger is very great at all times, and the fear and love of God are indispensable as safeguards, for often the missionary is the only man in the camp.

Life there is one long series of penances and humiliations; prayer, reading, writing, and work are the only preservatives; and the priest must always bear in mind that he is there for the Indians, and not they for him. He should not concern himself with the affairs of the Commandants, or clerks of the post; and never administer any public rebuke, or be importunate in his requests. Affability, civility, recognition of services, and praise for the smallest exhibitions of virtue, or even skill in hunting, canoeing, and the like, go far to gain the esteem of all. Nor should a missionary ever condescend to spend his time in fishing or trapping. It scandalizes both the French and the Indians. Anything like favoritism or familiarity with any one, either white or red, should be avoided. Long prayers in public are not to be recommended, and marriages of white men and squaws should not be performed without the approval of the bishop. No doubt he was thinking of Albanel's experience.

We have another brief sketch from his hand about missionary methods among the Montagnais. He signs himself, "an unprofitable servant of the Missions of Canada, from 1671 to 1697," the latter date completing his twenty-sixth wintering in the service of the Tadoussac mission and the fourth at the mission of St. Xavier. It was written at Chicoutomi, April 21, 1697.

"The life of a Montagnais missionary," he says, "is a long and slow martyrdom. Besides the sufferings in the cabins, and on the trail," he reminds those who are to come after him that " they are not to expect anything dainty at their meals. They must eat from a dish that is seldom washed, or, at best, is wiped with a greasy piece of skin or licked by the dogs. One eats only when something is offered, and the meat is commonly only half cooked and tough. As a rule, there is only one meal a day. The missionary never takes off his cassock or stockings, except to get rid of the vermin which swarm over every one, especially the children. On awakening, one finds himself usually among a pack of dogs. The snow is so dazzling that the missionary has often to be led by the hand. The cries of the children are annoying, and the stench is insupportable, especially when they are scrofulous. One has to sleep near them and eat out of the same dish."

Such are a few of the ordinary features of the life which this wonderful man led in the wilderness for twenty-eight years. He says nothing about the constant danger of death from exhaustion, disease, or hunger; or the perils of the forests, the lakes, the mountain torrents and the rest. He had had more than his share of them. At last, when shattered in health, he was summoned to Quebec, and it is not a little surprising that at his advanced age he was engaged in college work, even occupying the position of Prefect of Schools.

He died somewhere after October 28, 1702, at the age of sixty-four, leaving behind him the reputation of being one of the greatest apostles of the Indians.

ANTHONY SYLVIE

When Radisson handed over the Hudson Bay territory to the English, the French Canadians, aroused to fury, took up arms, although France and England were then at peace. The war was begun by La Martinière, who met some English sloops on the bay and put them to flight. But, like all the French victories, this exploit had no lasting result. The English forts at Moose, Rupert's River, and Albany were only slightly flurried when the news of La Martinière's exploit reached them. That was in 1685. In 1686 an overland raid was organized, than which fiction could not conceive anything more romantic. It is one of Canada's brilliant episodes of knight errantry in the forests.

. Towards the end of winter a band of thirty-three Frenchmen, arrayed in all the gay frippery of those days, accompanied by sixty-six plumed and painted Indians, might have been seen setting out from Montreal on snowshoes. They had no provisions with them; the guns on their shoulders and their pistols in their belts would bring down what game they met; or if they met none, they would go hungry. The blankets on their shoulders were all they had to protect themselves from the cold. At their head was the old Chevalier de Troyes; but more important than the commander was Pièrre d'Iberville, then only twenty-four, who was beginning his heroic career. With Pièrre were his brothers, Maricourt and Ste. Helène. The chaplain of the party was the Jesuit Father Sylvie.

Their route lay along the frozen Ottawa, past the long Sault, where Dollard had made his great fight twenty years before against seven hundred Iroquois; then up to the Rideau and the Chaudière Falls, around which they had to tramp, as they did when they reached the Calumet and

Chats, and the cataracts at Allumettes Island, where the Algonquins were gathered. On they went to Mattawa, and then turned north to Lake Temiscamingue, which they traversed, continuing their march till they came to Abbittibbi, at the height of land. There they waited for the ice to break, and to take time to build canoes for the descent to the Bay. They had traveled six hundred miles over the snow and ice, and no one had died or grown faint-hearted. They seemed to revel in their dangers and sufferings.

Before them was another three hundred miles, full of wilder adventure. It was a rush down cataracts maddened by the loosened floods which were tossing huge masses of ice through the foam and threatening every instant to crush the frail canoes like egg shells, or to crowd them against the rocks or giant trees which blocked the stream. Pièrre d'Iberville's canoe was swamped, and two of his men went down in the swirl, while two others were saved by d'Iberville himself, who, at the risk of his own life, dragged them ashore. Around the ice jams they had to portage their boats, or cut their way through with their hatchets, the men at times sinking to their armpits in the snowslush. At one stage of the journey they had to walk barefoot, dragging their canoes for eleven miles where the icy water was too shallow to float the boats.

They had left Montreal in March, and it was June when d'Iberville, who went ahead as a scout, sighted Fort Moose in the distance. "Hastily," says the author of " The Conquest of the Great Northwest," " all burdens of blankets and food and clothes were cast aside and *cached*. Hastily each raider fell on his knees, invoking the blessing of St. Anne, the patron saint of the Canadian voyager. Hastily the Jesuit Sylvie passed from man to man absolving all sin, for these men fought with all the Spartan ferocity of the Indian fighter, and thought that it was better to die fighting than to suffer torture in defeat."

It is not likely that Father Sylvie heard confessions in

LE MOYNE d'IBERVILLE.

that expeditious fashion, but that does not matter. He was in the fray, and prepared the men for possible death.

It was June 18, 1686, one of the longest days in the year, when there is no night, but when twilight merges into dawn. Not a sound disturbed the stillness when two figures emerged from the bush near the fort. They were d'Iberville and his brother. They measured with their eyes the eighteen-foot palisades, and saw the holes through which the inmates could thrust their muskets. The enclosure was a square, with stone bastions at each corner. In one of them were three hundred pounds of powder; in another the soldiers slept; in a third were the furs, and the fourth was the kitchen. Across the middle of the court were the two-story warehouse and the residence of the chief factor. These arrangements could only be guessed at by the two prowlers, who crept cautiously around in their moccasined feet, avoiding even to tread upon a twig. They found the main gate barred, but they saw to their delight that the fourteen cannon which protruded from the embrasures were all plugged. They pricked their ears to listen, but heard not a sound. Every one was buried in sleep, and then satisfied with what they had found, they quietly disappeared.

The next night the French surrounded the fort. De Troyes attacked, making a feint on the water-front, but meantime d'Iberville with his Indians scaled the pickets, and with a trunk of a tree were soon battering down the main gate. It yielded, and the sleepy guardian was sabred. Then a rush was made for the house; the door was partially shattered by their blows and d'Iberville leaped inside. It closed behind him, and he was alone in a darkened chamber; but he kept hacking right and left with his sword, making each blow tell. A soldier with a lantern appeared on the stairs above, and he was toppled over by a bullet from d'Iberville's pistol. Fortunately, the great door soon yielded under the blows of the battering ram, and the raiders were masters of the fort.

Then off these wonderful fighters started to the second fort, far up on Rupert's River, one hundred and thirty miles away. Sylvie was with them. They had remained at Moose only long enough to build a raft to carry Troyes and his prisoners along the coast. The rest embarked in their canoes. It was now the twenty-seventh of June. By July first, d'Iberville was in sight of Fort Albany. In the offing was a ship. Waiting for the night, the daring fighter took with him a half a dozen of his men and paddled out to the vessel. He reached the stern, and cat-like crawled up to the deck. Awakened by the noise, the man on the lookout awoke and sprang for d'Iberville's throat, but a stroke from the raider's sword laid him dead on the deck.

The men came trembling up from below, and three of them were sabred as their heads protruded from the hold. A fourth appeared. It was Bridgar, the Governor of the whole territory, and he surrendered helplessly. Then the signal was given to attack the fort. D'Iberville hastened from the ship and led the assault. In a trice he and his followers were on the roof of the principal house, hacking through it with their hatchets, and flinging hand grenades into the interior. As one of the explosives left his hand, says Laut, from whom we are borrowing this description, a terrified Englishwoman dashed up the stairs into the room directly under the roof. They shouted to her to retire. But it was too late. She was hit by the bomb, and the next moment d'Iberville and Father Sylvie sprang down the stairs dashing from hall to hall, candle in hand, looking for her. A plaintive cry came from one of the rooms. Followed by his powder-grimed raiders, d'Iberville threw open the door. With a scream there fell at his feet a woman whose hip was shattered. Lifting her to a couch, the priest and d'Iberville called in the surgeon, and, barring the door from the outside, forbade intrusion. It was the chief calamity in the assault. Fort Rupert was theirs.

There was still another post to take. It was Fort Albany, three hundred miles to the northwest. D'Iberville started out in his canoes; De Troyes followed in the ship with the traders and prisoners. They reached the open bay when night was coming on, and a fierce gale was sweeping down from the north tossing the ice floes about in the wildest confusion. It would be dangerous enough even for the stout ship that had crossed the ocean, but it would be madness to attempt to make such a passage in canoes, and so most of the Indians made for the land. The daring d'Iberville, however, with the men in two of his boats, refused to turn back or to stop. Though the huge white ice blocks were bearing down upon him, his two frail barks were paddled desperately forward. When the threatening ice could not be avoided, these desperate men leaped out upon the floes and carried their canoes across to the open water, or for hours held them above their heads to prevent them from being crushed to pieces. When morning dawned they kept on in spite of the fog, d'Iberville discharging his musket from time to time to mark the course for the men behind. For four days this fierce fight with the elements was kept up, and at last, on the first of August, the canoe-men landed below Fort Albany. Only some days later de Troyes arrived with the ship. With which section of the expedition Father Sylvie came at Fort Albany we do not know, but it is quite possible that the man who was with d'Iberville on the roof of the house at Rupert was with him in the canoes fighting the ice floes.

As soon as the ship arrived with the cannon, the French set about putting them in place for the bombardment. The fort had as yet given no sign of life, when suddenly its forty guns thundered simultaneously. The embankment, which the assailants had singularly enough been allowed to construct, appears to have prevented any one from being injured by this first cannonade, which was also the last that day. De Troyes mustered his troops, and with flag flying, went up to the fort and demanded its surrender. The Commandant refused, though his garrison was in a panic. For two days the firing was kept up, until just as the ammunition of the French was giving out the flag of truce was seen fluttering from the walls, and the raiders entered. They found 50,000 crowns' worth of peltries, but no food. The consequence was that the prisoners were all set adrift, and many perished from hunger or exposure. The raiders themselves hurried back to the St. Lawrence to avoid starvation, and a small garrison under Maricourt was left in the fort to defend it. Father Sylvie, as far as we can make out, remained, for he was only incidentally a military chaplain. His chief work was that of a missionary to the Indians.

In the following year d'Iberville was back again at the Bay. He came upon one of the vessels of the company and seized it. But that did not satisfy him. There was another ship at Charlton Island, and he sent out four spies to reconnoitre. Three of them were seized by the English and clapped in irons in the hold. In the springtime one was called on deck to help the sailors. He willingly consented to leave the fetid prison, but when he saw six of the men up in the rigging, he seized an axe, crept up behind two men who were working near him, brained them both, and then hurrying below freed his two comrades. They immediately seized the weapons that were at hand, and, keeping the men up in the rigging at pistol point, steered the vessel across the Bay to Rupert River, where d'Iberville was waiting. The capture of this vessel, which was well provisioned, kept him from starvation.

Rescue parties had come down from Nelson to attack the French at Fort Albany, but their two ships, the Hampshire and the Northwest Fox, were caught in the ice, and they sent their crews ashore, not suspecting that d'Iberville was waiting in ambush in the swamps nearby. No sooner had the eighty men been safely landed than, to the horror and consternation of the English, they saw d'Iberville boarding one of the vessels, and as the ice cleared he sailed away from Albany for Quebec.

But he was not yet out of danger. At the Straits he met two English vessels. Both he and they were caught in the ice and were within gunshot of each other. D'Iberville ran up the English flag and invited the captains of the two ships to come across the ice to visit him. They were actually on their way when the ice parted and away flew d'Iberville through a stretch of clear water which just at that moment left him a clear passage.

Father Sylvie, it would appear, remained at the Bay until 1693. He was not alone, however, for Dalmas was with him during the last fifteen months of that period. At last his health gave way and he returned to Quebec. What did he do there? Something that was as much a revelation of character as when he was at the side of d'Iberville in the wild raids of the Bay.

It must have been a very edifying sight indeed to see that battered old missionary undertake a class of mathematics in the college when he came back home. Then, for the last ten years of his life, he filled the position of Minister, and finally went to his reward in 1711, probably on October twelfth. He had reached the age of seventy-four. He had come to America in 1673, and had first labored for four years in the Far West with the Ottawas, where he was Allouez's companion part of that time. Subsequently recalled east in 1679, he was assigned to the work among the nomads of the Bay. It was only after seven years' toil in that difficult mission that he started as the chaplain of d'Iberville in his heroic efforts to win back Hudson Bay from the English. Very little is said of Sylvie in the " Relations," but nothing more was needed to show what a man he was.

ANTHONY DALMAS

After Sylvie withdrew to Quebec, Father Anthony Dalmas, who had been with him for a year and a half, was left alone in the frozen wilderness of Hudson Bay. There seems to be no doubt about this fact, though Father Marest, in a letter to de Lamberville written much later, makes quite a contrary statement. He tells us that Dalmas was the first priest to accompany d'Iberville in his attacks on the English. Evidently he had forgotten all about, or had never heard of, Sylvie's experiences. Indeed, Dalmas does not seem to have gone out with Iberville on any expedition, but was at Fort Albany looking after the French and Indians all the time that d'Iberville was fighting down at Schenectady, Maine, and Newfoundland.

Fort Albany, which had been captured by d'Iberville in 1686, was still floating the French flag in 1693, but the condition of its miserable little garrison was deplorable. They were starving to death. One by one they had dropped off, and Father Dalmas had read the Church's prayers over them as they were laid to rest in the snow. At last only eight remained.

The spring of 1693 had come, and the eyes of the unhappy sufferers were turned incessantly towards the great bay north of them to catch a glimpse of a sail coming to their relief. But none ever came. One day five of the little band started out over the snow to see if they could replenish their empty larder by capturing some chance game. There was some hope, for now the winter was breaking up. Father Dalmas, the surgeon, and the tool-maker remained in the fort. After five days the hunters returned. They found the tool-maker alone, and there were traces of blood in the snow. Murder had evidently been committed, and they seized the solitary wretch and put him in irons.

After a few days the prisoner confessed that he had killed the surgeon, and had thrown the body in a hole in the ice. What about the priest? Where was he? That was the saddest chapter of the tragedy. After killing the surgeon, the murderer returned to the fort and found Father Dalmas about to say Mass; but the priest, quite unaware of what had happened, spoke to him only afterwards. The unhappy man confessed his crime, and expressed the fear that when the others returned he would be put to death. "Not at all," he was told. "We are too few to think of that, and if the men attempt to do so, I give you my word, I shall prevent them. Fear, rather, the wrath of God, and implore His mercy for your horrible crime."

In order to forestall the anger of the others, the Father set out to meet them, with the consent of the assassin. But hardly had he left the fort when he perceived the wretch following him, armed with a hatchet and gun. He heard the cry, "Stop! You are going to betray me," and immediately a musket shot rung out and the ball entered the body of the priest.

The wound did not prevent him, however, from leaping on a cake of ice that was floating near the bank of the river. But his pursuer sprung after him, and buried his hatchet twice in the head of his victim, and then flung the body under the ice. Such was the story he himself told to his horrified associates. Their first impulse was indeed to wreak vengeance on him then and there, but they restrained their wrath, hoping that a ship would soon arrive from Quebec. Day after day passed and no help came. At last in the offing, to their consternation, a vessel appeared with an English flag flying at its peak. It was all over with them now, but they were not going to surrender without a struggle.

They had kept their cannon loaded for just such an emergency, and as the ship approached the shore it was met with such a murderous fire that it veered about and sailed away. The furious fashion in which they had been received created the impression that the fort was fully garrisoned. Shortly afterwards three vessels were seen bearing down on the fort, prepared for what they thought would be a desperate battle. Of course, the worn and emaciated Frenchmen were in no condition to resist such a force, and so, in the darkness of the night they quietly slipped away and disappeared in the woods, and then made for Montreal. Three of them perished on the way. Such is the French account. It is told, however, in a slightly different fashion by Laut in "The Conquest of the Great Northwest."

"Grimmington," the author says, "came out to Nelson in 1693, determined to capture back Albany for the English. Three ships sailed down from Nelson to Albany. The fort looked deserted. Led by Grimmington, the sailors hacked open the gates. Only four Frenchmen were holding the fort. The rest of the garrison were off hunting in the woods, and in the woods they were forced to remain that winter, for Grimmington ransacked the fort, took possession, and clapped the French, under Mons. Captain Le Meux, prisoners in the hold of his vessel. As the English captains searched the cellars, they came on a ghastly sight. Naked, covered with vermin, shackled hands to the feet, was a French criminal, who had murdered first the surgeon, then the priest of the fort. He, too, was turned adrift in the woods with the rest of the garrison." Such is the gruesome ending of Father Anthony Dalmas's missionary career. He was then fifty-six years of age, having been born in Tours, August 4, 1636. He had come to Canada in 1670, and was occupied almost all the time in the terrible Tadoussac missions. He was a martyr of the confessional. About his labors at Tadoussac there is nothing but the grim routine of hardship and dangers which always constituted the labors of that section of the Algonquin apostolate.

NORTH OF THE SAGUENAY.

GABRIEL MARET

Eight years of fierce warfare between the French and English had passed to get possession of Hucson Bay. Forts were taken and retaken by both sides, and finally the authorities at Quebec decided that there were no means of holding their posts in the south unless they dislodged the English from their stronghold on the Nelson River, far away to the north.

To effect that purpose, d'Iberville set sail from Quebec on August 10, 1694, with two frigates, The Poli and Salamandre. There was three hundred men on board. The chaplain was Gabriel Maret, who had just arrived from France. "They took me," he writes, "because I could not speak any of the Indian languages. As chaplain of the two ships, I could get along with French.

"We set sail," he says, "on the tenth of August, and cast anchor near midnight near the bar of Cape Tourmente. At seven or eight next morning we were sailing down the St. Lawrence, or attempting to do so, but the wind was against us, and for the next three days we made very little progress." Maret, however, profited by this enforced leisure to preach to the crew and to induce them to celebrate properly the feast of the Assumption, which was coming on. He spent the evening of the fourteenth and the morning of the fifteenth in hearing the confessions of the crew. Many of the sailors went to Communion, and lo! "just at the end of Mass the wind changed and the vessels were speeding down the river." On the twentieth they were becalmed again, and this time Maret went to the other ship, the Salamandre, to say Mass and to shrive the sailors.

On the twenty-first they were passing Belle Isle, which he says is two hundred and twenty leagues from Quebec, so that, all in all, they had made tolerably fair progress in those eleven days. The icebergs began to appear, and they seemed to him like mountains of crystal; some of them like glittering cliffs bristling with peaks. Calm and storm succeeded each other, and it was now the twenty-fifth of August. "The season was advanced, and we were going into a country where winter comes before autumn. We were only at the 56th degree latitude, and there was still a long distance to make, on a sea which was full of icebergs, through which we should have to force our way as far as the 63d degree."

On the twenty-eighth they had a good east wind, but on the thirty-first they were enveloped in a dense fog. At noon, however, the sky cleared, and "the 'Sugar Loaves,' all covered with snow, were before our eyes." About evening they were entering the Strait of Hudson Bay, which was choked with ice. They saw Button's Islands, which were in the 6oth degree and some minutes. Nearby deep bays were perceived, one of which was said to go as far as the lower end of Hudson Bay, "but," he adds, "this is very uncertain."

It took them four days, from September first to September fifth, to pass the straits, and on the seventh the weather became calm, "which," says the watchful missionary, "gave an opportunity to more than fifty persons to offer their devotions on the following day, the Feast of the Nativity of the Blessed Virgin." But the calm continued all along through the eighth, ninth and tenth, much to the worry and anxiety of the crew. Then Maret, who was always working miracles, proposed to the sailors to invoke the protection of St. Anne and to offer public prayers in her honor. Every one was delighted, and the very next night he says "a fair wind was drawing them along, and on the twelfth they described the North Land, but below the point where we wished to go."

Now a head wind sprang up, and the vessels kept tacking for several days; but as no progress was made they cast anchor. Meantime the cold was increasing, and the water was giving out. Again St. Anne was invoked, and the sailors approached the sacraments, d'Iberville and the officers setting the example. "The very next day," says the chronicle, "God gave us a favorable wind."

They entered the River Bourbon on Friday, September twenty-fourth, about six in the evening, singing the *Vexilla Regis* and the *O Crux Ave*, which they repeated several times, "to do honor to the adorable cross of the Saviour, in the country where it is unknown to the barbarians, and where it has been many times profaned by heretics who have overthrown with contempt all the crosses that our French had in former times set up." But did not the holy man mistake these overturning of the crosses as examples of religious hatred? The crosses were indeed thrown down, but, generally speaking, it was because they were marks of the French occupation. If there was any religious animosity, it entered at best only incidentally. For usually when a French cross was thrown down, an English one was set up in its stead. He was new in the country. "The Bourbon River," says Maret, "was called by the English in those days the Pornetton. Southcast of it, and emptying into the same bay, is the St. Theresa, the two streams being separated from each other by a neck of land only a league or two in width. On the St. Theresa the English had built their fort, and up that river d'Iberville sailed with the Salamandre, leaving the Poli to winter in the adjoining stream. The St. Theresa was called by the English the Nelson. The other was the Churchill.

On the night of their arrival, September twenty-four, a number of men were put ashore to attempt to take the fort by surprise. It failed, for the enemy were on the alert, and for four or five days afterwards d'Iberville continued looking for a place to pitch his camp. He finally went ashore about a league and a half above the fort.

It was now October 30. The moon was very nearly full, and, favored by the tide, the shallop, equipped with sixteen oars, towed the ship up the stream. As they passed the fort three or four volleys were fired at them from the shore, but the balls fell short, and the French replied with mocking cries of *Sassa Koues*, the savage shout of rejoicing. They continued up the river without further molestation. However, though they had passed the English, the elements were against them. On the night of the second of November, as they were striving to enter a harbor, a heavy snowstorm hid the shore from view, while a fierce northwest wind drove the ship on the shallows, and at ten o'clock the ice began to grind against the hull, opening it in three or four places. To lighten the vessel, d'Iberville threw his cannon out on the shoals, and did the same with whatever else would not be damaged by the water. On the third the wind subsided, and the whole cargo was taken ashore.

To add to the trouble young Chateauguai, d'Iberville's brother, who had been skirmishing near the fort, was fatally wounded. He died the next day in Maret's arms. Then came the news that the other ship, the Poli, in the Churchill, was having as much trouble as the Salamandre. It had been pounded by the ice, and much of its cargo and powder had been ruined, and to add to the distress its captain, de Tilly, had fallen dangerously ill.

Of course, the chaplain hastened over the intervening land to his assistance. " It was the first journey I made in the woods of America. The ground was marshy, and we had to go a long way around. We sunk knee deep in the half-frozen ground, but succeeded, nevertheless, in making five leagues through the woods, if you can call them woods, for there was nothing but thorns and brambles, with here and there an open space." When they arrived at the bank of the river they found the ship on the other side. The stream was a league and a half wide, and the current was swift and full of floating ice. At last they saw an opening and hurried with their canoe to the clear water. The sun was setting, but before darkness fell they were on board the ship.

After administering the sacraments to the dying man, and spending the next day visiting the cabins which the crew had thrown up on the shore, Maret made for the river again, and reached the other side very late at night. A shelter was hastily made, but they regretted their haste, for it snowed heavily for three hours, and they nearly perished before morning. On the eleventh the chaplain was again in camp with d'Iberville, who had meantime been making heroic efforts to begin the siege of the fort. A road had been built up to the defenses for the transportation of the cannons and mortars. They were in position on the twelfth, and on the thirteenth a message was sent to the garrison to surrender. They asked till eight o'clock next morning to consider. The next day they capitulated.

It is very edifying to be informed that in that desolate place, and sharing all the hardships and dangers of the soldiers, there was a Protestant minister, who came out to arrange the terms of surrender. He wrote them in Latin and Maret translated them into French. Unfortunately we do not know the good parson's name. He deserves to be remembered.

M. du Tas, with sixty men, took possession of the fort, which, Maret says, "was much weaker than we believed." It was a wooden structure and there was very little in it worth taking. Laut contradicts this statement. The defenders numbered fifty-three all told. They were a fine set of men, but we are informed that the Commandant knew more about driving a bargain than firing a cannon, which was the reason he surrendered so readily. It is noteworthy that this fort, on the St. Theresa River, was captured on St. Theresa's Day. D'Iberville called it Fort Bourbon, whereas he might better have chosen the name of the heavenly, instead of the earthly protector.

Of course, the victors celebrated their triumph by a banquet, but immediately after dinner Father Maret set out over land to see the dying captain of the Poli. When he reached the river it was impassable; so he and his party built a temporary shelter for the night, and the next day they started a great fire to announce the fall of the fort to the Frenchmen on the opposite shore. It was not until three days afterwards, namely on the eighteenth of October, that he succeeded in crossing the stream. There he remained till the twenty-eighth, when the sick man breathed his last. They made his grave in the snow.

When all was over Maret was eager to get back to the other river, so as to celebrate there the feast of All Saints, but it was impossible to cross the stream until the following day. His troubles, however, did not end there, for, though he reached the opposite shore in safety, he and his companions got lost in the woods and did not arrive at the other camp till the third of November.

That journey across the neck of land had to be repeated many a time after that, for both crews were attacked by scurvy, and the priest had all he could do to attend the sick on both rivers. Twenty men died. He attributed his own immunity from the disease to his enforced activity in going from one place to the other. The tramp was a hard one, but winter was now at its height, and both streams were frozen solid, so that it was easy to reach the ships. It was a disaster in other respects, for the Poli and Salamandre were imprisoned there from November till June. He notes that the Churchill, which was slow to freeze, took longer to break up, for, whereas the Nelson began its *debâcle* at the end of May, the Churchill was not open until two weeks later. No one seemed to mind it, however, and at the end of July both vessels went down to the mouth to fight any English ship that might appear; but none arrived to avenge the loss of the fort.

Meantime Maret had set himself to study the customs

and language of the natives. He tells us that three hundred or more canoe-loads of Indians came to the fort. There were among them representatives of seven or eight different tribes. The most numerous were the Assiniboels and Kristinons. The former lived at a distance of thirty-five or forty days' journey; the latter about twenty-four. They were allies and spoke each others' language. They were well formed and sturdy. The Assiniboels were heavily tattooed, and seemed to him to be a phlegmatic race; the Crees were more vivacious. They were both nomadic and consequently hard to instruct. In the judgment of the new missionary, they were " a base, cowardly, idle, churlish, and a wholly vicious set," a rather poor recommendation for the noble red man. The worship of the sun seemed to prevail among them, with the usual amount of jugglery and constant use of the pipe, which the good man fancied was a religious instrument.

" The land is marshy and unproductive," he says. " For more than thirty or forty leagues from the fort there are no real woods. Winter sets in about September and ends in June, but, though the snow is on the ground for eight months, it is never more than three feet deep. There is no rain, but only a powdery snow that sifts in everywhere. The short season of summer is unpleasantly hot, and the mosquitoes are a worse torment than in the more southern districts of Canada. Game of many varieties abound: geese, ducks, bustards, &c. The vast herds of caribou so frightened the sailors when they first saw them that those hardy adventurers, who would face all sorts of dangers, disgracefully fled from the deer.

The missionary made an offer at learning the language of the Indians. He tells us he had more trouble in understanding it than speaking it, and no doubt the Indians had a similar trouble in understanding him. He succeeded in baptizing three children, two of whom, he says, " have gone to heaven."

At the beginning of September, 1695, the two vessels set sail, but as they proposed to go directly to France Maret determined to remain with the eighty men who were left to garrison the fort. According to Laut, Nelson was a fine capture. It had a large square house, with lead roof and limestone walls. There were four bastions to the courtyard, one for the garrison's lodging, one for trade, one for powder, and one for provisions. All the buildings were painted red. Double palisades, with a trench between, enclosed the yard. There were two large gates, one on the waterside, one inland, reinforced with iron panels, and with huge metal hinges, showing the knobs of huge spike-heads. A gallery ran around the roof of the main house, and on this were placed five cannon. Three cannon were also mounted on each bastion. The officers' mess boasted a huge iron hearth, oval tables, wall cupboards, and beds that shut up in the wall.

Such a post was well worth fighting for, and apparently could have been easily held. But shortly after d'Iberville's departure Captain Allen swooped down upon it, and carried off the entire garrison to England as prisoners. Father Maret was, of course, among the captives. Perhaps he was on Allen's ship, and at one time his heart may have fluttered with the hope of rescue, for just as they were at the entrance of the straits, a swift sailing French privateer bore down on the whole fleet, and, singling out Allen's ship, which was separated from the others, raked it fore and aft with shot, killing Allen on the spot, and then sped away before the other ships could come to the rescue. Who was the enemy no one ever found out. But it was thought to be Serigny, d'Iberville's brother, who a little before that had been in the Bay.

The captives lay in prison at Portsmouth for five months. Maret's own account says Plymouth. Released at last, they hastened to France, where their spent and ragged condition excited the people to fury. Maret wrote an account of it to Lamberville, who was then in Europe as Procurator, but unfortunately the letter was lost. Possibly we can get an idea of the brutality that prevailed in England, and no doubt elsewhere at that time, from an old letter by Le Merceir, in 1652, who describes what was usual then, even in time of peace. It is concerned with the capture of Father du Perron.

The vessel on which he was going home was boarded somewhere in midocean, and all the passengers were unceremoniously plundered. The priest lost all his vestments and chalices, his breviary, and even his blanket. All his papers were rifled, and either flung overboard or torn to pieces and scattered over the deck. There was much valuable information about the missions in the documents, but that was of little consequence to the sailors. We are told that the best dressed among the Frenchmen were stripped quite naked and forced to cover themselves with whatever rags they could find. The nights were passed in the hold with no blanket but the dirt of the place, amid a swarm of soldiers, sailors, and passengers, and with bilge water beneath them, while the sea often broke through the portholes.

"At last," says the letter, "the ship was brought to Plymouth, where other Frenchmen were met with in the same plight. The vessel was immediately surrounded by small boats, and mobs of people poured over the deck to purchase the booty of the sailors." The Father saw his breviary put up at auction, and we suppose the rest of his belongings, though he does not say so; but everything appears to have been sold, so that the greater part of the passengers lost in one day what they had spent several years gaining in New France. Some of them said that the value of the ship itself might reach as high as 300,000 livres.

"There is no place in the universe, however," says the writer, "except hell, where there are not found some good people, or persons of good disposition," a reflection suggested by the presence of some Englishmen who approached the Father and gave him a small alms. It was very cruel after enduring the fatigues of the sea to be thus shipwrecked in port, and just at the moment when the travelers were looking to meeting their friends, to be captured again by their enemies. It was to this place that Maret was brought, but he was kept only a short time, and was then sent over to Havre de Grace, at the suggestion of some French captains, whose vessels had been also seized.

He did not remain long in France. He returned to the American missions, but instead of being sent among his Crees and Assiniboels, he was assigned to work in the Far West, among the Illinois, and we have a letter from him to Father Germon about that place. It was written at "Cascaskias, otherwise called the Immaculate Conception of the Blessed Virgin," and is dated November 9, 1712. It is very long, and we find in it none of the thrilling adventures that he met with in the earlier part of his career, for the conditions along the Mississippi were quite different from those in the north and east. The Indians were not as savage and not as brave. In fact, Maret had a very poor opinion of them:

"They are indolent, traitorous, fickle, inconstant, deceitful and naturally thievish and brutal; without honor; taciturn; capable of doing everything when you are liberal with them, but at the same time thankless and ungrateful. To do them a favor is to make them proud and insolent. They then fancy they are feared. Gluttony and love of pleasure are above all, the vices most dominant among them. They are habituated to the most indecent acts before they are old enough to know the shame connected with them. If you add to this their wandering life in the forests in pursuit of wild beasts, you will easily admit that reason must be greatly brutalized in these people and that they are very much adverse to the yoke of the Gospel.

"The country itself, with its great rivers, dense forests, extensive prairies and wood-covered hills, is delightful. There is abundance of game; oxen, hinds, stags and other wild beasts. We find here multitudes of swans, cranes, bustards and ducks. The wild oats, which grow freely on the plains, fatten the fowl to such a degree that they very often die, their fat suffocating them. Turkeys are likewise found here in abundance, and they are as good as in France."

There is some curious information about Missouri, "which is seven leagues below the mouth of the Illinois. It is called the Pekitanoui, or muddy water. It is extremely rapid and discolors the beautiful water of the Mississippi. It comes from the northwest, not far from the mines which the Spaniards have in Mexico." The Wabash, or *Ouabache,* as it was spelled, is also described, and then follows a detailed account of the natural productions of the country.

When Maret arrived in those parts many of the Indians had been Christianized, and the French were beginning to settle there. As elsewhere, hunting was the occupation of the men. The hard work fell to the women, and the missionary is of the opinion that "the feebler sex, being thus occupied and humble, are more disposed to accept the truths of the Gospel. In the lower part of the Mississippi," he continues, "the idleness which prevails among the women gives opportunity for the most shocking irregularities, and wholly indisposes them to the way of salvation."

The Manitou is the usual superstition, and the missionary was often in danger of having his head split open for his opposition to the practice, but the mission settlements finally expelled all the medicine men, and the most edifying piety soon reigned among the converted Indians.

Meantime the venerable missionary's younger brother, Joseph, had come out to America, and had been appointed General Superior. He lived chiefly at Mackinac, and thither Gabriel was sent to confer with him about the affairs of the missions, and incidentally to look after the Peoria Indians, among whom he had labored for some time, but who, for one reason or other, were not in the same good dispositions as formerly. He was accompanied by a few savages, one of them a catechumen. He had an excellent opportunity of measuring the extent of their courage.

The missionary's feet became swollen with the long journeys and he lagged behind on the trail. Finding himself in danger of being deserted, he cried out to his friends to come back to him. They, hearing his shouts, thought only of one thing, namely, that he was in the hands of some of their enemies, whose traces they thought they had seen a short time before. Instead of coming to his rescue they flung their packs from their backs and fled like deer in the opposite direction. At last, however, the catechumen, thoroughly ashamed of himself, crept cautiously back, and found poor Father Maret alone and crawling painfully along the trail. "You frightened us very much," said the valiant red man; "my companions had already fled, but I resolved to die with you." After that the missionary never lost sight of his guides.

He reached the Peorias, and found them repentent for their misdeeds. He remained a fortnight with them and promised to return to re-establish the old mission. Setting out then by way of the St. Joseph's River to the Mission of the Pottawatomies, he covered the seventy leagues in nine days. Part of the journey was by the river, which is full of rapids, and part across the country.

"As I was drawing near the village of the Pottawatomies," he writes, "some of the Indians, who were sowing their fields, saw me and hurried off to tell Father Chardon, who was in charge of the place. He made all haste to meet me, followed by another Jesuit. What a delightful surprise when I recognized the other Jesuit as my brother. It was fifteen years since we parted, never dreaming of seeing each other again, and we rushed to each other's arms. Of course, I had set out to join him at Mackinac, but here we were together three hundred miles from that place. Father Chardon gave us a great feast that evening."

GABRIEL MARET

The two brothers then proceeded on their way to Mackinac, and after remaining there some time Gabriel set out to see his rehabilitated Peorias, who received him with the greatest delight and promised to atone for the bad treatment the tribes had been guilty of towards Father Gravier. Maret promised to return and live with them permanently after he had settled matters in Kaskaskia, but when he announced that purpose at the latter place a tumult ensued. Neither the French nor the Indians would hear of it. Father de Ville was sent in his place and Maret remained in his old mission.

It is said of him that besides making the Indians good Christians he taught them to cultivate the soil, and raise live stock. He succeeded, indeed, in making them the most peaceable and industrious of the Western Indians. Gravier tells us that in 1707 Kaskaskia had a population of twenty-two hundred souls, all of them, with the exception of forty or fifty, being Christians. Maret was an accomplished linguist, but none of his MSS. are to be found. He died in Kaskaskia September 15, 1714. He was then fifty-two years of age, and had spent twenty years in the mission; the first part of his career being full of adventures, the closing years amid hardship, indeed, but in tranquillity and peace.

PETER LAURE

A few years ago an earnest seeker after historical treasures, while prowling around a garret in a certain city of Canada, happened to catch a glimpse of an old manuscript which had been tossed into a barrel with a number of other papers and newspaper clippings. In all probability it would have found its way to the cellar to kindle the fire of the furnace when the cold weather set in. It was yellow with age, and frayed on the edges. There were blots and erasures and omissions, and the writing was far from legible, but those were all good signs, and it turned out to be the original manuscript of a ten years' sojourn among the Saguenay Indians from 1720 to 1730. The author was Father Peter Laure, of whom his brethren knew very little, except that he had labored in those parts, and yet here in their possession, yet without being aware of it, was the most complete geographical and ethnographical account of those regions, as they were in the early days, that has ever been written.

Father Laure was born at Orleans, September 17, 1688, and entered the novitiate at Paris October 30, 1707. From 1709 to 1711 he studied philosophy at Louis-le-Grand and La Flèche, the finest colleges that the Society had in France. From La Flèche he went to Quebec, where he taught grammar, poetry, and rhetoric. He was also put in charge of the library, and a certain careful observer of such facts notes that it was the first time that such an office appears in the Jesuit catalogues of Canada. Perhaps the reason was that up to that time there was no library worth mentioning.

In 1717 he began his theology under a distinguished old professor who had won his laurels in France, Father Bertrand Gérard, and at the end of the first year we find him sustaining a public defense before all that was distinguished

in Quebec, both lay and clerical. It was a great event, and
reflected considerable glory on the defender. It was not
merely good enough for America in those rough times; it
was in reality an excellent performance, and the prelate
who presided was no less a personage than St. Vallier, who
was a doctor of the Sorbonne. He is described in the official
account of the event as *multum approbans*. In the following
year, the Prefect of Studies wrote to the Father General,
asking permission for Laure to attempt what is called the
"Grand Act," *ex universa theologia,* although ahead of the
usual time. The permission was granted and the defense
on that occasion is described as "brilliant." How did he
do it? Evidently he must have been a man of unusual
ability.

Besides aptitude for theology, he was also a painter.
The Father Minister at Quebec, writing to Rome, informs
the authorities that *"Magister Laure qui theologiae dat hic
operam, picturæ multum tribuit temporis."* The accomplish-
ment would be useful, no doubt, to amuse the savages, to
make maps, and to ornament his little chapels. His skill
as a mechanic also was of great service, as we shall see in
the sequel.

After all this glory he was told to go down to the
Saguenay, where there had been no possibility of sending a
missionary for more than twenty years. The old Indians
there could mumble some of their prayers, but the younger
generation was growing up with all the vices of paganism.
He went and remained among them for eighteen years, and
in the manuscript that was so luckily discovered we have
an account of the first ten years of that period. The other
eight were more or less a repetition of the preceding ones.
The narrative was written at the request of the Superior in
Quebec, and is characterized by the gracious and vivacious
manner which people were accustomed to in those days.

"You know, Rev'd Father," he says, "that we send
letters from here to Quebec only once, viz., in the winter.

But although I am late, I nevertheless beg of you [I conjure you, is the expression he uses] to accept the respectful homage which I presented to you with all my heart, at the beginning of this year, which I renew to-day, and which I shall always continue to pay to you till the day of my death. I send you a thousand good wishes. Whatever you desire is for me an order; but instead of commanding me, you almost entreated me when, with such extreme kindness, you accompanied me to the shore of the river on which I was to embark. You asked me to write to you whatever I might observe of an edifying nature among our Montagnais. I understood that you wanted a simple story of what occurred in our three churches in the nine years that Providence has confided them to my care. I obey; for could I hesitate a moment to satisfy your pious curiosity and to give you this feeble mark of my esteem for you, as well as my submission, and my gratitude for all the kindness of which I have been so long the recipient. Although you do not journey through the forests in search of the Indians, you are worth many missionaries because of the care which, as a true father, you take of your children, who, though they are scattered, are yet united in your heart. What could we not say, if we wanted to praise you? I am going, therefore, to give you a condensed account of these years, and would be only too happy if I had a crowd of true converts to present to your Reverence as a New Year's gift."

Chicoutimi, whither Laure directed his steps, was one of the four trading posts in what was called the King's Domain. The other three were Tadoussac, the Jeremy Islands, the Moisy River. The meaning of the term King's Domain is explained at length by M. J. Edmund Roy in his excellent little book entitled "In and Around Tadoussac":

"Long before the settlement of Canada, Tadoussac had been a great centre of trade. At least a hundred years before Columbus discovered America the Basque, Breton and Norman sailors had fished on the banks of Newfoundland and had visited the St. Lawrence in pursuit of whales, walruses and other cetaceous monsters, of which the seals of our days are but the degenerate and the bastard descendants. After fish came the search for furs, and there was a brisk trade in peltries at Tadoussac when Chauvin, and de

Monts, and Pontgravé, arrived with a royal grant, which gave them a monopoly of the latter commodity. The Basques resisted, and the dispute was finally referred to the King, who settled the matter in favor of his grantees, in 1613. From that out, instead of the great fleet of free traders, which could be seen every year at the mouth of the Saguenay, only two vessels arrived annually, and they belonged to the Trading Company. But it is recorded that in a single year as many as 22,000 skins were shipped. The value of a single cargo was from 150,000 to 200,000 francs.

"For more than twenty-five years one company succeeded another in this lucrative business. Chauvin had died leaving his powers to de Chastes. De Monts and de Caen succeeded him, but they quarreled in spite of Champlain's efforts to keep the peace between them. Finally, in 1629, Quebec was taken by the English, and that was an end of the French trading; but when the territory was restored to its former owners a number of the trading companies were formed, all passing through various vicissitudes, until the colonists formed an association of their own in 1645 and assumed the direction of the Tadoussac factory. In 1648 trading at that post had transactions to the amount of 250,000 livres, with a net profit of 40,000; a livre being nearly as much as a franc. Out of this, however, the expenses of the colonial government had to be defrayed.

"This great commercial success caused the old company of the One Hundred Associates, which had yielded up its claims to the "Compagnie des Habitants," to have a commission named, which reported that their supplanters had watered the stock and had 644,700 livres unsecured. The charge, however, was vehemently denied.

"In 1666 the West India Company came into possession; but in 1675 His Majesty the King appropriated the whole territory for himself, and it was known afterwards, until the time of the English domination, as the King's Domain, and became an integral part of the Combined Farms of France. In 1733 a survey was made and the limits laid out on the maps extended over no less than 72,000 square miles of territory. It reached from the lower extremity of the Eboulements to Cape Cormoran, a distance of three hundred miles. A straight line drawn from each of these extremities toward the north is the demarcation of the eastern and western limits of the reserve. On one side were the high lands dividing the waters of the St. Maurice and Batiscan from those which fall into Lake St. John; on the other were the still unknown regions where dwelt the Waskapis and the Esquimaux. Twelve principal trading depots were then in full operation within this network, of which Tadoussac was the centre and the rallying point. The reserve was so sacred that no one was allowed to approach nearer than ten leagues from the confines."

Into this Domain Father Laure entered in 1720. He had free access, for he was there only as a missionary and it was of great importance for the government agents that the red men should be kept in good order. His base of operations was in the north, at least sixty leagues from Quebec.

" The place has nothing to distinguish it," he says, " except that, from time to time, a number of savages go there with rich peltries, arriving from the little rivers which form the famous Saguenay, of which as far as I am aware no one has so far made a complete and reliable map. There would be curious things to tell your Reverence did my subject permit it. But I cannot refrain from giving you some idea of the surroundings."

It is to Father Martin that we are indebted for the information that in the portfolio entitled " Apparatus Français et Montagnais," 1726, consisting of 865 pages, and which is now in the Department of the Marine in Paris, there is an autograph map of Laure's, giving the countries north of the river. It is dedicated to the Dauphin, and the dedicatory letter is dated " Chicoutimi, August 23, 1731." In the same department there are two copies of this map, one of 1732 and another of 1733, with several additions. The latter has been executed and illumined with great care. All these maps are highly esteemed, even to-day, for their exactness. Other copies have been recently made of them. There is a large one which, made as it was in an Indian cabin, is quite a surprising achievement. But, besides that, Laure gives a word picture of the place, which for most readers will be more interesting than the map.

"The river," he says, "takes its source in Lake Piekoua-gami, which Father de Crespieul, who, with his apostolic sweat, watered these forests for thirty years, called Lake St. John." This is a piece of valuable information; for one would fancy that the name was given by Father Quen, who had discovered the lake. "The river," he continues, "is about twenty-five leagues in length from here to Tadoussac. It starts from a great bay, at the foot of a mountain chain, which is broken here and there by a great number of brooks and rivers. To the northeast is the Chicoutimi River, which starts with two cascades, and thus divides into two branches, forming the island on which we live. Uniting again below the island, it pours its volume of water into the salty Saguenay."

The official map of Bellini, drawn fourteen years after these words were written, has inscribed on it that it was based on manuscripts which were deposited in the Section of Maps and Plans of the Marine Department, 1744. Very likely Bellini's chief guide was Father Laure.

"At the mouth of the river," continues the narrative, "is the pretended capital of the Province of the Saguenay. I mean Tadoussac, which consists of one wooden house and a store. It must be confessed that the situation is very beautiful and quite suitable for the establishment of a city. The port is spacious, healthy, and safe. It is sheltered from every wind, and good sized vessels can anchor at high tide close to the shore. The English went there in old times to trade with the Indians, and you are shown a rock where they planted a post to moor their boats to. Two years ago an iron chain, about thirty fathoms long, and thick in proportion, was found on the sand."

Father Laure's conception of a great city was evidently not according to modern ideas, especially as he says:

"At that place the Saguenay rushes furiously into the St. Lawrence, and when the tide rises in the larger river the Saguenay fills up so rapidly that there is only about a quarter of an hour's difference between the rise of the water at Tadoussac and Chicoutimi, though the latter place is about ninety miles further up the river. This has been observed over and over again. Nor is it surprising, for as the Saguenay is nearly a league wide in certain places at its mouth, and is almost bottomless, the sea rushes, as it were, into a sort of gulf, the upper end of which is not so deep, and thus it keeps pushing back the water that comes down the stream, so that it is high tide at Chicoutimi, where the bottom of the river is more level and the banks closer together, almost as soon as at Tadoussac, at which place the water rises more slowly, for a greater volume of water is required to fill not only the great bays which are there, but the vast expanse of the river itself, which is eight or ten leagues wide at that point.

" The mountains between which the Saguenay flows are so high and steep that the gigantic trees which are on their summits appear from below no bigger than a man's legs. At 7 o'clock of a summer evening, unless you are quite out in mid-stream, you cannot read in your canoe. Here and there in clefts of the rocks, where the sun never beats, you may observe veins of very fine, white saltpetre. Every spring there are land-slides which come down with a sound like the roar of a cannon, and the atmosphere is filled with the smell of powder.

" The heat between these two mountain chains, which are for the most part bare and inaccessible, is so great that it melts the gum in the canoe, down to the water line. Although it is a dangerous stream, nature has left commodious havens for travellers. With the exception of a single stretch of four or five leagues, where it would be risking a good deal to venture without the greatest caution, and where in case of a sudden squall it would be impossible for a bark canoe to weather the storm, you find at intervals little stretches of sand where you can conveniently beach your boats. These landing places are mostly on the north shore. Almost everywhere there you find anchorage for larger vessels, and the ships in distress are happy to run into them. Thus, when the English were making their useless attack on Quebec, the French ships, which arrived too late to render assistance, anchored here. The ruins of the barracks and batteries which they built are still there.

"At low tide it is difficult to land. You have to carry your baggage a great distance over slippery stones, covered with slimy weeds, which we call goimon; but, on the other hand, Providence has so arranged that almost at every place we find wood to make our fires. There are also little streams which flow from the marshes, where the beaver builds his dam, and which leap over the crags into the river below. There the thirsty and tired traveller slakes his thirst.

"Only the north and northeast winds prevail in the Saguenay. The others are rarely felt, or, at least, are never violent. As long as I have been travelling over it, and my journeys have been frequent, I have not been troubled much except with those two; but they are extremely treacherous, violent, and lasting. As soon as one or the other blows you have to be on your guard, especially if it is cloudy weather and there is any appearance of a storm. Just as if you were on the high seas, the waves rise, toss, and foam, and the struggling of thousands of waves which chase each other, and then dash together, warns the people in the canoes to paddle with all their might to the shore. May I presume, Reverend Father, to tell you of one or two of my experiences?

"I had no knowledge as yet of the risk one runs on this capricious river. I was in a great hurry, for the call was urgent, and although we had only an old canoe for four, we had to travel all night. The weather was fine, and the moon was full, and there was no sign of a storm. My two red men, wearied with paddling, fell asleep. Tired of trying to keep them awake, I did not disturb them, and took a paddle myself to guide the boat, letting it go with the tide, which was setting down stream. After a little while one of my men, who awoke, seized his paddle. After the fashion of the savages, who are sovereignly independent of one another, to such a degree that they never urge their companions to work, lest the individual addressed would be offended, he asked me to arouse the sleeper. I did so and, being completely exhausted, I in my turn put my head and arms on one of the bars of the canoe and was soon in the land of dreams.

"Hardly had I done so when I heard some Montagnais words, and I thought my two men were quarreling. I started up, spoke and looked around. I saw neither the sky, nor the rocks, nor the water. All was darkness. A storm had arisen in the northwest. 'We are lost, Father,' cried the Indians. There was no shore visible where we might land, so dense was the gloom. Besides, we were out in the middle of the Saguenay, and we could see the gathering clouds and hear the thunder rumbling behind us. By the sheerest good luck we drew near a rock and as soon as we struck it I made an attempt to land, but my foot slipped and I went into the water. It was all over with me had not the Indian, who had only one arm, quickly stuck the stump under my arm-pit and flung me on the rock. There we hauled up our canoe. I could not help admiring my two companions, who after this adventure slept peacefully the rest of the night, while I, meantime felt the blood flowing from my leg, which had struck violently against the rock.

"I could not attend to the wound, for there was no means of lighting a fire. But I kept worrying about the canoe, lest the storm would carry it off, and then what would become of us? But God had pity on the father and his children, who were not yet ripe for heaven. The storm finally passed, and when morning came I was surprised to find that we were in a sort of niche, and I could not help laughing at what was, indeed, our lucky mishap. However, the receding tide had left us high and dry, ten or twelve feet above the water, and we had to carry our canoe, the provisions and the baggage over to a little runnel, in which we glided down to the river.

"We finally arrived at Tadoussac, and I gave the last sacraments to the sick man, who died a few days after. After that we started up the stream again for Chicoutimi. We were caught by a northwest wind, accompanied by a heavy rain, and we were so badly battered that two ribs of our canoe were broken. We were almost swamped, and I was on the point of giving absolution to my two men, who were more frightened than I, for they knew the danger and were begging me to make them pray to God as well as I possibly could. I confess that it was due to their faith and their confidence in the Blessed Virgin and St. Regis that we were saved. I quickly bound the canoe with my cincture and garters, the men steering, while I managed the sail, as we sped along, cutting through the waves, which were from time to time washed into the boat and threatening to fill it.

Finally we reached the shore and found an Indian hut. We emptied and mended the canoe, and my companions made a great fire, where we dried our clothes. I was delighted with the compassion which my dear neophytes had for me in our common misfortune.

"After that I considered myself fairly well impressed with the dangers to be met with on our river, and when I got to our little church I took the wrong resolution of being more cautious in the future. I say wrong, for in certain contingencies it is the part of prudence not to have too much of that virtue. Timidity will often make a man miss a good work. An hour's delay has often left travellers exhausted and famished when quite near the place of safety. I do not mean to say that one should not take proper precautions, for rashness has caused the death of many a Frenchman and Indian in these parts; but there are times when one can be too cautious."

After this story of his adventures, he turns to geography, and says:

"I had the honor to tell you in the beginning, Reverend Father, that the Saguenay takes its source in Lake St. John, but I want to give you a more exact idea of the place. Lake St. John is about thirty leagues from Chicoutimi, toward the west, and is situated in the depths of those mountains which you see north of Quebec. Its circumference is not more than thirty leagues. It is not deep, and in the summer, when the waters are very low, it has a beautiful beach of fine sand. It is full of fish, the surrounding country is beautiful, the landscape picturesque, the soil good, but most of the seed that is planted, especially corn, cannot ripen on account of the frequent northwest winds, which come early and are very piercing, sometimes bringing snow as early as the end of August. A part of the old missionary establishment is there yet. You can see that they had a large garden, and a chapel, where Brother Malherbe was buried. Over his grave I planted a cross."

It will be of interest to know that this is the Brother Malherbe who carried the remains of de Brébeuf and Lalemant to the tomb. His account of the mangled condition in which the bodies were is often cited by historians.

Charlevoix marks the site of the old mission in a map to be found in Volume VII of "Histoire de la Nouvelle France."

"At the top of the lake," continues Father Laure, "there is a river which is very curious on account of the little stones of all shapes which are found in its bed. Nature seemed to have studiously set about making models for all the arts. There are birds, animals, vases, and even tools for all sorts of trades, which are very recognizable. You can see them all in the water. The difficulty is to gather them. You have to make a journey there for that purpose and take time to gather them, for the Indians would not know what to choose. One who would fancy that sort of curiosity would only have to hire and feed two men, who would carry him there in a canoe. I have a specimen with me that is very curious. If, for instance, you hold it straight up, this little bit of hard grey stone looks like a monkey or an earless cat, squatted on its tail and paws, and holding a ball in its little mouth. If you lay it down it reminds you of a bird pecking, and on one side of the head is a spot which represents an eye fairly well. It is one inch wide and one and a half long. It is very singular that the stream carries none of these treasures down to Lake St. John, into which it flows.

"The river I am speaking of comes, like many others, from the mountain ridge which is the watershed of this part of the country. They all flow from Lake Kaouit-chiouit, and from there by a series of other lakes you can go to Lake Albanel, so called because Father Albanel discovered it. It is about 80 leagues E. N. E. of Hudson Bay and quite near Lake Mistassini, which receives the water of Lake Albanel, and empties into the North Sea.

"Here the Michtassini, or, in French, the Mistassini, dwell. The name is composed of *Mechta*, great, and *assini*, stone, given because of the great rock in the river. This is where the jewels I spoke of are made. The rock is held in great veneration, and it would be a crime for the Indian to pass near it without leaving some mark of superstitious respect for Tchigigoucheou, the god of good or bad weather, who, as they believe, has chosen to make his dwelling there.

"Usually the incense offered to him consists of a little tobacco or a cake, or, perhaps, only the bone of a beaver or

MODERN MONTAGNAIS.

fish. Sad to say, some of the less devout, or those who are
hungry for a smoke, often help themselves as they pass by
when this good or evil spirit is not quick enough to profit
by the piety of his worshippers.

"They tell you also that after the deluge (for they have
something of that in their tradition) the big canoe came to
grief on the high mountain which they point out to you.
Some of them assure you, as if it were an article of faith,
that they often saw an old man of immense height, armed
with bow and arrows, promenading on its summit and appearing to watch over the still very respectable wreck of
the great canoe. A few of its timbers are thought to be
preserved somewhere in those regions.

"These and a thousand other delusions do not, Reverend Father," says the deferential missionary, "deserve your
attention. Had Father Lafitau remained among us (and we
all deeply regret his loss), had it not been that his well-
known merit recalled him to France, he would have written about all these things in his marvellous manner. These
stories are so common hereabouts that there is not a child
who cannot tell you about the great canoe, and the gigantic Indian, the venerable grandfather Merchou.

"The tribe has dwindled down to an inconsiderable
number. Some of them come here for trade, in spring time;
some go to the English. They are such sweet tempered
and simple people that you can form no idea of their goodness. It would not be hard to make good Christians of
them if they were near a missionary, who could remain a
long time among them, and who would be left a certain
amount of freedom to instruct them." He was probably
alluding to the difficulties often put in the way of the missionaries by the civil authorities at Quebec.

"Unlike the other Indians, they have no liking for fire-
water, and if the French, who are more eager to plunder
them of their peltries than to help them save their souls, did
not, in spite of repeated royal prohibitions, force it on
them, they would never take it. When they do taste it
they make most ridiculous grimaces, and never of their
own account come back to the charge. To use their own
idiom, they do not like it because 'they lose their mind in
a shameful way once it has been killed by fire-water.'

"Along with this happy trait of sobriety, they display a
most admirable docility, no matter what it costs them.

Thus, for instance, some years ago, a missionary sent to a chief who was very old and not yet baptized, a little object of devotion, as a present, intending it also as an invitation to come to be instructed. In spite of his great age, the length of the journey, the fatigue of the canoe, and the difficulty of the portages, he obeyed and walked into the church, saying: 'Here, Father, is the old man you wanted to see.' Every day he asked for instruction so as to prepare for baptism. He wanted even to make his confession, so as 'to throw away,' as they are wont to say, all their sins. Thus at the end of his life he received the grace which he had travelled seven hundred and fifty miles to obtain; or, rather, the grace that went so far to find him. His confession was a source of great edification to every one.

"The Mistassini live on the fish which abound in their lakes. There are no beavers there, but droves of caribou make up for it. Almost all the popular superstitions are reduced to not allowing the dogs to eat certain bones, the impression being that the bones are profaned and the kind of animals they were taken from can never afterwards be caught by the hunters. Hence they are carefully thrown into the river or the fire. In reality this religious act has no other origin than the fear of having their dogs break their teeth. In old times hunters took that precaution and in the course of years it became a religious rite. Another custom is to throw a portion of what they are going to eat or drink into the fire as an offering for the dead. It is a sort of grace before meals which they teach their children.

"The most curious thing to be found in these forests is a cave of white marble near Wemiskou. You would imagine workmen had cut and polished it. It is easy to enter, is quite bright in the interior, and the style of the brilliant roof is quite in keeping with the columns. In a corner there is a rough mass of stone projecting from the wall, making a sort of a table which might serve as an altar. Indeed, the Indians call it a prayer and a council house, where the spirits assemble. On that account they never take the liberty of entering it; but the jugglers, who are, so to say, the priests of the tribe, do not hesitate to do so, to consult the oracles.

"I would not dare to assert that there are any genuine sorcerers among the Mistassins, nor among the other Montagnais. They are all little else than crude charlatans.

As far as I could make out, after watching them a good deal, their supposed powers are only tricks to inspire respect and fear. Although they have thirty different kinds of juggleries, they rarely succeed in doing what they propose. But, unfortunately, it is enough for them to make one lucky hit, to be forever in favor afterwards. Many of them do not believe there is anything in their ceremonies, and the most skillful among them have admitted to me that their art is only a fraud; that they have never seen the devil or the Atchene—that is, ghosts without any heads or hands, &c. They add that it is all only to humbug the ignorant, to give themselves importance, and to be regarded as privileged characters, that their ancestors invented those absurd fables.

" Others have assured me that they have seen extraordinary fires and supernatural monsters, but after becoming Christians they never saw them any more, although compelled very often to travel by night. One, more obstinate than the rest, insisted that he had seen the evil spirit, but being asked immediately what he looked like, whether he was black or white, he became confused and could not answer. By an admirable Providence of God these unfortunate sorcerers, real or sham, whose burdensome and impure practices are always to be condemned, usually die wretchedly. I have seen four instances of it. One of them I have already told your Reverence about. He was a famous juggler of the Lake who, while yet young, lost his life in a dreadful fashion, along with his wife, who was more superstitious than he.

" But you are tired," he says to his Superior, " of this wearisome story of mountains, and rivers, and rocks, and jugglers, and drunkards. Let me tell you about my first arrival here."

He then describes the lamentable condition into which the people had fallen; how licentiousness, polygamy, and all sorts of vice prevailed everywhere, because of the want of a missionary, but chiefly because of the scandalous lives of the French employees and woodlopers.

" When I left our dear, peaceful college, and arrived here, the general joy showed itself by a discharge of mus-

kets. It was a good omen for me, but after taking possession of an old chapel, which was falling to pieces, the first
sight that met my gaze was a lot of savages uproariously
drunk, others on the way to it, who in the most benign fashion came up to embrace me and to ask to go to confession.
You can imagine my feeling at this introduction to my new
field of labors.

"The Montagnais is a kind, gentle, peaceful creature,
who readily does what you ask provided you keep your
eye on him; he is credulous and never answers back; he
always accedes to what you wish. He is timid, obedient,
and, because he is ignorant of the riches he has in his
peltries, he is wretchedly poor, and is always looking for
some one to help him. They all readily do what I tell them,
except in the matter of drink. Yet it is surprising that
among all these different nations of Chicoutimists, Mistassins, Tadoussaciens, and Papinachois, I have never met a
drunkard who was brutal, in my regard.

"My only chagrin during the first stormy times was
that I could not easily make myself understood in this
strange land. Pure Algonquin was of no use to me; and so,
without a house, without help, without consolation, I was
withering up and growing pale, simply because I had no
way of showing them the bitterness of my heart. Worried,
and not being able to sow any seed in this fine field, I had
recourse to Father de Crespieul. I went frequently to the
church to ask the venerable man, long since dead, to send
me down from heaven his Montagnese tongue, as he no
longer had any use for it. But the saints want us to suffer
the same hardships as they did, so as to be in a condition to
glorify God. The plan I then adopted was to take as my
teacher a good squaw who had been a Christian for many
years. Old Mary, of whom I have already had occasion to
speak to your Reverence, after having happily assisted me
in finishing my Montagnais books, ended her days last year
by a precious death. She directed my studies like a professor, and at the very first word she heard me pronounce
she cried out to the others: 'It is all right; our Father has
spoken our language; I shall never speak a word of French
to him again; and in spite of my entreaties she kept her
word, with the result that by keeping me guessing at the
meaning of different expressions she had me in a condition
to preach at Christmas without paper."

It was a good result for six months' work. Mary was a great woman. We find in an old "Liber Miscellaneorum," or "Book of Scraps," which was dug up in the church archives at Chicoutimi, that she died in July, 1728, and over against the announcement of her burial is a eulogy written by Father Laure:

"Marie Outchiouanich, the wife of Nicholas Pelletier, died, as she had lived, in the odor of sanctity, after a sickness of a year. She was fortified by the sacraments of the Church. She was regretted by all, and will ever be mourned by me especially, who learned from her to speak the Montagnais language and to translate the prayers. She assisted me in making a grammar and dictionary, and deserved a longer life, if God had so willed. She was not yet fifty, I think. She had lived for seventeen years with M. Sauvage, at Quebec, where she learned French. When she felt the first approach of her sickness, which was as early as 1702, Father de Crespieul was dead, and there was no missionary at the post. She was so worried, and at the same time so fervent, that she went continually to the chapel to recite her prayers and weep, thus giving to her tribe a lesson of genuine compunction of heart. Her only regret in dying was that she could no longer help her Spiritual Father in his labors. May she assist him by her prayers in heaven. I buried her precious remains in the cemetery of Chicoutimi with all the honors of the Church."

It would be worth some traveler's while to find good Mary's grave.

There is another note in the "Scrap Book" which is not without interest. It is also the record of an interment, and runs as follows:

"29 Feb., 1729, Nicholas Pelletier, gallus natione sylvestris moribus, prope centenarius sepultus est." (On the twenty-ninth of February, 1729, Nicholas Pelletier, a Frenchman by birth, but a savage in his mode of life, and almost a centenarian was buried.)

This Indianized Frenchman was Mary's husband. The slight disparity of fifty years in their respective ages did not interfere with their happiness. He survived her only seven months. How pious he was we do not know, but a little over two years before his departure from this life, when Father Laure was building a new church, it is recorded that old Nick was the first one to go to confession in it. Whether he was prompted to secure that distinction out of vanity or piety is not set down. With regard to his family we know little, except that Father Laure gives special credit to a Charles Peltier, "who was conspicuous among the other Indians for his zeal in building the missionary's house." Evidently old Nicholas had wiped out all the French that was in him when his offspring were classed among the savages.

What became of the dictionary, and the grammar, and the sermon, elaborated in Mary Pelletier's wigwam, we do not know. Like many other precious things, they have been lost. At all events the Christmas sermon created a sensation, but, as aften happens with sensations, it produced no lasting effect. The people were as bad as before. But he kept on instructing them, taking the precaution, however, to have some old Indian sit near him to correct any blunder he might make in Montagnais. It was like St. Ignatius and Ribadineira.

When the people began to disperse in the woods for the hunt the hard-working priest set his hand to writing native hymns and a rudimentary catechism, but, exhausted by his new kind of life and chagrined also by his failures, he felt his health giving way, and so, at the beginning of spring, *au petit printemps,* as he expresses it, he went back to Quebec to recuperate. But he was hardly there when an irresistible impulse to return to his people took possession of him, and in spite of the entreaties of every one he was at Chicoutimi as soon as a canoe could carry him thither. Evidently the angel guardians of the Indians were urging him. He arrived just in time.

The people were returning from the woods and mountains after their winter expedition. They arrived at the post with their load of peltries, martens, beavers, and the like, the men carrying their canoes, and the women, with the privilege of their sex, everything else—babies, bundles of bark for building, faggots for the fire, tools, pots, kettles, and whatever else their lords and masters disdained to touch. After the savage fashion, they formed in a line before the chapel and saluted it by a volley of musketry. Then in cassock and surplice the priest received them at the altar. made a little address and said a prayer, after which they all betook themselves to the Company's warehouse for a feed. That being done, the building of their huts began, an occupation not left to the women, as among the other tribes, for the Montagnais were beginning to learn manners from the French. Unfortunately they were not building their houses, but their tombs.

A pestilence broke out, and the first victim was a great chief, who had not been baptized, but who had learned Christianity from the old missionaries, and was very observant of its practices. Scarcely had he begun to work when he felt himself growing ill. He kept on, however, and reproached himself with being lazy; but when the Father saw him a raging fever was consuming him. He had to be bled, an operation which the Indians usually performed by making an incision below the vein, which was lifted up and cut with a dull and perhaps a dirty knife, with, of course, deplorable consequences to the victim. When the French came, that sort of medical practice was changed, and in this case the chief had the advantage of saner treatment. The fever abated, indeed, but there was no one to take care of him. Not only that, but as some of his young men were fighting for liquor with the storekeeper, he got up to quell the riot. Then he insisted on going to the chapel, in spite of the terrible mosquitoes which were swarming there. Finally he died like a saint. " Knowing well," writes Father Laure, " what this infant church was losing by the death of

Maratchikatiq, or 'Bad Brow,' as he used to call himself, I
could only let my tears fall on my ritual during the
obsequies. In the bitterness of our hearts we could not sing
either in Latin or Indian. The French were weeping also,
as they gazed on the catafalque that had been erected in his
honor. The altar was draped in black, there were a number
of lighted torches, and on a beautiful funeral pall were
placed the sword and the musket of the dead chief in the
form of a St. Andrew's cross, and over it hung his ceremonial robe. A profound impression was made in every
one's heart that day."

"Alas!" moans the missionary, "it was only the beginning. We lost twenty-four adults." He was consoled, however, by many beautiful deaths. He informs us that the
Indians used the vapor bath against the sickness, but without the accompanying superstitious practices. In passing
we are told that the French had introduced an improvement
in this treatment by taking the steam from a caldron of
water, in which branches of balsam and other aromatic
trees had been placed. The head of the patient was kept in
the outside air—"a sovereign remedy," he says, "for lassi-
tude, rheumatism, swellings, pains in the side, nervousness,
&c." We quote it here as an illustration of medical practice
in the woods of the Saguenay.

"Happy was I to have returned from Quebec when I
did," he writes. "Had I got in the boat that would have
brought me to Chicoutimi I should have arrived when all
was over. But would you believe it? When the work was
finished I could not speak a word of Indian. I completely
forgot all I had learned. Perhaps God made me speak in
Montagnais only when I was needed. I make this remark
to recall to myself and others that an evangelical laborer
ought, if I can use the expression, tempt God for God; daring much, undertaking everything, not mistrusting too
much his own strength and fearing nothing so much in the
work of the Lord as pusillanimity."

The Indians were convinced that they had been poisoned

by the merchandise from the ship. As a matter of fact, only those who had bought any of the goods caught the fever. The clerk and others who opened the bales were the first victims. The cargo had been shipped from Marseilles, where there was a pestilence. It was fortunate that the Indians were not Iroquois, or there would have been no white men to tell the tale.

In describing this pestilence, he says that the pagan Indians took to flight and scampered off from the scene with the muzzles of their muskets pointed towards the village, which was the centre of contagion, as if to prevent the evil spirits supposed to be gathered there from pursuing the fugitives. When Laure recovered his Montagnais speech, he went down to Tadoussac, where he had been long awaited by both French and Indians.

" It was once a flourishing mission," he says reminiscently. " In former days 3000 people were gathered there and three Jesuit Fathers were assigned to take care of them, but now there are at most twenty-five families, and there is nothing very savage about the place. Situated on the shore of the sea [evidently he considers the wide St. Lawrence as being part of the ocean], the scene before you is very beautiful as you stand on the grassy bank, which is dotted down to the water's edge with a thousand flowers and diminutive wild trees. From the river comes the fresh breeze, and you see the canoes and vessels passing up and down the stream. The Indians at that place dress in the French fashion, though they are rather grotesque and dirty, but in their manners they are not quite as gross as their tribesmen in the interior. There are some old stone buildings, whose foundations and cellar, with the remnants of the oven and a battered gable, shows you where once stood a very pretty church and a comfortable dwelling. That chapel was dedicated to the Holy Cross on account of the veneration all the Indians along the shore used to have for the symbol of man's salvation. At least so I was assured by an old woman nearly a hundred years old, who used to know Father Briet [probably Druillettes] and Father Albanel. The grant of the land was made to the Jesuits by

237

the Queen Mother in the year " [here there is a blank in the manuscript] " the deed of which may be seen inscribed on parchment in the archives of the College of Quebec."

"I have not lost all hope," he continues, " that my immediate successor will succeed in getting from the Company of the Domain an order to have the church rebuilt. It is only sixty feet long; the stone and the old lime kiln are on the property, and it would redound to the credit of the King and of the agents to have it done. His majesty's principal post cannot very well do without a chapel and a house. They would not cost more than 1500 livres, and they would attract a multitude of Montagnais from the north and south, and so even in a worldly sense would be of service to this post, whose financial condition is on the verge of collapse.

"In this alleged Capital of the Saguenay there is now only a miserable chapel of bark, broken on all sides, which because of its wretched condition is incapable of giving these young Christians, who see only with carnal eyes, any idea of our mysteries, or of inspiring their hearts with any veneration for the holiness that should be there represented. Oh! if all the silks and furniture and precious stuffs that are piled up in out of the way corners of houses in France, only to be devoured by moths, were given to us, what could we not do in our poor little chapel in the forest? If I could but lift up again this cross of Tadoussac on its ancient ruins and give it a new splendor in making it shine once more over the restored sanctuary, very soon the walls would write its lessons in the hearts of these people who, although they are called savages, are not far from the Kingdom of God."

That winter he spent with the Indians at a place twenty-four miles nearer the Gulf. It was a seal station, and was known as Notre Dame de Bon Désir. For those who are interested in these poor Montagnais, who had so many good qualities which the other aborigines did not possess, it may not be unwelcome to cast a glance at them at this station of Bon Désir, which was soon to disappear from the map. They were no longer hunters and warriors, but degraded toilers for the French in the filthy work of manufacturing fish oil, and were as repulsive as the occupation could possibly make them.

"When a boat arrives," writes Laure, "the squaws and the children rush down to unload the cargo. The cleaning of the fish begins. First, there is a peaceful sharing of the choice cuts—the paws, the flippers, and the head. The heart is the least nasty portion. All are thrown into a boiler or toasted on prongs of wood planted near the fire and are then eaten, without salt or other condiment. They begin the work of getting the oil by skinning the carcass and then taking off all the fat, which is three or four inches thick. It is then thrown into a press and made to liquify gradually. It produces a rich oil which is good for tanning. Of course, the odor of this mass, melting and putrefying in the sun, is abominable; but such is not the case when the grease is put into the caldrons. That process gives a lighter and clearer oil, which is good for lamps and for making fritters; nor is the odor so foul. Placed in a phial, it has a whitish color, and is excellent for burns. When kept some time over the fire it turns red, especially if some other absorbent substance is put in to extract the impurities." Father Laure begs pardon for all "these greasy details," as he calls them.

"You can imagine," he tells us, "the frightful appearance of the people who are engaged in preparing these oils and how black and stifling is the smoke in which they are compelled to toil. It is done chiefly by the women, who with great skill and patience cut the fat into small pieces, which their husbands take for the boiling process. The Montagnais are unlike the other native races, who regard their squaws as slaves. These Indians help the women. Indeed, the man keeps what is hardest for himself and in times of want he will deprive himself of food so that his wife and children may not suffer. The distinction, however, is always kept that the food is first offered to him. In fact, the Montagnais women are queens and sovereigns compared with those of other tribes. They on their part pay the greatest deference to their husbands. All the family plans, projects, enterprises, journeys, and places of winter-quarters are left to the women."

Gentle and humble as they were, these Montagnais of

the Bon Désir post were courageous, even to rashness, especially in the dangers which they voluntarily faced on their journeys over the ice of the St. Lawrence. But their temerity had most frequently a backing to it of piety and trust in God. Among other instances, Father Laure tells us of a journey in quest of food made by a young lad and his aged mother. They were returning home over the cakes of ice when night overtook them. Huge blocks of ice were heaped up around them by the current, so that there was no possibility of their ever reaching the shore. As a signal of distress the boy discharged his musket. They listened, and it was answered from the village beyond. The people crowded down to the river and shouted. The Father was there and cried out to them to continue to pray. "We are praying," came back the reply over the intervening ice. "We are praying, and ask pardon of God for our sins." "Kneel down," said the priest to those around him, "and ask God for their deliverance." The poor Indians did as they were told, and there on the ice and snow, in the darkness of the night, went up their united supplications to the throne of God. They were heard. Almost immediately the piles of ice parted, and through the narrow passage came the little boy and his mother, who had been only a moment before looking into the eyes of death.

"Bon Désir should have never been given up," exclaims Father Laure. But it was. The agents of the Company did not want to be so much under the eyes of the priest. Indeed, they lodged a complaint that he was making his Indians pray too much, and that this interfered with their work. They then tore down his little chapel and hut during his absence, and so the mission ceased to exist. "But God vindicated us," writes the missionary, "for the Indians, knowing that they would never more see the priest waiting for them on the bleak rocks, as they returned from their labors of the sea, refused to go back to the post; and for four years after their expulsion three or four barrels of oil

was all the Company could get from the seals, whereas
before that, forty, sixty, and one hundred was the usual
outcome of the take. "There remains nothing now of Bon
Désir," he complains, "except the remembrance that Jesus
Christ was proclaimed there, and would have always been
served and glorified in what is now only a dilapidated and
unrecognizable station."

Father Laure must have been unaware of the destruction of his property at Bon Désir until he arrived among his
Indians for his usual winter stay. He writes that he left the
place on All Saints' Day, and started for the Jeremy Islands,
ninety miles nearer the Gulf, not far from the river of the
Bessiamites, which "is as deep as the Saguenay." He tells
us that from that place down to Labrador the people, who
are of the Montagnais stock, are called Papinachois, from
the Indian word which corresponds to their character:
"*Ni-papinach*—I laugh a little; or, *Poupapinacheouets*—I like
to laugh a little. On account of their unalterable gayety they
are a most attractive people, and would to God they could
communicate something of their temperament to their
intractable neighbors, the Esquimaux, who will never be
evangelized short of a miracle. Buried in the hollows of
impregnable rocks, where they breathe only by a little hole
which serves for both door and window, they allow no one
to approach them, not even the Basque, although, according
to the common conviction around here, a Basque fisherman
was their unfortunate Adam. He and some hideous Eve
were shipwrecked on these coasts in the long ago."

We do not know if the Americanists have taken note of
this tradition.

"I have talked too much, Reverend Father," he says.
"I have now only to communicate to you a new design
which I think comes from God, because it can only tend to
His glory, and it has held possession of me for a long time.
It is to let me extend the limits of my mission. Tadoussac
and Chicoutimi, and the Isles, are too restricted a territory.

The new commercial establishments at Lake Mistassini and Lake St. John will prevent many Indians who are half Christians from coming here, and I think you ought to let me go to Labrador, where, I am told, there is much to be done. It could be arranged without abandoning this post, or, if you so wish, a new missionary can keep my place here. The effort is worthy of your zeal in propagating the Faith. But it is my duty to propose and yours to decide. Perhaps this information, which I take the liberty of giving you, will influence the natural tenderness of your heart. If you do not consent, do not fear to tell me so. I make the proposition because of the fear that has long worried me lest a single savage in Labrador, old or young, should one day reproach me because he had lost his soul. I am only satisfying the demands of my already agitated conscience. Send here the first Father that comes from France; then I shall embark for the gulf and I shall always have the honor to be, as at Chicoutimi and everywhere else, with gratitude and respect to your Reverence,

"Your very humble servant,

"Laure."

He did not go to the Gulf, but continued his painful and perilous journeys from Chicoutimi to Tadoussac and the Jeremy Islands until the year 1737, when we find in the "Repertoire Général du Clergé" that he was made Curé of the Eboulements, and died there November 22nd of the following year, at the age of sixty-four.

Glorious Father Laure! and yet we should have known nothing about him had it not been for the poor old discarded bundle of paper which had been lying for years in the dust of an unvisited garret in Quebec, and which is now safely pigeonholed among the other valuable Jesuit archives in Montreal.

MASSACRE ISLAND.

JOHN AULNEAU

CHAPTER I.

WITH DE LA VERENDRYE.

If you glance at a map of the great Canadian Northwest you will see before you a vast region intersected in every direction by lakes and rushing rivers. Near where the territory approaches Minnesota you will notice a vast expanse of water called Lake of the Woods. It is one hundred miles long and fifty wide. Its shores are indented on all sides by deep bays and inlets, and its surface is dotted with thirteen thousand islands, few of them very large, some mere rocks, but others spacious enough and covered with gigantic pines and firs, where eagles, even to-day, build their nests undisturbed.

It will be remarked that in the lower reaches of the lake the boundary line between the two countries is broken in a very singular fashion. Instead of continuing west, as it had been doing so far, it suddenly deflects to the north, then veers west again, entering what is called the Northwest Inlet, which it divides in two as far as there is anything like possible navigation. The northside of the Inlet is Canadian, the south, American. The latter, though still a wilderness, has suddenly leaped into fame. It was one of the outposts in the pioneer development of the continent.

In the Canadian section of the lake, however, twenty-one miles from Northwest Inlet, though forever to be associated with it in thought, lies a wooded island to which a deep religious interest attaches. It has a gruesome name and history. It is called Isle au Massacre. Even the pagan Indians make the sign of the cross as they approach, and then paddle furiously by. They never land on its shore, and never even point at it. Red men do not easily recoil from bloody memories, but a priest was murdered there in 1736, and crimes of that nature make even savages shudder. At present a cross keeps guard over the once haunted island. Another rock in American waters once disputed the distinction of the massacre, but measurements, Indian traditions, and recent discoveries have settled the matter beyond dispute. Canada owns the horrible but sacred place.

The priest who was murdered there was Father Aulneau, a young Jesuit. He had gone out with the famous de la Verendrye, in an attempt to find a way to the West Sea, as the Pacific was called in the early days. The road lay through a mysterious country, where people who wore white beards, and owned horses and cattle, and domestic fowls were said to live. The learned men of those days were sure there must be in those parts a great river that ebbed and flowed; for, they argued, if the St. Lawrence went east, and the Mississippi south, why was it not likely that there was another going west through those unexplored regions? The balance had to be preserved.

De la Verendrye never saw the white beards nor the river. He did not even succeed in going further than the Mandan country, at the headwaters of the Missouri; but the wonder is that he had the courage to go so far after the tragedy that carried off twenty-one of his men, among them his son and the priest. They were on their way to Mackinac and, unsuspicious of danger, had encamped on an island in the lake, but the Sioux crept up behind them, murdered them in cold blood, and then, cutting off their heads and taking their scalps, disappeared over the lake. Hence the name Isle au Massacre. The mangled bodies were found there later and transported to the fort. De la Verendrye meditated vain things against the foe for some time, and then resumed his weary tramp through the wilderness, towards the sea which always receded. A record of the massacre was inscribed in the "Archives Coloniales de la Marine," of Paris (1679-1759), but it only rehearsed the story told before that by a voyageur, named Bourassa, who seemed to be conspicuous in those days.

Two years later Father Lafitau wrote from Paris a brief account of it to the General of the Society in Rome, and that was about all that was known, for a long time, of the bloody ending of the missionary's career. As years went by even the trappers forgot where Verendrye's fort had stood. The northern storms rapidly battered it to pieces. Its timbers rotted, and when its masonry crumbled and fell the weeds hastened to cover the wreck. In the same way poor Father Aulneau's memory faded away from men's minds. To a great extent even his own Order lost sight of him, not out of negligence or unconcern, for it is very solicitous about its records, but many dispersions and the general suppression of the Society, had swept away mountains of precious documents, some of which are only now beginning to be found.

As a matter of fact, neither his famliy nor his birth-place, nor the college where he studied, nor the province he belonged to in the Society, was known until our times. Even his full name was a matter of dispute, until, after many years, the delvers in archives and the decipherers of frayed and forgotten manuscripts made it certain that he was Jean-Pierre Aulneau de la Touche. In Garneau he appears as Arnaud, which is not surprising when we see, in the exquisitely beautiful and careful handwriting of the Jesuit, Father Pothier, the very phonetic rendering of Aulneau as *Ono*. Pothier was often facetious, but he was serious in this instance. But now, in a very unexpected fashion, the grave has given up its dead and revealed a hero and perhaps a saint.

It happened in this wise: In 1889 three Jesuits were giving a men's retreat in La Vendée, in France. Among the six hundred who followed the exercises was a venerable old man named Aulneau. He had never before met a Jesuit, but in the course of a conversation with one of the missionaries he chanced, or perhaps the Lord prompted him to say, that there was a precious heirloom in his family—a package of letters written by a relative, a Jesuit priest, who had been slain by the savages in the wilderness of North America, one hundred and fifty years before. The letters were examined, and the joy of his spiritual brethren was as great as that of his kindred in flesh.

It was only then that the details of his life became known, and we can now put down as history that he was born April 21, 1705, at Moutiers-sur-le Hay, where the Aulneaus, or the Seigneurs de la Touche, as they are called, still reside. It came out that one of his brothers was also a Jesuit, another a Sulpician, and that there was a sister, a nun. His first schooling was at Luçon, and he entered the Novitiate when he was only fifteen. He was making his fourth year of theology when Father de Lauzon, Superior of the Canadian Mission, came to France seeking help. Aulneau offered himself and was accepted. He was only twenty-nine years of age when he embarked on " the King's ship," otherwise the man-of-war Ruby, commanded by the Chevalier Chaon, and bound for America. With him was an illustrious company, for, besides his three Jesuit companions, the Ruby carried Mgr. Dosquet, the fourth Bishop of Quebec, with a number of ecclesiastics, who were to fill the vacancies in the ranks of the diocesan clergy. In the group there was also the famous Sulpician Piquet, who was to build the Indian mission of La Présentation at what is now Ogdensburg, after the English had driven the Jesuits out of New York.

It is gratifying to get a glance at the young missionary's qualities of mind and heart from the letters so fortunately found in the château. One addressed to "My Dearest Mother," is dated Quebec, October 10, 1734. It is a description of his journey over the Atlantic, and may serve as a remonstrance against our cowardly fashion of crossing the deep in modern times:

"Quebec, Oct. 10, 1734.

"My Dearest Mother:

"On taking leave of you, I promised to write as often as possible, and to inform you of whatever should take place during my journey and even of what might happen later on. It is with pleasure that I now begin to fulfill my promise, and this is the first letter I write since my arrival in Canada.

"We embarked on the 29th of May, at two in the afternoon. Adverse winds obliged us to lie in the roadstead the 30th, so that it was only on the 31st, at three o'clock in the morning, the wind having become favorable, that we weighed anchor and set sail. We lost sight of the shores of France that same day, and we made such headway that all on board began already to congratulate themselves at the prospect of a quick voyage. Their satisfaction was but short-lived, as contrary winds soon set in. We consoled ourselves, however, with the hope that they would not last. The sequel convinced us but too well that our hopes were vain. We took forty-seven days to reach the great Banks of Newfoundland, and during that long run, with the exception of a few days of calm, we encountered fierce head winds from the northwest, which more than once forced us to let the vessel scud before the gale. Mass was not celebrated on board, either on Pentecost, or the Octave, or on Saint Peter and Saint Paul's day, as the storm was so violent and the rolling and pitching of the ship so heavy that it was impossible to stand. Our rations on those days were biscuits and dry bread, of which each one secured a supply as best he could.

"The pleasure we experienced the morrow of our arrival on the Great Banks, watching the sailors fishing for cod, compensated us for our late fatigues. In less than two hours the crew caught more than two hundred. Some were salted and the remainder distributed amongst those on board. That same day they were served up at the table, and were much relished by some, others found them insipid, myself among the number. Once on the Banks we began to catch sight of different varieties of birds, which I do not think are to be seen in Europe. The kind

247

most frequently seen the sailors called 'Tongeux.' It is
a bird shaped somewhat like a goose and nearly as large.
Its breast is pure white, and the tips of the wings black.
We saw numbers of 'Happefoix,' 'Godes' and 'Pelyngoins.'
They are a kind of a small duck, which never abandon the
vicinity of the Grand Bank.

"There arose during the night which followed our catch
of codfish, a dense fog, accompanied by a breeze strong
enough to enable us to set sail. We, therefore, got under
way and began tacking as we had done heretofore. We
sailed at haphazard, and if the fog had held out an hour
or two longer a misfortune would have befallen us, for
after beating about for twenty-four hours in the darkness
we were surprised when the mist cleared away to see land
about a league and a half distant. It was the island of
Newfoundland, whose coasts loomed up high before us.
We had drifted imperceptibly with the current towards the
island, and found ourselves at the entrance of Placencia
Bay, an English settlement and the capital of the island.
We immediately put about and took a whole day to keep
out from land. As soon as we thought that we were at a
safe distance we continued our run along 'Cavert Bank.' *
It is a bank of sand about fifteen leagues long, where
large quantities of codfish are caught. We did not stop,
however, to fish for any. We were delayed by another fog,
which rose and forced us for three entire days to beat
about Cavert Bank.

"Meanwhile a great many on board had fallen sick, and,
seeing the winds always unfavorable, our officers began to
grow despondent, and thought seriously of putting in to
Louisburg, a town of 'Isle Royale' (Cape Breton), which
belongs to the French, and is situated at the entrance of
the Gulf of the River St. Lawrence. Had they done so,
we should have been obliged to take shipping in some
smaller craft to make the two hundred leagues which yet
remained before we could reach Quebec. Providentially,
the winds having become a little more favorable, the officers abandoned their project, and determined to go as
far as that port. We consequently entered the Gulf of the
St. Lawrence, leaving on our left Isle Royale and St. Paul's,
and on our right, the islands of St. Pierre.

"It was at about this date that we began to notice fre-

---

* Cap Vert, at present Green Bank.

quently on our masts and yard-arms a kind of bird called
the cardinal, very likely because its plumage is red, with
the exception of the tail and the tips of the wings. It is
about as large as a chaffinch, but its beak resembles that
of a parrot. Several were captured by the sailors and
caged.

"It was also about this time that we had to change our
foretopmast, which was split in the late gales. In spite
of these delays we made some headway towards the
mouth of the St. Lawrence, but before reaching it, we witnessed a spectacle, which, I am sure, many in Europe
would set down as a pure invention. In the middle of the
gulf are two small islands, the larger of which might be
about half a league in circumference. They are not named
without reason Bird Islands. Never in all my life did I
see as great a number of birds as were on these islands,
though they are completely denuded of trees. The ground
was actually alive with them, and the sky darkened. It
was one of the kinds of birds of which I spoke to you
above. Our captain fired a cannon twice in their direction
as we passed, but as we were not near enough, both shots
fell short of their mark. During the remainder of our
journey up the gulf we caught sight of Brion and Mag-
dalen Islands (to the southwest of the Bird Islands). Porpoises of a prodigious size, whales, blowers and sea-cows
awakened, if they did not entirely satisfy our curiosity.
Finally we reached the mouth of the river two months
after leaving France. We entered it on the south side,
with the Island of Anticosti on our right. The river here
is more than forty leagues wide, and is one of the greatest
and most beautiful of the world. The wind soon obliged
us to bear away from the southern towards the northern shore, which is of the two the less dangerous. Both
are formed of very lofty mountains, which extend along
the river almost as far as Quebec. For several days we
struggled on against the violence of the winds, which
tossed us about even more boisterously than they had
done heretofore, but finally we made an island lying midway in the stream. It bears the name of Isle Verte.

"A dead calm succeeded when we were abreast of it,
and this gave us an opportunity of sending a boat ashore
in quest of refreshments, of which we stood in great need,
as for many days we had lived on nothing but salt beef,

while the number on the sick list had considerably increased. Since we left the Grand Bank five had died, and were buried at sea. The boat, which we had dispatched to the southern shore, for the settlements begin about here, took a day and a half to make that little trip, and when she again joined us we had already been two or three hours under sail, the wind having sprung up again while she was away seeking fresh provisions. She brought back but a small supply, but what little she did bring was received with satisfaction by all on board. We proceeded on our way with more caution and dread than ever, for though we had escaped many dangers already, we had still greater ones to guard against.

"We shortly made for another island, which bears the name of Isle-aux-Coudres. Near this island there is a whirlpool, which makes it the most dangerous spot throughout all the passage from France to Canada. It was there that we realized for the first time that we were in summer, for since our departure from France we had all along experienced wintry weather. The sick had suffered much from it. I can say that in all my experience I never endured such intense heat.

"For two days we rode at anchor near the whirlpool without being able to pass it, as we were wind-bound. This delay brought us a further supply of fresh provisions, and gave us a chance to admire at our leisure the snow-white porpoises and numbers of seals. At last a northeast wind sprung up about two o'clock in the afternoon, and we successfully cleared the whirlpool, but again cast anchor two or three leagues beyond.

"On the morrow we proceeded as far as the cape called Maillard, and there I left the King's vessel. From the time we reached the whirlpool I had suffered from violent headaches, and this led Father Superior to apprehend that I had caught the ship-fever. He, therefore, bad me take the launch, which a Jesuit had brought down from Quebec to receive those among us who might be ailing. But fifteen leagues remained to reach that port. The evening of the day on which I left the ship, I supped at the Island of Orleans, and travelling all night, I arrived the following morning at six o'clock in the bark canoe, which, to journey more expeditiously, we had taken at the Island of Orleans. I had up to this enjoyed good health. I had not even been seasick during the passage across, though it had taken us seventy-five days. Three days after landing at Quebec I was taken down with ship-fever. Twice it brought me to death's door, but, thank God, I have now quite recovered.

"Beg the Father of Mercy, my dear mother, to grant me the grace of devoting to His service my health and my life which He has restored to me, and that I may bring the poor Indians also to serve and love Him. I have already seen a few of almost all the tribes, and there is no more repulsive sight, but they have been ransomed by the blood of a God. How happy shall I be if He deigns to make use of so unworthy an instrument as myself to bring them to love and adore Him in spirit and in truth.

"I am to spend the winter in Quebec. It is a town perched on the top of a mountain. There are houses pretty enough, but they are built, to some extent at least, as necessity required; without order or symmetry. The Island of Orleans, the environs of Quebec, and either shore, for a stretch of more than a hundred leagues beyond, are under very good cultivation, and with the exception of wine, everything that is found in France may be found here.

"Once more, my dear mother, implore our Lord that I may have the grace to draw profit from the grand examples of virtue which I have before my eyes. I am here in a college made up of former missionaries, who have sacrificed their health and strength to win for Him the love of souls. Father Nau, who is in excellent health, sends his compliments.

"I am, dear mother, with the tenderest affection for now and for life,
"Your servant and son,
"AULNEAU, J."

Although Father Aulneau refrains from describing all the horrors of that ocean voyage, his companion, Father Nau, in a letter to his Superior, lifts the veil, or rather opens the gangway of the hold of the Ruby:

"The mere sight of the gun-room was a revelation," he says. "It is a room about the size of the Rhetoric class-room at Bordeaux. There was a double row of frames swung up in it, which were to serve as beds for the passengers, subalterns and gunners. We were packed into this dismal and noisome place like so many sardines in a barrel. We could make our way to our hammocks only after repeated blows on our limbs and head. A sense of delicacy forbade our disrobing, and our clothes in time made our backs ache. The rolling and pitching loosened the fastenings of our hammocks, and hopelessly entangled them. On one occasion I was pitched out sprawling on a poor Canadian officer, and it was quite a time before I could extricate myself from the ropes and wraps. Meanwhile the officer had scarcely breath enough to give vent to his profanity.

"Another disagreeable feature was the company we were thrown in with, day and night. We had to shun them as much as possible. But the worst of all was the stench and vermin. There were on board about a hundred soldiers, freshly enrolled, each of whom carried a whole regiment of 'Picardies' [a euphemism for insects as unpleasant to name in English as in French].

"In less than a week these ravenous 'Picards' migrated in all directions. No one was free from their attacks, not even the bishop or the captain. Every time we went on deck, we could see that we were covered with them. We found them even in our shoes.

"Another source of infection were eighty smugglers, who had already passed a twelvemonth in jail. They sent out swarms of the marauders. These wretched men would have caused the heart of a Turk to melt with pity. They were half naked, and covered with sores; some were eaten alive with worms. All that we could do was unavailing to prevent the outbreak among them of a pest which attacked all, indiscriminately, and carried off twenty of our men at a stroke."

Such were our missionary's surroundings during those three months on the wild Atlantic. And yet, while the ship fever was burning him up, we find that he was assiduous in caring for the unhappy wretches in the hold of the Ruby. He was hurried ashore on her arrival, and when the crisis was over he had a bad relapse. He finally recovered and was told to prepare for his fourth year examination in theology, of which he acquitted himself with ease.

JOHN AULNEAU

Here enters the explorer de la Vérendrye. The world was crazy at that time about the mysterious land of the west. The court of France was very anxious to have it mapped out, but, on the other hand, was unwilling or unable to advance the necessary funds, and so the discovery was left to private enterprise.

The man who did most in that direction was undoubtedly de la Vérendrye, one of Canada's most notable heroes. His real name was Pierre Gaultier de Varenne, and before he started out on his travels he had been commandant at Nepigon, north of Lake Superior. He had seen service in two American campaigns, one in New England, the other in Newfoundland, and he afterwards fought in Flanders. He won the grade of lieutenant, at Malplaquet, thanks to the nine wounds that left him for dead on the field, and at the end of the war he returned to America, but without his rank and without a penny in his purse. Appointed to a little trading post near Three Rivers, he supported himself as best he could, and married a wife. Governor Beauharnais, who was his friend to the last, made him Commandant at Fort La Tourette, near Lake Nepigon, which was regarded as being " at the end of the world."

Though poor and with no future before him, he was dreaming of eclipsing Marquette, Joliet, de la Salle and the others in discovering new territories. At Mackinac he met Father de Gonner, who had been out among the Sioux, and whose brain was seething with similar projects. Together they dreamed and schemed about the Far West, and when de la Vérendrye drew up his plan, de Gonner journeyed down to Quebec to plead for him, and later on crossed the sea to France for the same purpose. Subsequently, de la Vérendrye showed Beauharnois a map made for him by a savage, which, because of the artist, must have been a marvel of elementary cartography. Everything was ready but the money, and that could not be extracted from the French Court, so de la Vérendrye was given a post at Winnepigon, with permission to sell furs, to see if he could get rich enough by that means.

At last, on May 19, 1731, he started for Mackinac with fifty men. With him was Father Mesaiger, whose name Garneau, Margry, and B. Sulte spell " Messager," though the autograph signature is very clear. They reached the Grand Portage of Lake Superior August 26, and wintered at Kaministigoya. The next year they arrived at Rainy Lake, and in 1732 built a fort on the shores of Lake of the Woods, which was called St. Charles, after the chaplain, Charles-Michel Mesaiger, who, however, soon collapsed, and had to return to Quebec. Some one had to take his place to care for the garrison, a charge which was only incidental to announcing the Gospel to the Assiniboels or Assiniboins, the Cristinaux or Cris, and the Oua Chipoüanes, who are none other than the Mandans, with whom Catlin made us familiar at a much later period. Who was to go? The young priest lately ordained and scarcely over his almost fatal illness, Father Aulneau.

The proposition filled him with horror. Without counting the uninterrupted series of terrible journeys in the wilderness, and the privations to be endured, he did not know a single word of Mandan, Cris, or Assiniboin, nor could any of his fellow travelers teach him. Moreover, he was to be absolutely isolated from all religious assistance, two or three thousand miles from Quebec. There was to be no missionary near him to afford any help. " I assure you," he wrote to Father Fay, " it is the hardest trial of my life, and I cannot face the situation without fearing for my salvation. The Superior has appointed me for this mission without any warning, and without any regard for my intense aversion to it. I assure you it has cost me the greatest struggle to make up my mind to obey. May God deign to accept the sacrifice of my life and of every human consolation which I have made in this act of submission."

True to his heroic instincts he wrote as follows:

"May God be blessed! Henceforth, He will be my entire comfort and consolation. I have no other help than what Jesus dying on the cross will give me. What inspires me with confidence is that it is not of my own choice that I am exposed to so many dangers. From this out, I must think only of the souls of the savages. The more I reflect on the sufferings before me, the more joy I feel that God has called me for the missions of that wretched country. My joy, however, would be complete if I had another Jesuit to go with me. Implore God to give me the grace not to be unworthy, by my sins, of His protection and mercy. Let us love God always, and Him alone. Le us do all we can to be like His adorable Son dying on the cross. Happy are those whom He has judged worthy of dying for Him."

No one could talk in that way, when face to face with terrible sacrifices, unless his soul was illuminated and fortified in a wonderful way by supernatural grace. He went forward with grim determination. Meantime, it is very comforting to find that the affections of his heart were not deadened or blunted. When he was in Montreal, on June 12, already on his way to the West, he writes to his mother: "To-morrow I leave here with no other sorrow than that of going too far away from you to be able to write to you often." The "dearest mother" must have been happy and proud in her grief. She was like the mother of Father Jogues. Indeed, there are very strong points of resemblance between those two young apostles, though they were separated by a whole century.

It took him till October 23 to reach Fort St. Charles. We have only one note of that long journey, and it was written the following year.

"From the end of Lake Superior to Fort St. Charles," he says, "we traveled 300 leagues. Almost all the time our road led through fire and stifling smoke. We never once saw the light of the sun. The savages in hunting had set fire to the forest without dreaming of such a horrible conflagration. We saw nothing but lakes and rocks, for-

ests, savages and wild beasts. It was too late to reach
Winnipeg, so we passed the winter in Fort St. Charles.
It is a long quadrangle, consisting of four rows of palisades,
twelve or fifteen feet high, inside of which are some miserable cabins, made of wood and mud, and covered with bark.
Next summer I am going to the Assiniboins, who occupy
all the land near Lake Winnipeg. At All Saints, if it be the
will of God, I propose to go with some Frenchmen who
are ready to face the same perils as myself, and start for
the Assiniboins, who every year, as soon as the ice forms,
go to the Mandan country for their supply of corn.

"As for the Indians who dwell here, I do not believe,"
he continues, "unless it be by miracle, that they can
ever be persuaded to embrace the faith; for even not taking into account the fact that they have no fixed abode,
and that they wander about the forests in isolated bands,
they are superstitious and morally degraded to a degree
beyond conception. What is most deplorable is that the
devil makes use of the very men who should endeavor
to break their bondage, to rivet their fetters more firmly.
Both English and French, by their accursed avarice, have
given them a taste for brandy, and have thus been instru-
mental in adding drunkenness to their other vices. Yet,
notwithstanding the shameful degradation of these poor
infidels, God has allowed them still to retain certain notions, which, perhaps, may help to determine them to range
themselves on the side of religion. They acknowledge the
immortality of the soul. After its separation from the
body it goes to join those of the other deceased Indians;
but they have not all the same dwelling-place; some in-
habit enchanting prairies, where all kinds of animals are
found. The departed souls have no trouble in slaying them,
and with the viands of the chase they are perpetually re-
galing one another. Everywhere on these plains, we are
told, you see kettles swung over the fire, and dances and
games. That is their paradise.

"But before reaching it, there is an extremely dangerous place, a wide ditch which the souls have to cross. On
one side of it there is a stretch of muddy water, offensive
to the smell and covered with scum; then there is a pit
filled with fire, which rises in fierce tongues of flame. The
only means of crossing is a pine tree, the ends of which
rest on either bank. Its bark is ever freshly moistened and

besmeared with a substance, which makes its as slippery as ice. If the souls who wish to cross to the enchanting plains have the misfortune to fall at this dangerous passage, there is no help left; they are doomed forever to drink of the foul, stagnant water, or to burn in the flames. Such is their hell, and such their obscure notion of what efforts must be made-to secure heaven.

"I leave untold a thousand other vagaries, of which, from the little I have said, you may form a faint idea; nor am I sufficiently versed in the matter, having but a very imperfect knowledge of the language. If it be pleasing to you, I may revert to the subject later on.

"I am the first missionary who has yet undertaken to systematize the language of the Kristinaux. I am not very skillful at it, for I have picked up only a little of it during the winter, because the Indians have been out on a warlike expedition against the Maskoutepoels or Prairie Sioux. They destroyed some lodges of the enemy, and have returned with a few scalps. This war was the occasion of much suffering during the winter, as we had no other nourishment than tainted pike, boiled or dried over the fire.

"The Kristinaux are not so numerous as the Assiniboels, but they are much braver, or, rather, much more fierce and cruel. They massacre one another on the most trivial pretext. War and the chase are their sole occupation. They are averse to teaching their language to others, so that what little I know has been picked up in spite of them. I hope, nevertheless, before my departure for the Koatiouaks to announce the gospel to them.

"The devil is the only idol they acknowledge, and it is to him that they offer their outlandish sacrifices. Some have assured me that he has visibly appeared to them. They are in great dread of him, as, according to their own avowal, he is the author of all the ills that befall them. It is for this reason they honor him, while they do not give a thought to God, since He sends them nothing but blessings. They acknowledge having received everything from Him, and that He is the author of all things. Wherefore, they manifest no surprise when told of His wondrous works. Even the raising of the dead to life would not astonish them. One day a Moussouis, listening to the story of Lazarus, exclaimed: 'Wonderful that God raised him to life! He had already given life to him once. Could He not give it to him a second time?'

"When we speak of Christianity to them, one of their standing reasons for not embracing it is, that the Indians were not made for that religion. But the true reason, which they do not wish to avow, is their fear of the devil, and the necessity in which they would be placed of renouncing what they call their incantations, which they imagine they could never abandon without immediately being stricken with death."

This was the last letter he ever wrote. He ends with a thought that would indicate something of a premonition of death: " The issue of my project is known to God alone. Perhaps instead of hearing that I have succeeded, you may hear of my death. Let it be as God pleases; with all my heart I will make the sacrifice of my life."

The end soon came. Provisions were giving out at the fort, and three canoes with a party of men were sent down to Mackinac for supplies. Father Aulneau went with them. One of the motives of his going was that because of his extremely delicate conscience he was anxious to go to confession. To be sure of making the journey quickly, he asked for young de la Vérendrye as a companion. Permission was given, and on June 8 twenty men and the priest left Fort St. Charles, never to return.

The Sioux were then at war with the Cris, who were allies of the French, and when Aulneau and his party were only about twenty miles from the fort a band of Sioux swooped down upon them. Was it in the early morning, or at their camp-fire in the evening, or when they were all asleep? No one can tell. There are several accounts of it, and they all differ. Not one of the party was left to tell the tale. Some, it is said, were drowned, but in view of recent discoveries, that is unlikely. In Father Du Jaunay's letter from Mackinac to Aulneau's mother, three years later, we read that the majority of the Indians were averse to killing the priest, but that a crazy savage, careless of the consequences, struck the

JESUIT CAMP.

LAKE OF THE WOODS.

blow. " I have heard also," continued the writer, " that scarcely had the deed been perpetrated than a deafening clap of thunder struck terror into the whole band. They fled from the spot, thinking that heaven was incensed at the deed." Of course, this may be pure invention. Stories grow with the imagination of the narrators.

We gain some additional information from de la Vérendrye's Memoirs. It appears that on June 20 a party of voyageurs, with thirty Cris Indians, gave him the news of the massacre. On July 29 it was confirmed by four other Frenchmen, who arrived at the fort. Alarmed at their long absence, he sent a canoe with eight men to verify the facts. They found young de la Vérendrye lying face downward, his back gashed with knives, a hoe imbedded in his loins, and the head separated from the trunk. Father Aulneau was kneeling on one knee, his left hand supporting the body, his right raised in the air. An arrow had pierced his side, and there was a deep gash in the breast. It is not said that he was decapitated. Indeed, it was reported that the Indians were afraid to touch his body, but whether the posture in which he was found is a fancy picture, or whether he was really in that attitude after the butchery, must be left to adepts in surgery or anatomy to quarrel about. The skulls, we are told, were wrapped in beaver skins. All the skulls and some of the bodies were transported to the fort.

Father Martin relates that M. Belcourt, a missionary at Pembina, visited the island in 1843, and saw a mound, about seven feet high, which had been built over the bodies. A grave was impossible there, for the island was all rock, and hence stones were merely piled on top of the remains. One is tempted to ask why Father Martin did not visit the tomb himself. The explanation is not hard to find. A journey to that remote place is even now a matter of great difficulty and expense. It was out of the question in his time.

CHAPTER II.

FINDING THE FORT.

De la Vérendrye left Fort St. Charles in 1737. On October 3, 1738, we find him at Fort Maurepas, which he built, and a few months later he was away in the Missouri country among the Mandans. In 1740 he returned to Montreal, to appease some clamorous creditors, and in 1741 he was at Mackinac. Subsequently he made his permanent abode at Fort la Reine, and from there directed the explorations of his sons, who valiantly sustained the family traditions. They established forts in many places, and in 1742 started west. They reached the Upper Missouri, followed its course as far as the Yellowstone, and on January 1, 1743, pitched their tents at the foot of the Rocky Mountains, sixty years before the arrival of the American trail makers, Lewis and Clarke.

During all this time, the elder de la Vérendrye was the victim of jealousy and hatred. Blamed by the Quebec Government (though Beauharnois was always true to him), accused of illicit trading, and disgusted by the ingratitude of those who had profited by his sacrifices and labors, he resigned his position as Commandant of the Northwest, and withdrew from public life. He was reinstated, however, in all his honors, and others were added, but his toil, his misfortunes, and especially the attack on his reputation, had shattered his constitution, and he died on December 6, 1749. Canada owes much to de la Vérendrye.

Meantime the world began to forget all about Fort St. Charles, and, of course, Father Aulneau passed out of man's memories. It is true that the untiring Father Martin wrote about him, but even he makes a mistake of four years in recording the date of his arrival in America, putting it at

1730 instead of 1734. In 1890, however, immediately after the discovery of the Aulneau letters, the cloud began to lift. The Jesuits of St. Boniface College, Manitoba, visited Isle au Massacre and erected a cross upon it. They were accompanied by Captain Laverdière, who knew the lake by heart, and besides had all the traditions of the Indians at his finger tips. There could be no mistake about the location of the island, and subsequent developments showed that no error had been committed in its identification.

In 1902, Mgr. Langevin, the Archbishop of St. Boniface, who, like his predecessor, had been for years intensely interested in the question, organized an expedition at his own expense to make another discovery, viz., the site of Fort St. Charles. He and those associated with him in the enterprise left Rat Portage September 2, on the steamer Catherina S, and in the afternoon stopped at the Isle au Massacre to say a prayer at the foot of the cross which the Jesuits had planted there two years before. From thence they went to Flag Island, where they took on board the great chief Powassin, who said he knew all about Fort St. Charles. He led them straight to what he said was the place, having told them first the kind of ruins they were going to find. They saw there, indeed, remnants of a chimney, with a quantity of ashes, calcined bones, etc. Besides, everything seemed to correspond with the accounts of which de la Vérendrye has left about the locality, and on the site they solemnly erected a cross, with the inscription:

FORT ST. CHARLES.

Founded 1732.

Visited 1902.

Great enthusiasm reigned among the happy explorers on their return home; but after a while doubts began to arise about the advisability of accepting their find as conclusive. The stones and the ashes were scarcely a firm enough foundation to build on. The old chief Powassin had told them he was sure of it, but he might have been mistaken. It is true that another chief, whose name we fear all the printers of the world will gag at, for it is nothing short of Andakami-gowinimi, agreed with him about Frenchmen having been there, but from time to time he alluded to a fort on the other side of the inlet. His casual utterances did not attract much attention then, but they afterwards proved to be a very valuable clue. So the conviction gradually began to force itself on the minds of those interested that Fort St. Charles had not yet been discovered.

In 1908 another expedition was organized. The archbishop's absence in Europe explains why he did not lead it. It started on July 10, and was composed of Jesuit priests and lay brothers. They embarked at Kenora, or Rat Portage, in an autoboat of their own construction. With absolute trust in Divine Providence and serious doubts about the boat, they started out on the lake, singing the *Ave Maris Stella*. At two o'clock in the afternoon they arrived at American Point, down at the entrance of the lake. The next morning they began investigations, as usual, along the north shore, but several hours' search ended in complete failure. Providence, however, came to their rescue by an accident. Father Paquin had cut his foot very badly the night before while driving tent pegs, thus rendering him unfit for work. He did not sulk in his tent, however, but while nursing his foot occupied himself meditating on de la Vérendrye's memoirs, and studying the maps and notes, which he had gone over a hundred times before. The vague hints of the old Indian with the unpronounceable name also came back to him with unwonted force, and it then suddenly flashed on his mind that they had all along been following the wrong scent. The fort, he felt sure, was on the south, and not on the north, shore. Accepting his suggestion, the searchers, the next day, traveled two miles up the inlet in the direction indicated, and arrived at a bay which the old chief had spoken of. There, stretching out in a long line, each man being responsible for five feet on either side of him, and meantime making a wide clearing through tangled brushwood, and fighting the dense swarms of mosquitoes, which were as thirsty as Sioux for white blood, they were all suddenly summoned by a cry to the side of one of the party.

He had come upon a number of flat stones carefully laid upon each other. The spades were quickly at work, and the great discovery was made. They had struck the large chimney of the fort, without a doubt. Digging deeper, they unearthed, among other things, a carpenter's chisel about eighteen inches long and covered with rust. The next day was Sunday, but on Monday, the thirteenth, they uncovered a heap of bones. Among them were scissors, nails, etc., and a blade of a knife, with a name on it, "Alice D." By Tuesday they had found the two other chimneys of the fort, after seventy poplar trees had been felled to clear the ground. The next day it rained, but by Thursday night three lines of palisades had been laid bare.

The joy of the explorers was now at fever heat, but the time for their annual retreat had arrived, and they all had to pack off to St. Boniface for their eight days' seclusion. Why did they not make their retreat there? The reason was that they had brought only ten days' provisions, and even holy men must eat. But when the retreat was over they returned to their work with renewed energy.

With them was a distinguished historiographer of the locality, M. Prud'homme, who had been working for years at the problem. Before two weeks had passed they had turned up nineteen skulls. De la Vérendrye's account was startlingly verified. In addition they found five bodies, two of which were in a box, side by side; one with the *os sacrum* broken slantingly, precisely as the wound of young de la Vérendrye had been described one hundred and sixty years ago. At the feet of the other skeleton were beads of a rosary and a bunch of keys. Between the two was a cutlass. Both bodies were headless. There could be but little doubt that the Jesuits of 1908 had found their brother, who was murdered in 1736.

With the greatest reverence all these precious relics were transported to the College of St. Boniface. Photographs of everything were taken. The picture of the skulls represents them just as they were found, viz., carefully placed in layers, one above the other. It is unnecessary to reproduce them, but the base of one may be given as a curiosity. It shows an arrowhead still imbedded in the bone. It is curious, indeed, but may it not be something more? Garneau, quoting Bourassa, says that " Father Aulneau was struck by an arrow in the head." May not this skull, so singularly marked, be the head of the priest?

Such was the sudden and unexpected result of a search taken up, at intervals, during nearly twenty years. It is a discovery of the greatest interest to the students of the history of the Church in this country, for it tells us exactly where one of the great missionaries who had gone furthest into the interior of the country, was killed, and where he was buried. Of course, there is no desire to claim that he was a martyr of the Faith; for hatred of Christianity does not enter into the cause of his death. He was, however, a great confessor and apostle, and as such should be honored and revered.

Independently of religious considerations, the discovery of the site of Fort St. Charles is also a notable achievement in historical exploration work. It has revealed the line of de la Vérendrye's discoveries.

It will be a satisfaction to Americans to know that the United States Government has recently made the place a National Park. The Canadians, however, have the better place, namely, the island where the heroes were murdered. They also can claim the honor of having discovered both sites, and to have given us one.

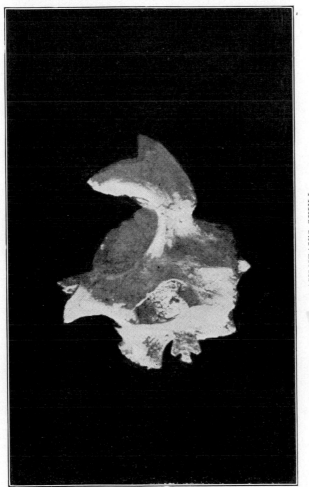

AULNEAU'S SKULL.

SEBASTIAN RALE

CHAPTER I.

WITH THE OTTAWAS

On the banks of the Kennebec, about thirty miles above Augusta, there is a secluded and beautiful spot which is without doubt the most sacred place in New England. It is called Indian Old Point. To reach it you follow your guide along narrow and winding paths in the dense woods, and when at last you emerge into the open you see before you a perfectly level and treeless stretch of twenty or thirty acres extending from north to south along the river. You are on the site of the old Abnakis village of Narantsouac, or "the place of those who travel by water," and you notice that here and there the soil has been dug up by people who have come to hunt for Indian relics.

As you enter the plain from the north you have the river on your right, while deep forests on the three other sides shut it in completely from the outer world, as if to make it a sanctuary. A decaying farmhouse in the distance is the only sign of human occupation in the past, and the stunted pine woods on the opposite bank, whither the Indians once fled to escape the murderous fire of their foes, are apparently unfrequented by any living creature. All is still, and only the splash of water on the rocks or the occasional rumble of a distant train, disturbs the silence. As you look towards the further extremity you are almost startled to see, though you knew it was there, a shaft of grey stone, surmounted by a cross, outlined against the background of the trees, and standing as the lone watcher in the solitude. With feelings of awe you approach the monument, which bears the marks of many a rude northern winter. It is slightly out of perpendicular, and the cement has fallen from the seams where the obelisk rests upon the base, and also from the stones of the base itself, on which there is an inscription still legible, if you stand where the sun may help you to decipher the letters. It is written in Latin and tells us that reposing beneath the monument lies:

"The Reverend Sebastian Râle, a Frenchman by birth, and a missionary of the Society of Jesus, who after evangelizing the Hurons and Illinois, became the apostle of the Abnakis, keeping them for thirty-four years in the faith and love of Christ. Unterrified by the perils of war, and often testifying his readiness to give his life for his flock, he died the best of shepherds, on this very spot, amid the slaughter of his people of Narantsouac, on the 23d of August, 1724. To him and to his children in Christ, who died along with him, Benedict Joseph Fenwick, Bishop of Boston, built and dedicated this monument August 23d, 1833. A. M. D. G."

The mind of New England has passed through three stages in its appreciation of Father Râle. It was first under the spell of the extravagant ideas expressed in the poem of "Mogg Megone," by Whittier, who represents the great missionary as the malignant Jesuit plotting to establish "Romish" domination in the New World, and to attain that end, availing himself of the most degraded and fiendish passions of the savages. Râle, according to him, was the son of Belial, and was very justly slain by the outraged and virtuous Puritans. In after life Whittier considered "Mogg Megone" as one of the sins of his youth.

Converse Francis, the Unitarian Minister, who wrote a "Life of Father Râle" for Jared Sparks' "American Biography," is fairly typical of another and more liberal view. Though not intentionally unfair, Francis cannot entirely divest himself of all the prejudices of his class, and whenever there is question of veracity, even though Râle may have been an eye-witness of the event, he is set aside, and others, whose testimony is necessarily biased, or who were not even present at the occurrences in dispute, are preferred. Unfortunately also, being a Unitarian, Francis could not sympathize with, or even comprehend, the motives which actuated the subject of his sketch.

At the present time there is a saner and more rational view taken by historians of the character of the great apostle of the Kennebec Indians, and there is even a tendency to accord him all the honor which his heroic life deserved.

Sebastian Râle was born on January 4, 1657, in the little town of Portalier, which is situated on the Doubs, a tributary of the Saône. Portalier appears in history as early as the fifth century, and in the course of time it passed successively under the domination of the Saracens, Hungarians, and Germans. It is now a well-laid-out city of eight thousand inhabitants, with its hospital, municipal buildings, public library; and the college, where, long ago, Râle went to school, is still there. He made his whole course of classical studies and then two years of philosophy. The Jesuits had a novitiate at Portalier, and the boy sought admission to it at the age of eighteen. From there he went to Carpentras and Nimes, where he taught the usual classes of grammar, humanities, and rhetoric. In both of these cities he devoted all his leisure time to the spiritual needs of the laboring people. He began his theology at Lyons, and before he was ordained a priest he was Director of the Sodality of Laborers and Porters. Those who saw how devoted he was to his work were not surprised when the news came that he had asked for the Indian missions.

He left La Rochelle on July 23, 1689, and after three months of what he calls " a sufficiently happy voyage," arrived at Quebec; but as he needed very little to make him " sufficiently happy " in any surroundings, we have no means of knowing how unkindly the ocean treated him.

Though remarkably gifted as a linguist, and very readily acquiring a knowledge of a number of words and phrases, he soon saw that he could never grasp the meanings attached to certain turns of expression and tones of voice, unless by daily contact with the savages; so he betook himself to a Christian village about nine miles away, on the other side of the river, somewhere in the vicinity of the Chaudière.

The difficulty did not, however, immediately disappear. Among other troubles he tells us that the gutturals formed his chief obstacle. They were uttered without the slightest movement of the lips, and, though he sometimes caught the sound, he more frequently succeeded with only half of it, to the great amusement of the Indians. However, at the end of four months, he could express himself with tolerable accuracy, and then with the assistance of five or six of the most intelligent savages, he constructed a grammar and a catechism. We are not aware that these valuable books are extant at present.

Years afterwards, when he was master of many tongues, he wrote that the Indian modes of speech contained much genuine linguistic beauty, and were particularly remarkable for strength of expression. They had no affinity with any European language that he was acquainted with, and it was hard to trace any relationship even with the speech of the other tribes. To illustrate this he gives us in a letter to his brother the first verse of the *O Salutaris Hostia,* in Algonquin, Huron, Abnakis and Illinois. To the ordinary observer there is not a word common between them.

He is at one with other scholars in regarding Huron as the most majestic of all the Indian languages, but at the same time as being the most difficult, not merely because of the gutturals, but because of the multiplicity of the accents which give a totally different meaning to the same word. He recommends Chaumonot's Grammar as the most helpful for beginners, but adds the very discouraging information, that even with its assistance, ten years of unremitting labor will be needed to speak it with elegance. Once acquired, however, it will be easy to learn the five cognate Iroquois tongues. It will be a surprise to most people to hear that there could be anything like elegance in the language of the savages.

The Indians with whom he resided at the Chaudière quite captivated him. They were all Christians, and lived in a well laid-out stockaded village. They were decently clad, and he notes that they showed a passion for red and blue in their apparel. They were attached to their children, but all, even the girls, were deplorably addicted to tobacco, and would give their own weight in gold for a supply of the weed. The men were sturdy, agile, bronzed, and beardless. Their hair was straight and black. Their teeth were white as ivory. They decked their locks with strings of many colored shells and pebbles, which fell over their ears and down the back of their heads. Similar bands did service as belts, collars, and garters; all of them were decorations as precious to the savage as gold and jewels to the European.

As elsewhere, the women were the workers. Their lords and masters waged war, or tracked the wild beast in the forest. He tells us how they hunted the moose in those days and from all accounts the same methods still obtain. The hunter set out on snow-shoes, and when the huge beast was wearied with plunging in the drifts, his pursuer approached with a knife fastened to the end of a stick and despatched him. How much fighting occurred at that moment is not said. We have also a glimpse of the table manners of his friends. The etiquette was at first too much for him and he merited a reproof for his weakness. To have a lump of half-raw meat dragged from the pot and passed around for each one to bite, was something he was not used to, and he hesitated when his turn came. The Indians reproached him and said bluntly: "You are a patriarch, and you pray. You must overcome yourself." He accepted the advice, and from that out never balked at the foulest mouthfuls.

He had lived nearly two years in the village when he received orders from Quebec to prepare himself for the Illinois mission. He immediately returned to Quebec, and began the study of the new language which he should henceforth have to employ in the far west. On the thirteenth of August he was in his canoe, making for the country of the Illinois which, on account of the way he had to travel was eight hundred, but Martin says this is a copyist's error for five hundred leagues away. He saw the great lakes for the first time, but apparently made no attempt to cross them, for he writes: "We landed each night and were happy to find a flat rock on which to stretch our limbs." On the way up, some of the canoes were shattered in the rapids; but though his own struck the rocks again and again, no harm resulted. It had been supposed that game would be found as they journeyed on, but none was met with, and the travellers were reduced to such a state of hunger that they had to resort to the *tripes de roches*, a sort of lichen, which was made into a stew or roast. Râle, who by that time was a connoisseur in Indian delicacies, pronounced it "disgusting."

When they reached Lake Huron, a storm scattered the boats. That meant death for some of the travellers; for starving as they were, there was now no hope of reaching Mackinac. Fortunately Râle was able to keep on his course. "I reached the fort," he said, "ahead of the others, and sent provisions back to them. They had been seven days without food, except for a cow which they had killed more by accident than skill. They were so weak that they could not stand up."

At Mackinac he found two missionaries; one in charge of the Ottawas; the other of the Hurons, and he remained with them, for the season was too far advanced to attempt to reach the Illinois. Fortunately the delay has to some extent helped our knowledge of the Ottawas. He tells us they were grossly superstitious, and firm believers in their medicine men, who were nothing but charlatans. The manitou superstition prevailed there, as elsewhere, with the usual sacrifice of tobacco, pots, etc., which were thrown into the water to insure protection against the rapids, or to insure a prosperous hunt. The nation was composed of three families, the chief of which was descended from The Great Hare. The Hare was a giant so tall that when in former times he entered the lake to gather his nets, which were eighteen fathoms down, the water came only to his armpits. In the time of the deluge, he is said to have sent out a beaver to find land, but the beaver never returned. Then the otter was dispatched on the same errand, and soon appeared with a clod of earth covered with foam. After a while the clod expanded into an island and then began to extend in all directions. Having done this much, the Great Hare took his flight to heaven, but before doing so ordered his descendants always to burn their dead; otherwise their country would be covered with snow and ice.

Shortly before Râle's arrival a cunning old squaw availed herself of the popular delusion to increase her reputation. The winter had been exceptionally hard, and the starving family of The Great Hare were in consternation. "It serves you right," said the prophetess. "You have no sense. You know you were told to burn your dead, and to throw their ashes to the wind, and yet there is a body here for several days, and you have not burned it." "Mother!" they said; "you speak the truth;" and forthwith twenty-five men were deputed to perform the sacred duty. They took fifteen days to accomplish the task, but by that time the thaw had set in, game was available and the old woman's name was forever after in veneration.

The second Ottawa group claimed an accommodating carp as their parent. It had spawned on the banks of the river, when lo! a ray of sunlight fell on the eggs, and produced a woman, who became the mother of the tribe.

The third family sprang from the paw of a bear. The

genesis was not explained, but the persuasion of its truth was so profound that when they killed a bear, accidentally or otherwise, they were profuse in their apologies to the carcass, reminding the animal that it was a glorious thing to be eaten by one's children, who otherwise might have starved to death.

The Great Hares had the monopoly of cremation. The others buried the corpse, and followed the common practice of filling the grave with everything that might be useful to the warrior when he arrived at the happy hunting grounds. While the interment was in progress the relatives kept up a lugubrious chant, and with measured strokes waved the ceremonial sticks in the air. On them were hung little bundles of rattles to increase the expression of grief.

At the opening of spring, Râle started for the Illinois Country. It took him forty days to reach the Illinois River, and then he had to travel fifty leagues before he arrived at the first village. It consisted of three hundred cabins, all of them with four or five fires, that is to say, with eight or ten families in each. There were ten other such villages belonging to the nation. On his way he had met the Maskatings, the Takis, the Omikones, the Tripegonons, the Outogamis, etc. They all had their own language, but in other respects were like the Ottawas. A missionary from Baie des Puants, or Green Bay, looked after their spiritual interests.

On the day after his arrival, a great chief paid him a formal visit to invite him to a banquet which had been prepared to do him honor. It was a very splendid affair, and as several dogs had been sacrificed for the occasion, it was regarded as a feast of the upper set. The usual flow of oratory was let loose, and when the long discourses were over, esquires ("ecuyers," Râle calls them), were sent around with the meats, one bark dish being assigned to every two guests. Fortunately for the missionary, they were not, as in the east, compelled to eat everything, but could carry off the remnants to their lodges. He tells us that the Illinois were not as reserved as the men of the east. They went naked, from the waist up, but atoned for their absence of garments by all sorts of fanciful tattoos. At church, however, and in winter they put on their furs. Plumes of various colors adorned their heads, and they daubed their faces chiefly with vermilion, though other colors were permitted. They wore collars and earrings of cut stones, of various shades, and usually displayed a porcelain breastplate. They were convinced that all this finery added to their beauty, and exacted proper respect from those they dealt with.

When not fighting or hunting, they were gambling, or dancing, or eating. The dances were chiefly for joy or sorrow. The latter were mostly funeral rites, and lasted as long as the provisions held out, or the character of the presents to the afflicted family seemed to demand. Any one could join in these ceremonies who came bearing gifts. But it does not seem to have been the case with the dances of rejoicing. They were select affairs; for, as among civilized people, there were class distinctions among the Indians. Unlike the Great Ottawas, they did not burn the dead, but wrapped them in skins and hung them by the head and feet to the branches. The men made arrows, bows, calumets, and the like, while the squaws did the tilling, tanning, and net-making, and provided the food supplies of the wigwam. When a brave shot a bear or a deer, he left it where it fell, perhaps miles away from the village, and the squaws had to go and find it, and bring it home and skin and dismember it.

Of all the Indian tribes none lived in greater plenty than the Illinois. Their rivers were swarming with wild ducks, swan, and the like. Great droves of turkeys roamed over the plains, some of the birds being thirty or thirty-six pounds weight. Bisons covered the prairies, as far as the eye could see, and were slaughtered by the thousand every year. Râle found the meat somewhat salty, but so light that even when eaten raw no bad consequences ensued. Only the fat ones were taken; the lean kind were left to rot, the savage contenting himself merely with the tongue.

Firearms had not yet been introduced to any great extent. The arrow, which he says was shaped like a serpent's tongue, was their great instrument for hunting and warfare. The accuracy and rapidity of their aim was marvelous. A hundred arrows would leave the bow while a European was loading his gun. They concerned themselves very little about fish-nets. The abundance of fish made it unnecessary, but occasionally, when fancy prompted, they went out in their canoes, and standing up for better aim, darted a spear at the fish and rarely missed their aim.

As elsewhere, the savage was esteemed only for his prowess as a hunter or warrior. To kill a man, or make a captive, they would travel as much as four hundred leagues at a time, in spite of the danger that met them everywhere, and the starvation that faced them, especially when they neared the enemy's country. There they could not hunt; for if they missed the beast, or only wounded it, the lost arrow would betray them. Scalps were certificates of martial greatness, but more valuable were the captives who were brought in alive.

They tortured their victims, but Râle attributes the particularly fiendish methods employed, such as eating the flesh and rubbing powder into the wounds and then setting it on fire, to the teaching of the Iroquois. The practice of resuscitating the dead by giving a captive to a household which had lost one of its inmates, was in vogue, as in the east.

We sometimes hear of Eliot's converts in Massachusetts as "The praying Indians." The same word was in use among the Catholics. They were not said to have embraced Christianity, but "the prayer." All were eager to hear about "the prayer," but their polygamy and licentiousness prevented them from embracing it. The Illinois Christians went morning and night to the chapel, and even the medicine men sent their children to be instructed and baptized. Of course, the missionaries gladly availed themselves of this opportunity, especially as many of those children were almost sure to die after a few years. Their mothers had no idea of how to take care of them. The remoteness of the Illinois from civilization fortunately preserved them from fire-water, which in the east was almost as much as impurity an obstacle in spreading the Faith.

CHAPTER II

INDIAN WARS

The journeys undertaken by those heroic old missionaries were amazing, and Râle had his share of such trips. He had been two years among the Illinois when he received orders to return to his Abnakis in Maine. He was in his canoe immediately, paddling back over the same route that he had traversed such a short time before. He says nothing about the hardships of the journey. It was merely a repetition of what he had already suffered, but he eagerly tells us that by a special providence he found a poor Indian girl, about sixteen years of age, who was dying near a French settlement about one hundred and twenty miles above Quebec. As a matter of geographical detail it is of interest to know that there were already twenty-five French families there, with a resident parish priest; but he does not give us the name of the settlement.

Unfortunately the priest of the place could not speak the language of the sufferer, and hence on Râle's arrival they both made haste to visit her. A few questions brought out the fact that she had been thoroughly instructed in the Faith by some missionary, but for some reason or other had not been baptized. "Do not let me die without baptism," she begged very piteously. Râle assented, and appointed the following day for the ceremony. To his amazement, early next morning the sick girl walked into the chapel. Her joy had given her superhuman strength, and she would not let a moment of the day pass before baptism was given her. She returned to her miserable cabin after the ceremony, and two days afterwards Râle knelt at her side, as her soul took its flight to heaven.

We do not know the exact date of his arrival at Quebec,

but Gilmary Shea tells us that during his brief stay there he put his hand to the incomplete autobiography of Father Chaumonot. Indeed the manuscript is in Râle's handwriting. Shea adds that this precious document is, at present, in the archives of St. Mary's College, Montreal, but a long and careful search has failed to discover it.

In 1693 Râle again found himself among his beloved Abnakis. With the exception of a hurried visit to France in 1700, of which we know nothing beyond the fact that he went there, the next thirty years were passed on the banks of the Kennebec at Narantsouac. Every moment of that time was a preparation for its tragic end.

The Indians were all Catholics, and most devoted to their faith. Every one assisted at Mass in the morning, and eagerly listened to the instruction that followed. They would have done so, in any case, but Râle had a remarkable power in fixing their attention, the old people showing as much pleasure as the children in answering the questions that were proposed. After Mass, up to midday, his house was crowded with applicants for advice on every conceivable subject, temporal as well as spiritual. The afternoon was given to the sick, or in assisting at the interminable councils of the Indians, to determine questions of public policy.

He had scarcely time to attend to his own spiritual duties, and after a while was compelled to forbid them to speak to him from night-prayers until after Mass next morning, except for some very urgent reason. Being handy at tools, and somewhat of a painter, he devoted himself to making his chapel as beautiful as possible. The structure he found there on his arrival, and which was burned in 1705, was "the rude, unshapely" thing that Whittier speaks of, "built in those wilds by unskillful hands." The one that replaced it, he used to tell his friend, was very beautiful and they would be proud of it in Europe. He was plentifully supplied with means by helpers in France for that purpose.

At the services the altar was a blaze of light, for he found means of making wax from the bay-berry. Twenty-four pounds of wax obtained by boiling the berry was sufficient to make a hundred candles a foot long. They may not have been strictly in accord with the requirements of the ritual, but bees were not busy in those parts at that time. He had trained forty altar boys for the service of the sanctuary, and also to give splendor to the procession through the woods and village streets, on the great festivals. He called his acolytes "the junior clergy"—an expression which Francis takes seriously. Besides the village church, there were two other chapels, about three hundred feet from the village, one dedicated to the Blessed Virgin, the other to the Guardian Angel. They were placed on the paths that led to the fields and the woods. The women took great pride in adorning them.

Besides these permanent chapels other temporary ones were erected for the conveniences of the tribe when out hunting and fishing. Such expeditions occurred at least twice every year. First, after planting and hoeing their corn, they all went down to the mouth of a river to fish for herrings, which were found there in great numbers. In fact had there been means at hand, he says, 50,000 barrels might have been filled with the catch. But the poor Indians could only dry a certain number, and they spent eight or ten days at that work. This stock had to support the village till they gathered the corn, and with that they tided over the intervening period until winter. Then they went down again to the sea, and gathered an abundance of shell fish, and shot the wild fowl and game which were there in abundance. Their own immediate territory had, long before, been exhausted by the thoughtless slaughter of all the bears and moose of the place.

When they arrived at the hunting grounds the first thing they did was to select an island and build a chapel. The priest was always with them, his attendance being in-

variably requested at a solemn council held for that purpose. He brought his chalice and vestments and all the
services were as carefully carried out as they would have
been in the village. It was on one of these journeys that
he was seriously injured. He fell on the ice, and fractured
his thigh and leg, and had to be carried to Quebec to have
his injury attended to, for there were no surgeons at Narantsouac. On that terrible fifteen days' journey, he suffered
excruciating torture while being carried through the woods,
and over the lakes and rivers, and by the time he reached
the St. Lawrence the bones had knitted, and had to be
broken again. He underwent that operation, of course without anesthetics, but gave no sign of the agony it caused him.
"Groan, at least, Father," said the physician; "it will give
you some relief."

During the thirty years he remained at Narantsouac his
food was nothing but corn sweetened with a little of the
maple sugar, which the squaws obtained from the trees—an
item of his table *menu*, by the way, which is useful in the
history of maple sugar making, for it shows us that the art
was not discovered by the whites, but was already known
to the red men. Indeed even to-day, the process seems savage enough, for the same kind of bark receptacles for the
sap are employed which the old Abnakis squaws had invented.

The holy anchoret never drank wine, even on his visits
to Quebec. He washed and mended his miserable garments,
and looked after his little garden to obtain his needed supply of corn. His religious exercises were performed with
the same regularity as if he had been living in some great
establishment of the Society, and every year the first week
of Lent found him entering Quebec to begin his annual retreat. That time was sacred for him. He would never put
it off, for any consideration. "Otherwise," he used to say,
"I might neglect it altogether," a disaster which only
he himself could have apprehended. At every spare mo-

ment that he would get in his daily work he was working at his Abnakis Dictionary, or writing spiritual works in the native language, to read to his neophytes. Only a very few hours in the night did he give to his needed rest.

Such a life might seem ideal for a heroic missionary like Râle; but in that village on the Kennebec other scenes were occurring that filled him with horror and dismay. Over and over again his Abnakis, who were terrible fighters, came back from the warpath stained with English blood, and carrying reeking scalps at their belts. But after all, they were fighting for their country. The English claimed that side of the Kennebec and the Abnakis said they were defending their homes.

Here the tragic part of Râle's life begins, and we must cast a glance at this protracted struggle between the English and the Abnakis in order to vindicate him from the charge which almost every English author lays at his door, of being the chief instigator of these bloody reprisals.

As a matter of fact, the war with New England was already in progress when he arrived at Narantsouac. It was known as King William's war, which begun in 1688, and lasted until 1698. It was the *"decennium luctuosum,"* or "doleful decade," as old Cotton Mather described it. Hence it was in full swing before Râle had left France, for it was not until 1689 that he sailed out of the port of Rochelle. Indeed he had to make the long journey to the Illinois country in the very midst of that terrible strife, and at the risk of meeting the fierce Iroquois, who were allies of the English. That war was surely not of his making.

These bloody battles in America were only repetitions, on a small scale, of what was going on simultaneously in Europe in the fight of the allied powers against the ambition of Louis XIV. William of Orange, Tourville, Noailles, Vendome, Catinat and Luxembourg were all on the warpath, and were covering Europe with blood from Spain to the Netherlands. It was not until the treaty of Ryswick had been signed in 1698 that these European Indians buried the hatchet.

During that period the Iroquois had perpetrated the horrible massacre at Lachine in 1689; Le Moyne d'Iberville had fought his heroic fight among the icebergs of Hudson Bay, and lowered the English colors at Pemquid on the sea coast. In 1690 Frontenac had made his triple raid on Schenectady, Salmon Falls, and Casco, and the English colonists had attempted a counter invasion of Canada, by land and sea; Cadillac also was fighting at Detroit. The part the Abnakis took in the fray was relatively inconsiderable; and, moreover, they had withdrawn from the struggle before the others; for in 1693, the year of Râle's arrival, they made a treaty of their own with their English neighbors. "All the charms of the French friar, then resident among them [Râle] could not prevent them," says Cotton Mather, "from suing to the English for peace."

Unfortunately the peace was broken in the following year. The rupture was, of course, ascribed to the recovered "charms of the French friar," and it may not be out of place to remark that the "charms" here referred to may not have been in Mather's mind mere graciousness of manner, but a diabolical influence. The old New England divine, who was a firm believer in Salem witchcraft, was quite convinced that the devil had his hand in the troubles between the English and the Indians, though the explanation of the strife was much simpler and more mundane. The English at Pemquid had seized Chief Bomaseen and sent him to Boston as a prisoner. That was sufficient to enkindle the wrath of the savages for they remembered how, seventeen years before, one hundred and fifty of their people had been captured, in the same treacherous fashion, and sold into slavery at Boston. War was therefore begun not by the devil but by the English.

Unfortunately Bomaseen had helped the delusion in Boston about the priests. The popular conviction was, according to Francis, that "Frontenac had four special Jesuit agents to stir up the Indians; namely, Thury, the two Bigots, and Sebastian Râle." It mattered little that Thury was not a Jesuit at all. Râle was, and that was sufficient; and Cotton Mather specifically names him as "instigating the Indians against their own inclinations." Probably to make his chains rest easier on his limbs, Bomaseen assured the magnates of the Massachusetts Colony that they were correct in their assertions. He told them, and they were delighted to hear it, that the French priests had taught them that the Blessed Virgin was a Frenchwoman, and that the English had murdered Christ, who, on ascending into heaven had said that his favor could be gained only by unceasing war against the English.

As the good people of Boston were convinced that the captive, Bomaseen, was far gone in these errors, they determined to enlighten and convert him. "Hence," says Francis, "a minister, availing himself of such a symbolical mode of instruction as he supposed would best suit the savage mind, took a tankard of drink standing on the table and told the Indian that Jesus Christ gave us a good religion, like the good liquor in the tankard, but that the French had wickedly poured poison into the good liquor." Bomaseen was conquered. Lifting his eyes and hands to heaven, he declared for the real article. What was in the tankard is not specified; but Bomaseen was ultimately released. The miserable deceiver, however, was not really converted. For, years afterwards, we find him giving up his life to defend Father Râle. His bones rest at the side of the martyr today, under the cross at Narantsouac.

As four other Indians had already been seized in the same manner at Saco, and four more at Pemquid, though the latter had presented themselves under a flag of truce, which John Pike, an officer of the garrison disrespectfully describes as "a white rag," the natives had sufficient reason to dig up the hatchet and keep it raised until the general treaty of 1798. During that time, it was, of course, impossible for the missionary to restrain them, and one cannot refrain from smiling at the affected horror of Bancroft when he says that "before setting out on the warpath, the braves went to confession, and prayers were said every day in the village for their success in battle."

But, after the peace of 1798, though the Indians along the Kennebec accepted the treaty like the rest, they were always discontented, for their land was being rapidly invaded by English settlers. Matters were drawing to a crisis when Governor Dudley summoned them to a conference. It took place at Casco in 1703.

At the request of his Indians, Râle was present, but kept in the background. Dudley noticed him, however, and approached to speak to him, but the red men immediately formed in a body around the priest. They were apprehensive of treachery, for three years before that, the General Court of Massachusetts had passed a law, making it death for "a popish priest to persist in remaining on New England soil," and similar legislation had been forced through the unwilling Assembly of New York, by the bitter Orangeman, Governor Bellomont. Indeed, the New York decree was worse than that of New England, for whereas the latter inflicted death for persistency in remaining, New York had determined to hang any priest who would voluntarily enter the Province, which Smith, in his "History of New York" (p. 160), says, without any regard for the feelings of the clergy, "is a law that ought forever to continue in force." To which Bancroft, who is generally credited with kindness of heart, subjoins (III, 193): "This is a commentary of a historian wholly unconscious of the true nature of his remark." And yet we look benignly on Bancroft.

Whether or not Dudley intended to seize the priest on that occasion, we do not know. In any case it would have been very unwise for him to have attempted it, so he contented himself with merely urging Râle to use his influence in keeping the peace, to which Râle answered: "My religion and my priesthood both counsel me to do so." But when Dudley urged the Indians to break with the French they cried out: "No! the French have always treated us well. If you lift the hatchet against them we shall lift ours against you, and hasten to strike." The Governor returned to Boston disappointed.

Penhallow, who was not present on this occasion, gives quite another account of what occurred, and informs his readers that the Indians had intended to turn the friendly conference into a massacre. He makes no mention of the presence of Râle. "Nevertheless," says Converse Francis, "Penhallow's account is more credible." Why it should be so, the historian does not state. The rejection of Râle's testimony in this off-hand fashion is certainly a reflection on his honesty. For, although he wrote his account twenty years later, he could not have forgotten the details of such an important event, and there can be little doubt, moreover, that the report which he then sent to France was only a transcript of his notes made in 1703.

This conference was evidently convoked because Dudley expected a renewal of hostilities. As a matter of fact war had already begun, and another "dolorous decade" had been inaugurated. Marlborough, and Eugene, and Villars, and Berwick were in the field in Europe, and when the news arrived in America the Indians willingly went out on the warpath. "Within six weeks," says Bancroft, "the whole country, from Casco to Wells, was in a conflagration. On one and the same day several parties of Indians and French burst upon every house or garrison in that region." It was at this time that Deerfield was destroyed and its inhabitants massacred. "Such cruelties," continues the historian, "inspired our fathers with a deep hatred of the French missionaries." It was unjust, however, to accuse the missionaries with having caused the uprising. However, it was impossible to convince the New Englanders of the contrary, especially after two hundred and fifty braves had set out from Narantsouac in their war paint. "I counseled them," writes Râle, "to observe carefully all the laws of war, to practice no cruelty, to kill no one except in the heat of battle, and to treat their enemies humanely." That he was so considerate would, of course, never be credited, and, indeed, Converse Francis informs us that Râle "recounts with an air of triumph the service which these two hundred and fifty warriors rendered in the work of desolation among the English settlements, and that when they finally returned to their village each man had two canoes loaded with the plunder they had taken."

Such an account was indeed found in Râle's letter to his brother, but it was written long after, and the unprejudiced will, with difficulty, discover "any air of triumph" in the narration. Perhaps, after all, Converse Francis was not sufficiently conversant with French, for we find him making a very curious mistake when describing the tragedy of Râle's death. The French text has it *"il fut enterré à la même place ou il avait celebré la Messe la veille."* Francis reads this: "He was buried in the same place where he had celebrated Mass the *evening before*," which is not only a linguistic, but an ecclesiastical, blunder. For a minister, at least, the latter mistake is unpardonable.

That it was chiefly Râle who kept the Abnakis faithful to the French was, of course, true, and that was a sufficient reason for the authorities of Boston to determine to capture him. Hence, "in the winter of 1705, when the snow lay four feet deep on the ground, and the whole country was like a frozen lake, Captain Hilton, a man of some distinction, was sent, with two hundred and seventy men, with provisions for twenty days, to Norridgewock, with the intention of surprising the enemy in their headquarters. The dreary and severe march on snowshoes was accomplished with much spirit. But the expedition failed of the main object. When the party reached the place they found only a deserted settlement. The large chapel, and the vestry at the end of it, and the wigwams, they burned to the ground." The invaders then withdrew, leaving the fugitives, wherever they were, to camp out in the snow. Râle's account of this devastation is merely that it was " a sudden irruption by the English when the Indians were absent from the village." Very likely he means the fighting population. The women were probably hiding in the woods.

The war went on, and three years later Haverhill, which Charlevoix spells " Heiveruil," was destroyed; not, however, by the Abnakis, but by other Algonquins and the French. Port Royal, after being gallantly defended by Subercase, fell into the hands of the English in 1710, and in the following year Sir Hoveden Walker sailed up the St. Lawrence with a fleet to capture Quebec; but, though it was the month of August, he was afraid that the St. Lawrence, whose depth he fancied was at least a hundred fathoms, would freeze solid under his hulls, and so he returned exultingly to Boston without even having seen Quebec. Eight of his ships had run ashore far down the river, but he regarded the mishap as providential, as he had saved the rest by returning home.

Thus the war continued with alternate triumphs and defeats, on both sides of the Atlantic, and finally the fighters, both in Europe and America, laid down their arms and the treaty of Utrecht was signed.

Unfortunately the treaty failed to determine the limits of the English and the French possessions and the unrest and discontent continued. To prevent a new outbreak, Dudley again invited the Indians to a conference. The meeting took place at Portsmouth on July 11, and Penhallow declares that " a treaty was made, in virtue of which the English were to quietly and peacefully enter upon, improve and forever enjoy all properties and possessions within the eastern parts of the province of Massachusetts Bay and New Hampshire, and be in no wise molested therein, saving unto

the Indians their own ground and free liberty of hunting,
fishing, fowling, and all other lawful liberties and privilege."
The historian adds that " the Indians confessed that they
had been unfaithful to their previous engagement, and then
eight sachems affixed their marks to the document."

Râle's account contradicts that of Penhallow. He says
that the Governor informed the Indians that the King of
France had given the territory to the English; whereupon
the Indians replied that he had no right to give what did
not belong to him; the land was theirs; and they immediately sent a deputation to Quebec to inquire if any such
transfer had been made. The answer was in the negative.
But as the Abnakis were weary of war, they went no farther than to protest.

CHAPTER III

Raids on Narantsouac

After the war the Abnakis set themselves to repair the village, and their first care was to build their church. To accomplish that as soon as possible they applied for workmen from Boston. The request was eagerly acceded to; and the Governor volunteered to build the church for them, provided they sent away Râle and accepted a Protestant minister. The proposal was received with contempt, and by means of some help from Quebec the new church was erected. In a letter to his brother, Râle says "it would have been admired even in Europe."

The building of the church aroused the fury of the New Englanders. It was an invasion of their territory, and had been done in a particularly offensive manner. It was also to stand as a reminder that they had burned the one that stood there. Angry protests were made against allowing it; and at last, yielding to the popular clamor, Dudley sent two hundred men to overawe the Indians. He would have succeeded but for the presence of Râle. Indeed, but for him the Abnakis from that day would have been subjects of Queen Anne, religiously as well as politically.

When "great Anna" departed this life she left her earthly kingdoms to the good German, George I, and his dealing with his colonists, through his deputies, furnishes the first chapter in Râle's life in which we are permitted to smile.

The new Governor was named Shute, who in order to follow in the footsteps of his predecessors summoned an Indian council. The place of meeting was at Arrowsick, at the mouth of the Kennebec, where a new municipality had been established, and was already called Georgetown, in honor of his Majesty. Thither the red men came in their

288

canoes, and Shute offered them a British flag and a Protestant Bible. The Indians accepted both. They appreciated the flag as an ornament for their boats, but were puzzled about the Bible. Shute explained that the flag represented their allegiance to the crown of Great Britain, and the Bible the new faith which they were to adopt.

The Indians asked for time, and went off to consult Father Râle. On the next day they returned saying that they accepted the flag, for they had no objection to submit to King George, provided he guaranteed them their rights; but they objected to the change of religion. " Every one," said they, " loved their ministers, and it would be strange if we also should not love those who come from God. Hence we must return the Bibles, as God has given us teaching already, and if we should desert that we should displease God."

There is a very important point in this reply which throws light on Râle's attitude in dealing with the Indians. He was not a rabid Frenchman, determined to keep his Indians devoted to France, at any cost. His purpose was to save their souls. He accepted the English flag, and he did not speak unkindly of the ministers, though he was well aware that they were the chief fomenters of the trouble.

Shute seems to have dropped the subject of religion, for the moment, and addressed himself to that of the land. He produced a deed signed by six Indian Sagamos, making over the whole territory to Richard Walton; but the Indians protested they had never heard of it. They were willing to say nothing of the west bank of the Kennebec, but the eastern one was theirs. The dispute became very hot, and, throwing down the English flag, they tramped back to their own quarters.

In the evening they again presented themselves, with a letter from Râle to the Governor, which stated that when Vaudreueil was in France he had asked the King if such a cession had been made, and was assured that nothing of the kind had been done. Shute read the letter, and denounced it as unworthy of notice. Hutchison says: " He let them know he highly resented the insolence of the Jesuit." Baxter adds a little color by informing us that " he would not buckle to them." Shute then pretended to make for his ship in anger. The Indians, who were easily fooled, and who dreaded another war, ran after him, and in the language of the pompous historian of the day " apologized for their rude carriage of yesterday," and it was finally stipulated that if they would remain at peace " they should be provided with two or three warehouses and a smith to mend their guns." A formal treaty was then made, in which the hope was expressed that " it would prove of mutual and reciprocal benefit advantage to them and to us, and that they should cohabit with us."

Having thus arranged the land question, Shute now set himself to adjust the religious difficulty. He commissioned the Reverend Joseph Baxter " who was said to be of the family of the famous Richard Baxter, as well as a man of distinction in the ministry and in the Colony," to establish an Indian school at Old Town, a village on an island of the Penobscot above Bangor.

The school was indeed begun and a number of letters were exchanged between the minister and the missionary. In these communications not a little of *odium theologicum* is displayed on both sides, particularly by Baxter, who found, after a while, that he could do nothing with his little copper colored scholars. So he went back to Boston and the incident was closed.

Josiah Flynt, to whom Râle had also written in 1720, finds that " Friar Sebastian Râle affords in this instance evidence of excited feeling and resolute defiance, not unmingled with a tone of arrogance." Flynt was irritated by Râle's threat to suspend some of the Indians from the church and he took offense especially at the phrase: " a missionary is not a cipher like a minister, and a Jesuit is not a Baxter nor a Boston minister." That sentiment is put down as evidencing "the braggart dignity of a churchman." His animadversions on the episode are to be found in the "Massachusetts Historical Collection" (2d series Vol. VIII, p. 253). Râle's expostulations do indeed seem to have been written in a somewhat overwrought state of mind, as presented by Flynt, but perhaps the context, if we had it, might convey a different impression.

In the Flynt collection there is reference to a book which Râle declared he was writing for the King's enlightenment, but it has never been produced. He seems to have also communicated with Dudley and Shute. In the reply of the latter the priest is roundly rated for his lack of charity in dealing with his fellow ministers, and then Shute pours out the vials of his wrath against "the spiritual Babylon which is drunk with the blood of the saints and of the martyrs of Jesus. The English could live in amity with the Indians were it not for the instigations of the Popish missionaries." From these writings, and indeed from all the histories of those times, it is evident that Râle was held responsible for all the Indian uprisings, while the English are regarded as guiltless.

As the solemn promise of providing warehouses for the Indians had not been kept the authorities gave permission to some private individual to build a store near the village. The Indians made no objection at first, until another and another storekeeper arrived, and then the red men opened their eyes and saw that they were being quietly dispossessed. Râle had foreseen what was coming and had already exhorted his people to emigrate to Canada, and leave their lands to the English, which is another evidence that he was not actuated by any political, much less by any warlike, purpose. His sole object was to preserve the faith of his neophytes. On the other hand it seemed as if the colonists were deliberately provoking an outbreak by these encroachments. Thus, for instance, on one occasion a party of twenty Indians had gone into an English house to trade or to rest; they suddenly found themselves surrounded by a troop of two hundred men.

The Indians seized their arms, and were about to fight for their lives, but were pacified by being told that the soldiers were a Boston delegation, coming to make amicable arrangements with them. Accepting this assurance as truthful, they commissioned four of their number to go down to Boston to talk to the Governor. On arriving there the envoys were thrown into prison, and when the tribe protested, the answer came back that the four were not prisoners, but hostages, for some damage that had been done, and that they could be redeemed for two hundred pounds of beaver skins. The ransom was sent, though the depredations were denied; but the prisoners were not released.

Thereupon a delegation was sent to Vaudreuil, to ask him if he would help them to drive out the English. The question was embarrassing, for France and England were then at peace; and so the non-committal answer was given that "rather than abandon them to the English he would lead them himself."

Again they asked for a conference with Shute. He appointed the time and place, but failed to appear—a discourtesy which made the Indians both angry and suspicious. Father de la Chasse, Râle's Superior, had come down from Canada with a French officer, and a letter was written by de la Chasse to Shute. It was dated July 21. It was in Latin, Abnakis, and English, and respectfully submitted: First, that the Abnakis did not understand why their deputies were kept in prison; secondly, why their lands were seized, and thirdly, they requested an immediate release of the prisoners.

The presence of de la Chasse and the officer was considered a defiance of the English; and it may have been the reason why the English answered only by another outrage, viz: the capture of the young half-breed chief, Castine, who had been at the conference. He was decoyed on board a ship, and kept in durance, in spite of the remonstrance of Vaudreuil, whose letter was not even answered. Castine was set free, only after six months' imprisonment. An explanation was sent subsequently that he had been taken by soldiers who misinterpreted orders. But that could scarcely explain the duration of his confinement.

In the face of all these provocations, it is idle to accuse Râle of inciting the Indians. In fact, Francis says he can find "no good evidence that Râle used his power as a confidential adviser of the Indians to promote wanton and bloody outrages, or to incite unprovoked invasion of the property and lives of the English." The charge was only the outcome of that hatred of priests which had caused so much bloodshed in the mother country and which was expressing itself in America.

Nor can Vaudreuil's demand for the liberation of Castine be adduced as a cause of the outbreak. His letter was written on June 15, 1721, and already in November, 1720, a resolution had been passed by the House in Boston, ordering one hundred and fifty men under Colonel Walton to proceed to Norridgewok, to seize the priest and bring him to Boston. If he could not be found the Indians were to be summoned to produce him. If they refused they were to be arrested and carried to Boston as a guarantee for the surrender of Râle.

The resolution was not indeed carried out, for the Council and Governor regarded it as a declaration of war. But Hutchison thinks that the House would have been glad to seize that opportunity of extirpating or subduing the Indians; for just because of the peace then existing between France and England, the French would not have dared to interfere. He also admits that it was not certain that the Indians were aware that they had ever promised submission to the English (II, p. 270).

In the following year the capture of Râle was again discussed, and it was voted by the House and assented to by the Governor, to send three hundred men under Colonel Thaxter to demand the surrender of the Jesuit and other incendiaries, but it happened that good old Judge Sewall, who had imposed a penance on himself for his stern judgments in the Salem witchcraft cases, declared against the measure, because he thought the Indians were the remnants of the lost tribes of Israel, and so the matter was dropped for the time being.

As the legislative proceedings were a matter of public knowledge, the Indians heard about them and were stirred up to bitter hatred. Indeed they would have already been on the war-path, had it not been for " the incendiary Friar Sebastian Râle." The English desired to avert that calamity, for the Abnakis, though mild-mannered in time of peace were terrible warriors. Every one in the colony remembered how, when thirty of them were surprised in their sleep by six hundred Englishmen, sixty whites fell in the fray that followed, and the rest fled in confusion, leaving the colonel dead on the field. It was precisely this dread of the Indians that prompted the stealthy tactics adopted in all the attacks by the English on Norridgewok. They were invariably made in the winter, while the braves were away or as, in the last raid, when success attended their efforts, it was by creeping secretly up to the village and opening fire, without a moment's warning. Even then the village was almost deserted.

The efforts of the colonists to capture Râle only made his Indians more resolute in protecting him. In a letter to his brother we are told of two instances of this devotion. They are well worth referring to.

The tribe was down at the sea when a report came that he had been taken prisoner. They assembled immediately, and it was agreed to rescue him at all hazards; but they first sent off two braves to see if the report was true. They arrived at the village, late at night, and found the priest occupied in writing the life of a saint. "Oh Father!" they exclaimed; "how glad we are to see you!" "But what brought you here, and in such frightful weather?" "We heard that you had been captured, and we came to find the trail. If they had carried you to the fort we would have attacked it." "You see, my children," he said, "your fears are groundless. But your love for me fills me with joy, for it shows how sincerely you are attached to your religion. You must remain here to-night, and to-morrow, after Mass you will hurry back to tell your fellow warriors not to worry about me."

Another false alarm was the occasion of a great deal of suffering and danger to the missionary. He was out with his people on one of their hunting expeditions, when the report came that the English were only a half a day's march of them. "Father you must leave," they said. "We shall wait here and fight if necessary, and our scouts have already gone to watch the enemy. You must return to the village and here are some men to guide you. When you are safe we shall be at rest."

"At day-break," says Râle, "I started with ten Indians, but, after a few days, our provisions gave out. My guides killed a dog, which had been following us, and devoured it. After that they began to chew some of their bags, which were made of the skin of a seawolf. I was not able to join them in that. From time to time we ate a sort of wood, which, when boiled, is about as tender as a half-cooked turnip, except the core, which remains hard and has to be thrown away. The rest had not a bad taste, but was very difficult to swallow. It is an excrescence to be found on trees, and is about as white as a large mushroom, but when stewed, does not taste like it. At other times, we dried green oak-bark in the fire, and made a stew of that also, as we did with the lichen that we could gather, but the mess made by the latter is very black and disagreeable to the taste. I took my share of it however, for a hungry man will make a meal of anything.

"As we were very weak with such fare, our progress was slow. However, we reached a lake where, unfortunately, the ice was beginning to thaw, and indeed, it was already covered with three inches of water. We had to cross it, but as our snow-shoes are made of strips of hide, the leather began to swell, and made the shoes heavy and the walking difficult. Although an Indian went ahead to sound the ice, I sunk once up to my knees, and the man at my side, to his waist. 'Father I am done for,' he cried. I strove to help him, but we only went deeper in the slush. Finally after a good deal of difficulty, for we could not get our snow-shoes off, we reached the solid ice. However, I ran less risk of drowning than of freezing to death, while crossing the lake.

"New dangers awaited us next morning. We had to cross a river on floating ice. We succeeded in reaching the other side, however, and finally arrived at the village. I dug up some Indian corn, which I had buried in the house, and was eating it raw to allay the pangs of hunger, and meantime the poor Indians were hurrying around to procure something else. They gave me a real feast. First, they presented me with some corn stew; the second course was a small piece of bear's meat; and then some acorns and a corn cake, baked in the ashes. Dessert consisted of an ear of corn, or some of the grains roasted in the fire [our modern pop-corn]. When I remonstrated with them for making such a fine spread for me, they exclaimed: 'Why, Father! You have eaten nothing for two days. Could we do less than give you a feast?'

"While I was resting from my fatigue another alarm came. One of the Indians arrived from the sea-coast, and not finding me around, was sure that I had been captured, and he hurried back to apprise the fishermen. On the river bank he stripped off the bark of a tree, and with a piece of charcoal, made a picture of a party of Englishmen cutting off my head. Putting this crude drawing on a stick he planted it near the bank. A little while afterwards some Indians coming up the river in their canoes saw it at a distance, and paddled over to read it. They were overwhelmed with grief. 'Alas!' they cried, 'the English have killed the Father, and have cut off his head.' Without saying another word the whole party unloosened their long hair, and, letting it hang down on their shoulders, sat speechless

around the stick till next morning. They then resumed
their journey, and when about half a league from the village
they sent a scout to see if the English had burned it down.
When the Indian appeared on the other side of the river
I was walking along the stockade saying my breviary.
'Oh, Father!' he cried, 'how glad I am to see you! My
heart was dead, but it lives again. We saw the writing
which said the English had cut off your head. How glad
I am that it lied!'

"When I wanted to send a canoe to take him across
the river, he said: 'No! It is enough to have seen you.
I must go back with the news, and we shall soon return
to visit you.' That same day the party arrived at the village and were all consoled to find me alive."

What they did to the artist who made the picture is not
recorded.

The alarms, however, soon ceased to be false. Late in
January, 1722, Râle was alone in the village with a few sick
and old people, the others being away on the annual hunt.
They were unaware that Captain Westbrooke, and a party
of armed men, had just set out from Boston to take him
prisoner. We have an account of the affair in Râle's own
words:—

"All the Indians had gone off hunting, and it was
thought to be the best time to lay hands on me. For that
purpose the English sent a detachment of two hundred
men. Two young Abnaki braves, who were down at the
sea, heard that the enemy had already entered the river, and
they hurried over to see if it were true. They caught up
with the party about two leagues from our village. [That
must have been at Cousinoc, the present Augusta.] Strap-
ping their snow-shoes on their feet they made all haste to
Narantsouac to warn me of the danger, and to have the
old and sick people conveyed to a place of safety. I had
scarcely time to consume the sacred species, to hide the
chalices and vestments, and make for the woods. The
English arrived at night-fall, and finding no one around
they waited till morning. [Meantime the old and sick
were freezing to death in the snow.] When morning came
they began the search in the woods, following the tracks

which the Indians had made. We saw them about a gun-shot away. I had not been able to go far, for I had not time to get my snow-shoes, and my legs were crippled by the accident of a few years ago. All I could do was to crouch behind a tree. They came within eight paces of me. Naturally, they could not have failed to see me, for it was winter, and there were no leaves on the trees. But suddenly, as if repelled by some invisible hand, they retraced their steps, and returned to the village. It was the special Providence of God that saved me. However, they pillaged the church and my little house, and so left me to starve."

Francis tells us that the troops carried off all the Indian provisions, the intention being, of course, to let the people die of hunger, for it was the dead of winter, and there was nothing to eat, except the few things that had been stored away to tide over that season of want. Before supplies could have been obtained from Quebec the whole village would have died of starvation.

It was on this occasion that Râle's famous Abnaki Dictionary was seized. There is no doubt about it, even if on the first page there is an inscription in English which would imply that it was taken in the following raid. The inscription reads: "This book was taken in the fight at Norridgewock." But that is an error. That particular treasure had already been seized before Râle's murder. What labor had been spent on that work may be appreciated by another note on the same page in Râle's hand: "*Il y a un an que je suis parmi les sauvages; je commence à mettre, en ordre, en forme de dictionnaire, les mots que j apprens.*" Thus he had begun the work in the second year of his stay on the Kennebec.

This valuable book is now in the possession of Harvard. It is divided into two parts; the first is a dictionary in French and Abnaki, the French word being given first. It consists of two hundred and five leaves, a small number of which have writing on both sides. The second part is de-

RÂLE'S RELICS.

voted to the *Particles*, the Indian word being placed opposite its French or Latin equivalent. It has only fifty pages.

In 1818, Mr. John Pickering published an account of this manuscript, and expressed a hope that it would soon be printed. Von Humboldt was also anxious to have it done. But it did not appear until 1833, and is now to be found in the first volume of " The New Series of the Memoirs of the American Academy."

Râle tells us that besides his book he was robbed of his strong box. No doubt it is the one that is now exhibited in the Portland Museum. It is about eighteen inches long, is covered with embossed brass, and fastened by a rough iron hasp. It has two compartments, the lower one requiring a knowledge of its mechanism to open it. Possibly he kept his chalice in it. The upper section has an ink-well and an old-fashioned sand blotter.

In the Museum there is also exhibited Râle's cross and a small well-printed volume of Busembaum's " Moral Theology." This book proved conclusively to the parsons that Râle believed that the end justified the means. In the Catalogue of the Museum it is noted that all these articles were once in the possession of a Catholic priest, the Rev. Father Waldron, a descendant of Westbrooke, the commander of the troop. Although repeatedly asked by the Jesuit Provincial to bestow them on those whom one would naturally suppose to be the owners, Waldron refused, and made them over to the Museum. Prior to that they had been in the custody of the Museum of the Massachusetts Historical Society.

It is alleged that in the strong box were found very compromising letters from Vaudreuil. As the Governor of Quebec had to do his best to keep the Indians attached to the French, and as the limitation of territory had not yet been officially made, it might very easily happen that an Englishman would find Vaudreuil's letters very inflammatory without involving any culpability on the part of the

Governor. It all depends in the point of view, and no good can result in discussing the tenor of the letters.

It is unnecessary to state that Westbrooke's expedition, even if it failed, did not diminish the exasperation of the Abnakis. On the contrary, they immediately resolved to avenge it. They dispatched messengers to the other Indian tribes, and the war song was sung by the Hurons in Lorette and in all the Abnakis villages. Narantsouac was given as the rendezvous, but, before any allies arrived, a descent was made on the settlements at the mouth of the Kennebec. They destroyed three or four houses at Merry-meeting Bay and then coming up the river burned several others, but did no harm to the inhabitants personally, beyond taking five hostages to secure the deliverance of their own men who were still languishing in chains in Boston. Their moderation, however, had no corresponding effect on the English, for soon afterwards Captain Harmon, finding sixteen Indians asleep on an island of the Kennebec, fired at them, killing five and wounding three others. Francis says "he slaughtered a large number." The devil was let loose then, and Shute, though restrained for some time by men of influence who protested that the Indians had not only been unjustly treated, but had been plied with rum by New England traders, issued a proclamation of war on July 25, 1722. The ceremony was somewhat superfluous, for Westbrooke's raid in the preceding winter was itself the beginning of hostilities.

It was not, however, until February, 1723, that the first expedition ordered by this proclamation was sent out. Harmon, the midnight murderer of the year before, was in command. But it never reached Narantsouac, for the country was flooded, and the rivers were filled with floating ice. He was too late, and returned ingloriously to Boston.

Nothing more was done until the following winter, when Captain Moulton reached the village but found it deserted. He merely seized some more compromising letters from

Vaudreuil, which would go to prove, if it were true, that Râle must have been a singularly careless man about his correspondence if he left his letters lying about in a hut so that the usual winter marauder had nothing to do but to pick them up.

During all this time the devotion of the Indians to him never failed to display itself. A prize of £1,000 sterling was offered for the missionary's head, but that part of his anatomy still remained on his shoulders. Francis says it was only £500 and was afterwards cut down to £200; but less than that was enough to tempt the average savage. Not only did they not accept the offer, but were insistent in begging Father Râle to withdraw to Canada, and his Superiors also left him free to do so if he judged fit. But he answered that he was not a coward to desert his post in time of danger. He had not to wait long.

In the beginning of August, 1724, one thousand one hundred men, partly English, partly Indian, started out to perform the final act of the tragedy. Counting the expedition of nineteen years before, this was the fifth attempt to capture him. The English historians cut the number of men in this raid down to two hundred and eight, but Charlevoix and de la Chasse vouch for the first figures. There were two commanders this time: Harmon and Moulton.

On the nineteenth of August they left Fort Richmond on the Kennebec; and on the following day they arrived at Teconnet. Leaving there forty men to guard the nineteen whale boats, which had transported the party thus far, they began their march to the village on the twenty-first, diverting themselves on the way by shooting at two Indian women, killing one and taking the other prisoner. The murdered squaw was the wife of Bomaseen, the chief who had been assiduous in his efforts to conciliate the English and who was supposed to have been converted at Boston when his religious difficulties were discussed over a tankard. The murder would soon matter little for Bomaseen, for he himself and his son-in-law were killed two days afterwards at Narantsouac.

About midday the invaders were near the village. Like Indians they crept cautiously through the woods, and at three o'clock stood before the silent wigwams. Not a soul was seen. Then at a given signal every musket blazed and a shower of bullets pierced the thin walls of the houses. Hutchison denies this, and says the Indians fired first, though he admits that the settlement was surrounded before any one was aware of what was happening. There were only fifty warriors in the place, and they seized their weapons and rushed out to cover the flight of their women and children, who were already making a mad rush for the river. Where was Râle? He was already facing the foe. He was the only one whom the English wanted, and he knew that if he presented himself it would divert their attention from the fugitives. He was not mistaken. A loud shout greeted his appearance. The man they had so often failed to find was before them. Every musket covered him, and he fell riddled with bullets at the foot of the cross which he had planted in the centre of the village. They crushed in his skull with hatchets again and again, filled his mouth and eyes with filth, tore off his scalp, which they sold afterwards at Boston, and stripped his body of his soutane, which they wanted as a trophy, but as it was too ragged to keep they flung it back on the corpse. Meantime the fire was kept up on the fleeing Indians, who were endeavoring to reach the shelter of the woods on the other shore. Some were slain before they reached the river, others were killed in midstream, and others before they reached the protecting forest.

When the slaughter was over, the soldiers retraced their steps to the village and began the work of plunder. They desecrated the Blessed Sacrament, and defiled the vessels of the altar. Then putting the torch to the buildings, they withdrew in the glare of the conflagration. They were laden with booty, and Hutchison tells us that the New England Puritan thought it no sacrilege to take the plate from an idolatrous Roman Catholic Church; which he supposes "was all the profaneness offered to the sacred vessels." There were also some expressions of zeal against idolatory in breaking the crucifixes and other imagery which were found there. So died Sebastian Râle. The "inflammatory friar" would flare up no more.

The raiders were received with enthusiasm at Boston. There is little doubt that the missionary's white scalp was put up at auction and duly knocked down to the highest bidder. Harmon received a promotion, and Moulton was awarded the thanks of a grateful country. The Rev. Dr. Colman, of Boston, declared that Râle's death was "the singular work of God. The officers and soldiers piously put far from themselves the honor of it; and he who was the father of the war, the ghostly father of those perfidious savages like Balaam, the son of Beos, was slain among the enemy after vain attempts to curse us." The Reverend Doctor would have been a good war chief.

After having outraged Râle's body, his enemies set to work to besmirch his reputation. When Vaudreuil asked for an explanation, Lieutenant Governor Dummer replied, "that the priest was killed in action, associated with the open and avowed enemies of the English, and that more than once he had shown himself at the head of the Indian troops,"—"an accusation," says Francis, "which might be urged against any army chaplain." The New England Courant accused him of "making the offices of devotion serve as incentives to the ferocity of the savages," and urged as a proof that "the flag which was brought to town on which were portrayed five crosses, one in the middle, and one at each corner, had been hoisted by Râle as a help to devotion and courage, when he granted them absolution before any considerable expedition." As a matter of fact he hoisted it for precisely the opposite reason: viz., to subdue their ferocity. However the Puritans had a dislike for the cross on a banner. Endicott had long before cut it out of the royal standard.

Attempts to palliate the deed only added new calumnies. It was said that Moulton had given orders to spare the priest, but that Lieutenant Jaques was so exasperated at seeing Râle firing from a wigwam that he broke in the door, and shot him through the head while Râle was loading a gun, and shouting that he would neither give nor take quarter. It was further alleged that, in the wigwam with Râle, was an English boy who had some time before been taken prisoner by the Abnakis. Râle shot him through the thigh, and stabbed him in the body. Captain Harmon testified to the truth of this ferocious act under oath. But apart from the unthinkableness of such a deed, the fact is that Harmon arrived at the village only after the battle was over. The witness's bad reputation would in any case discredit his testimony.

Another charge was based on a letter which was said to have been written by Râle on the very day he was slain. The French original, if there were ever one, is not produced, but only what purports to be a translation. It is for the most part unintelligible, and if the writer's knowledge of French was no better than his English the document might be tossed aside as valueless, but at the end of it we can divine its purpose. Râle is made to express his thanks to some one whose name is not given, for the great quantity of wine that was sent him. " I have now enough for a twelve month, and I will keep it in my cellar, with what I already have. I take a glass after Mass, but I prefer brandy."

As there could be no cellar in an Indian cabin, and as Râle never tasted wine, it is unnecessary to call attention to the malice of the insinuation. But he was not merely a drinker. He was a profligate as well. In Belknap's " New Hampshire " (Volume II, p. 57), and in the "Massachusetts

Historical Collection " (2d Series, Volume VIII, p. 257) the paternity of young Castine is ascribed to him, on the authority of a certain Hugh Adams. As Castine was perfectly well known, both to the French and English and to the Abnakis, and as he had also solemnly declared himself, before the judges in Boston, to be the legitimate son of Baron de Castine by an Indian mother, this attempt to blacken the reputation of a holy man like Râle cannot be too bitterly reprobated. Young Castine himself had just been killed by the English a month before at Oyster River. His lips were forever dumb and could not refute the calumny.

Quite different from those disgraceful scenes at Boston were those that took place at the same time on the plateau of Narantsouac. The day after the massacre, the Indians crept cautiously back to the desolate village. The men cleared away some of the ruins, and then sat down to weep over the dead; the women meantime scoured the woods for herbs to heal the wounds of the braves. The body of their beloved priest was found horribly mangled. They kissed it again and again, and then took it up tenderly, and after washing it, laid it in the place where for thirty years he had offered the Holy Sacrifice. His altar was his grave. Around him in a circle they laid the bodies of the seven warriors who had died in his defence. There was Mogg, the Indian whom Whittier has defamed. His wife and children had likewise been killed. There, too, was Bomaseen, who probably died before he knew that his wife and daughter had been murdered. His son-in-law was placed near him in the grave and also Job, Carabasset and Wessemenet. The name of the seventh hero is not known. The Indians carried the bloody cassock to Quebec, but what became of that sacred relic cannot be discovered. The chapel bell, of course, was uninjured, and it is said that an Indian lad took it, and hid it some distance up the river. He lived many years after the tragedy, but would never tell where he had placed the treasure. When asked about it, his only answer was: "Maybe Indian need it some-time." He died with his secret, but after some time a wood-cutter found the bell in the hollow of a large pine that had been uprooted in a storm. It was taken to Norridgewock and from thence to Brunswick. It is now in the Portland Museum.

Narantsouac never rose from its ruins, but remained in the desolation in which the destroyers saw it as they turned back for the last time to gaze at its flaming wigwams. Relic hunters occasionally visited the place to dig up its soil. But the village had disappeared forever. There is, however, one interesting record of how it appeared fifty-two years after the tragedy, and singularly enough it is from the pen of no less a personage than Benedict Arnold. Fortunately it was written before the cloud of dishonor had settled on his name. Indeed he was then an ardent patriot and on his way up the Kennebec to capture Quebec. It was the year 1775.

"At a place below Norridgewock Falls," he writes, "was a wide and beautiful plain, once the site of an Indian village, from which the falls took their name, and memor-able in the annals of former days, as the theatre of a tragical event in which may of the tribe were slain, in a sudden attack, and among them Father Râle, the vener-able and learned missionary, who had dwelt there for twenty-six years. The foundations of a church and an altar in ruins are still visible, the only remaining me-morials of a people which was once feared, and of a man who had exiled himself from all the enjoyments of civiliza-tion to plant the cross in a savage wilderness, and who lost his life in its defence. Let history tell the story as it may, and let it assign such motives as it may for the conduct of the assailants; the heart of him is little to be envied who can behold the melancholy vestiges of a race extinct, or pass by the grave of Râle without a tear of sympathy and a sigh of regret."

After some years a wooden cross was erected over Râle's

RÂLE'S MONUMENT.

remains, but some one cut it down. Later on a rude memorial in stone was placed there, and finally on August 23, 1833, the one hundred and ninth anniversary of the massacre, a throng of people, among whom were Penobscot, Passamaquoddy and Canadian Indians, gathered around a granite shaft about twenty feet high which the second Bishop of Boston, Benedict Joseph Fenwick, had erected to commemorate the glory of the hero. The great bishop thrilled his hearers on that day with the story of Narantsouac. Fenwick himself was a Jesuit.

During the time of the Knownothing excitement the monument was thrown to the ground, but was put in its place again soon after. It has stood there ever since, and the railroad guides indicate it as one of the points of interest for travellers in that part of Maine.

In spite, however, of its solidity, the storms of seventy years had opened the seams of the pedestal, and undermined the foundation. The shaft was out of plumb, and the ruin of the monument seemed imminent. To avert the disaster the Bishop of Portland, the Right Rev. Louis Sebastian Walsh, who regarded the custody of the place as a sacred duty, had the foundation strengthened and set the obelisk again squarely on its base. Meantime excavations were made in the hope of finding the precious remains beneath, but without success. The danger of undermining the monument prevented a very thorough search.

When all this was done, a pilgrimage to the holy place was announced, and although Indian Old Point is really in the woods, and affords no shelter in case of a storm, six or seven hundred people assembled to do honor to the martyr. A rustic altar was constructed at the base of the monument, and in the sanctuary were the relics that had been loaned for the celebration by the Portland Museum. Distinguished men were present and the speaker of the occasion happened to be the present writer, who could not help feeling the emotion that arose from the fact that he was standing on the very spot which was once dyed by the blood of Father Râle. The sacred remains of the great missionary and martyr were still there mouldering beneath the monument, and on the altar steps were the bell, the book, the strong box, and the cross, which had been familiar objects to the faithful who knelt there in the days when Narantsouac was a Catholic village. The bishop, whose name, by a happy coincidence, is like Father Râle's, Sebastian, and who rejoiced in the possession of a treasure more precious than any other diocese of North America can claim, addressed his people with emotion, which he did not attempt to conceal. Benediction of the Blessed Sacrament was given and then the multitude wended their way through the woods to the train which carried them back to their homes. The scenes of that day will never fade from their memory.

The entire plateau has since been purchased at a price not much greater than Bishop Fenwick paid for a single acre in the times when religious bigotry stood in the way of Catholic ownership, even if it were to be in the midst of a forest. It is now a burial place for the dead, and is thus secure against desecration. The people of Maine are particularly blessed in possessing such a sanctuary. They could not find a better place to lie down in the sleep of death than at the side of their apostle, Father Râle.

INDEX

309

INDEX

INDEX

311

INDEX

Imprimi Potest

JOSEPH F. HANSELMAN, S. J.

Præp. Prov., *Md.-N. Y.*